Medicine for Law

Medicine for Lawyers

Edited by

Roy Palmer

HM Coroner, Greater London (Southern District);
Governor, Expert Witness Institute; formerly Secretary &
Medical Director, The Medical Protection Society 1989–1998

and

Diana Wetherill

Forensic Physician; Police Surgeon, West Yorkshire

The ROYAL
SOCIETY *of*
MEDICINE
PRESS *Limited*

Published by the Royal Society of Medicine Press Ltd
1 Wimpole Street, London W1G 0AE, UK
Tel: +44 (0)20 7290 2921
Fax: +44 (0) 20 7290 2929
Email: publishing@rsm.ac.uk
Website: www.rsmpress.co.uk

British Library Cataloguing in Publication Data
A catalogue record for this book is available from the British Library

ISBN 1-85315-548-9

Distribution in Europe and Rest of World:
Marston Book Services Ltd
PO Box 269
Abingdon
OXON OX14 4YN, UK
Tel: +44 (0)1235 465500
Fax: +44 (0)1235 465555
Email: direct.order@marston.co.uk

Distribution in the USA and Canada:
Royal Society of Medicine Press Ltd
c/o Jamco Distribution Inc
1401 Lakeway Drive
Lewisville, TX 75057, USA
Tel: +1 800 538 1287
Fax: +1 972 353 1303
Email: jamco@majors.com

Distribution in Australia and New Zealand:
Elsevier Australia
30–52 Smidmore Street
Marrickville NSW 2204
Australia
Tel: + 61 2 9517 8999
Fax: + 61 2 9517 2249
Email: service@elsevier.com.au

Phototypeset by Techset Composition Limited, Salisbury, UK
Printed in Great Britain by Bell and Bain Ltd, Glasgow

Contents

List of Contributors

Iain M Breckenridge ChM FRCS FRCSE FRCPE
Consultant Cardiac Surgeon, University Hospital of Wales, Cardiff

Roger V Clements FRCS (Ed) FRCOG FAE
Obstetrician and Gynaecologist; Editor - Clinical Risk; Founding Governor of Expert Witness Institute

John H Coakley MD FRCP
Consultant Physician and Medical Director, Homerton University Hospital, London

Frances Cranfield MB BS LRCP MRCS DRCOG DipFMS DMJ FRCGP
General Practitioner; Expert Witness; Assistant Deputy Coroner, Hertfordshire

Roger Evans FRCP
Consultant in Emergency Medicine, University Hospital of Wales, Cardiff

Beverley Gordon
Clinical Governance Lead, The Ipswich Hospital NHS Trust, Suffolk

Peter Harvey MA MB FRCP
Emeritus and Honorary Consultant Neurologist to the Royal Free Hospital, London

Tom EJ Healy BSc (Hons) MD LLM MSc FRCA
Emeritus Professor of Anaesthesia, University of Manchester; Consultant Anaesthetist, Manchester Royal Infirmary, University Hospitals of South Manchester and Hope Hospital, Salford

Charles J Hinds FRCA FRCP
Senior Lecturer in Intensive Care Medicine, Queen Mary University,
St Bartholomew's Hospital, London

CDR Lightowler MBBS FRCS
Consultant Orthopaedic Surgeon; Chairman of the Senior Fellows Society,
Royal College of Surgeons of England; Past President of Section of
Orthopaedics, Royal Society of Medicine

Harvey Marcovitch MA FRCP FRCPCH DCH
Consultant Paediatrician

John O'Grady MB BCh FRCPsych
Consultant Forensic Psychiatrist, West Hampshire NHS Trust

Roy Palmer LLB MB BS LRCP MRCS DObstRCOG Barrister-at-law
H M Coroner, Greater London (Southern district); Governor, Expert Witness
Institute; formerly Secretary & Medical Director, The Medical Protection
Society 1989–1998

John H Scurr MB BS BSc FRCS
Consultant Surgeon, Lister Hospital, London

Margaret F Spittle MSc FRCP FRCR AKC
Consultant Clinical Oncologist, Meyerstein Institute of Oncology,
The Middlesex Hospital, London

Lewis Spitz PhD FRCS
Nuffield Professor of Paediatric Surgery, Department of Paediatric Surgery,
Institute of Child Health, London

Gareth Thomas MD LLM FRCOG
Consultant Obstetrician and Gynaecologist, The Ipswich Hospital NHS Trust,
Suffolk

Diana Wetherill MB ChB MMedSc DMJ(Clin.)
Forensic Physician; Police Surgeon, West Yorkshire

Robin CN Williamson MA MD Mchir FRCS
Dean, Royal Society of Medicine, London

Preface

This book is derived from the series of lectures for lawyers given at the Royal Society of Medicine (RSM) in London. The lectures were planned in response to requests by lawyers, not only by those specializing in medico-legal fields of practice (such as civil personal injury and medical negligence), but also by coroners, for some basic guidance in the various medical and surgical specialties that they encountered. Many of those who attended the lectures asked for them to be put together in written form and that is what this book attempts to do.

Each chapter has been written by acknowledged experts in the relevant fields, usually by those who gave the original lectures on the RSM course. Many of these authors are experienced in advising lawyers and the courts. The opinions expressed are those of the individual authors and not necessarily those of the editors or of the RSM. The editors are aware that not every medical specialty has been covered (nor were they covered on the lecture course) and indeed it would be impossible to do so in this book. Some lectures were based on specific cases and so could not be included for reasons of medical confidentiality, and some illustrative cases were (or remain) *sub judice*.

Physiology (how the body works) has a separate chapter but the lecture on anatomy (the structure of the body) is not included because the many illustrations required would make the cost of the book prohibitive. Relevant anatomy has therefore been considered within the various chapters, with some line drawings to aid clarity. Standard anatomical texts, with drawings in colour, are available from medical publishers and also from Internet websites (for example www.medtropolis.com/VBody.asp). A brief glossary of technical and medical terms is included but it is not intended to be comprehensive and a medical dictionary should be consulted for further definitions and clarification.

The editors hope that this book will provide insight into some of the problems and pitfalls encountered in current medical practice and that, having read this book, lawyers will be able to commission an expert witness to write a medical report and will be able to interpret it, using their greater knowledge and a better understanding of the practice of medicine.

Roy Palmer
Diana Wetherill

1 Basic medicine: physiology

Robin CN Williamson

Human physiology is the study of how the body works. Thus, anatomy is concerned with structure and physiology is concerned with function. Strictly speaking, only normal function is included; the abnormal function seen in disease is termed pathophysiology. Innumerable chemical processes are involved in the day-to-day working of the body, so some knowledge of basic biochemistry is an important part of physiology. Whereas anatomy is based on the structure of individual organs, physiology requires a more integrated concept of the major organ systems of the body, as follows:

1. Circulatory system, i.e. heart, major arteries and veins, and capillaries, with particular regard to blood flow.
2. Respiratory system, i.e. airway and lungs, including the mechanisms and control of breathing, and the transport of oxygen in the blood.
3. Nervous system, i.e. brain, spinal cord, somatic and autonomic nerves, which exert a controlling influence on the function of muscle, skin, and internal organs.
4. Alimentary system, i.e. the gastrointestinal tract and its major appendages (liver, pancreas, biliary tract), with particular regard to the digestion, absorption, and metabolism of food.
5. Renal system, i.e. kidneys and their ability to excrete waste products and to maintain both normal fluid balance and the correct pH (acid–alkaline balance) of the body.
6. Endocrine system of ductless glands, which produce hormones, including those involved in male and female reproduction.

This chapter can only summarize the principles that govern the function of these major systems. Organs of special sensation—the eye and ear—cannot be tackled within the space available. The human body is wonderfully complex in the organization and control of its many functions. Readers who seek a fuller understanding are encouraged to consult an undergraduate textbook of physiology (see Further reading).

Circulation

In primitive organisms the substances necessary to support life can reach their target by simple diffusion, but in higher animals a sophisticated transport mechanism is needed. The circulatory system exists to transport oxygen and nutrients to the vital organs—brain, kidney, heart, and gut—and the crucial transport medium is *blood*. Blood contains three types of cell (red cells, white cells, and platelets) suspended in a fluid called plasma. Red cells (erythrocytes) carry oxygen, white cells (leucocytes) are concerned with immunity and the fight against infection, and platelets play an important role in clotting. Red cells and platelets are synthesized (made) in the bone marrow and are eventually broken down in the spleen; red cells have a lifespan of about 120 days. Chief among the white cells are polymorphs and lymphocytes, both of which are able to ingest bacteria and other foreign material, a process termed phagocytosis. There are two main types of immunity: humoral immunity depends on the formation of antibodies to antigens, such as bacteria and viruses, while cellular immunity depends on the formation of T lymphocytes which destroy the cells that triggered their development. In brief, humoral immunity is a defence against acute (recent onset) infection, while cellular immunity is a defence against chronic infection, such as tuberculosis, and is also responsible for allergic reactions and the rejection of transplants.

Haemoglobin is the oxygen-carrying pigment contained in red blood cells and gives them their characteristic red colour. It is a combination of haem, which contains iron, and globin, a polypeptide (protein component). An adequate supply of iron and certain vitamins (B_{12}, folic acid) is necessary for proper synthesis of haemoglobin (erythropoiesis); supplements of iron and folate are usually given to pregnant women who need extra supplies of blood for their fetus. Oxygen binds to the iron atoms in haem to form oxyhaemoglobin. When oxygen is released in the tissues the colour of blood changes from bright red (as in the arteries) to a duller bluish-red colour (as in the veins). It is the avidity of haemoglobin for oxygen that makes blood such an effective transport medium.

It is necessary for blood to flow freely through the circulatory vessels, yet an effective mechanism is required to staunch its flow if a vessel is injured; otherwise the individual would bleed to death. When a small vessel is breached, *haemostasis* (control of bleeding) is achieved partly by contraction of the vessel wall and partly by thrombosis—a complex process that involves several clotting factors in the blood together with calcium and platelets. The result is the formation of a fibrin clot that plugs the hole in the vessel. This clotting tendency is balanced by a similarly complex process called fibrinolysis. Imbalance in these processes can lead to either an excess tendency for venous thrombosis—especially if blood flow is sluggish, as in bedridden patients or those on long-haul flights—or a tendency to bleed, as in haemophiliacs who have a congenital deficiency of one important clotting factor (Factor VIII).

The *heart* is the muscular pump that drives blood around the body. It has long been known that blood will spurt from a cut artery under high pressure, but it was thought to oscillate to and fro until William Harvey showed that blood circulates from small arterial branches through tiny vessels in the tissues (capillaries) before being collected by veins and returned to the heart. The dynamo behind this circulation is the heart, which contracts 60–80 times per minute throughout an individual's life. The heart contains four chambers and is responsible for two separate circulatory systems (Figure 1.1). The systemic circulation supplies all the organs in the body with oxygenated blood, while the pulmonary circulation delivers exhausted blood to the lungs where it is replenished with oxygen. The heart chambers comprise two atria which collect the blood and pass it through valves into the two ventricles, which contract forcefully to distribute blood throughout the body. The cardiac cycle consists of diastole, the phase of filling, and systole in which contraction of the atria is immediately followed by contraction of the ventricles.

Blood pressure comprises two components—systolic and diastolic pressure—both of which can be measured by inflating a cuff on the upper arm and then slowly releasing it while listening with a stethoscope placed in the crook of the elbow for the return of blood to the brachial artery. Nowadays more sophisticated, electronic blood pressure measurement devices are in common usage, but the traditional method remains perfectly valid. The normal pressure of blood in the systemic circulation is about 120/80 millimetres of mercury (mmHg), which means that there is a background (diastolic) pressure of 80 mmHg rising to 120 mmHg with each contraction of the left ventricle. The left ventricle has a much thicker wall than the right ventricle, as the latter only has to pump blood a short distance to the lungs at a much lower pressure. The maintenance of a relatively high diastolic pressure is necessary for a consistent blood flow to the tissues. It depends upon a competent aortic valve, which guards the outflow from the left ventricle, plus the elastic recoil in the wall of the aorta and its major branches to the head, abdomen, and limbs. Incompetent valves or septal defects (abnormal

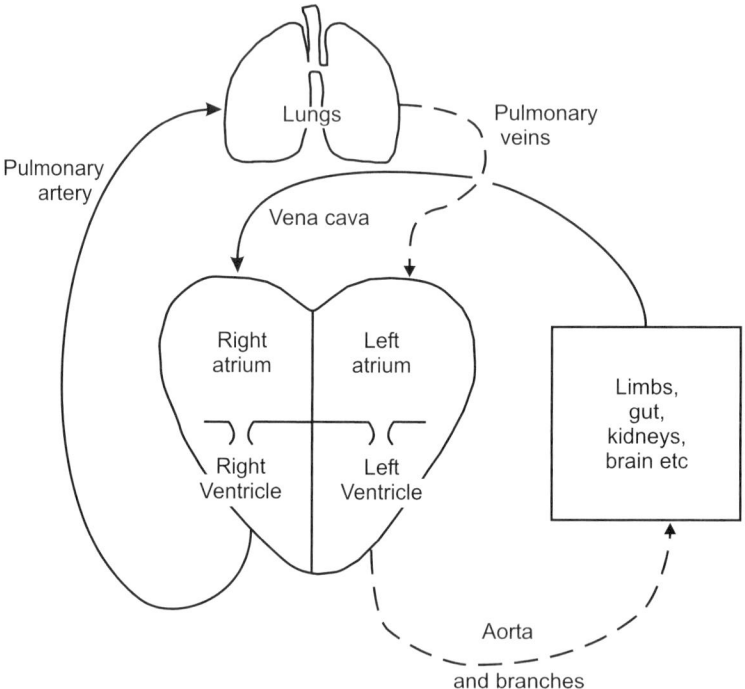

FIGURE 1.1 Schematic representation of the two circulatory systems, pulmonary and systemic. Oxygenated blood (– – – –) returning from the lungs passes through the left side of the heart and is distributed by the arterial system throughout the body. Deoxygenated blood (——) returning from the tissues passes through the right side of the heart and from there to the lungs.

communications between the left and right sides of the heart) reduce the effi-ciency of the pumping mechanism and can lead to heart failure.

Like all muscle, the myocardium or cardiac muscle is an excitable tissue, influenced by electrical impulses but with an inherent contractility. Its most excitable part is called the sino-atrial node, which acts as the natural pace-maker of the heart; its rate of electrical discharge governs the *heart rate*. If its conducting system is damaged, the heart beats at a much slower rate than normal (about 40 beats per minute as opposed to 60–80), which is inadequate to support normal activity. This condition of heart block may be controlled by inserting an artificial pacemaker. The electrical activity of the heart can be studied by means of an electrocardiogram (ECG). The ECG pattern is disorganized by the death of muscle after a myocardial infarct (heart attack), which is precipitated by thrombosis of the coronary arteries, i.e. the heart's own blood supply. One consequence of a heart attack can be the development of a cardiac arrhythmia, i.e. loss of the normal regular rhythm as judged by feeling the pulse and looking at the ECG. Extra beats or extrasystoles, when the pulse seems to skip a beat, may be relatively harmless. Atrial fibrillation (the loss of a concerted atrial contraction) can be more troublesome, while ventricular fibrillation is fatal unless the heart is shocked back into a normal rhythm by means of a defibrillator.

Blood is distributed throughout the body by a system of *arteries* that progressively diminish in size as they branch repeatedly. If the sole supply to an organ is via one artery, then thrombosis of that artery will inevitably lead to death (infarction) of all or part of that organ; the coronary circulation is one such example. Blood is returned to the right atrium by a matching system of *veins*, which increase in size as they get nearer the heart. Veins have much thinner walls than arteries, and blood returns to the heart partly by the pumping activity of muscles in the limbs and partly by a process of 'negative pressure' as the chest expands with each breath and sucks blood into the heart. Venous valves preserve a one-way flow. As the blood is squeezed through the narrow capillary bed in each tissue, some fluid permeates through the vessel wall into the tissues. This tissue fluid or lymph is returned to the venous system by a collection of tiny colourless vessels called *lymphatics*. Cancer cells have a peculiar tendency to spread via the lymphatic system.

Respiration

There is a two-fold purpose to breathing: absorption of oxygen and expulsion of carbon dioxide. The body produces energy by oxidizing carbohydrate, fat, and protein; water and carbon dioxide are the by-products of this process. The respiratory system comprises the lungs where the crucial gas exchange takes place, the air passages leading to them, the muscles that cause the chest to expand and draw in air, and the brain centres and nerves that control this activity. The *lungs* are elastic structures. They glide easily over the chest wall, stretching as they are expanded by the intake of air and then collapsing during expiration.

The tidal volume is the amount of air inspired and expired with every breath, and in a healthy adult at rest is about 500 ml. The normal resting respiratory rate is 12–15 per minute. Of the tidal volume, only about 350 ml reaches the alveoli of the lungs where *gas exchange* takes place; the rest occupies the upper airways, an area that is regarded as dead space. One reason that patients with respiratory insufficiency may be given a tracheostomy (an artificial opening directly into the windpipe) is that it greatly reduces the dead space. Air is warmed and humidified as it passes through the nose and pharynx. From there it passes through the larynx (voice box), trachea (windpipe), and then the right and left bronchi and a system of branching bronchioles to reach the alveoli (or air sacs). At this point only the thin alveolar membrane and the wall of the pulmonary capillaries separate the outside air from the blood. Oxygen is exchanged for carbon dioxide by diffusion across this double membrane.

The main muscle of respiration is the diaphragm which forms a continuous sheet separating the chest and abdominal cavities. Most quiet breathing is effected by the diaphragm, but during exercise or chest disease, when increased inspiratory effort is required, extra muscles can be recruited. Chief among these are the intercostal muscles which run between the ribs. *Respiratory capacity* is measured by a process termed spirometry; the subject breathes in and out through a tube connected to a gas chamber, with a floating drum in the chamber to record the volume of air moved. The vital capacity or maximum volume expelled after a deep inspiration is about 4.5 litres in healthy individuals.

Breathing is controlled by a respiratory centre in the brain stem. A rise in the carbon dioxide concentration of the blood stimulates this centre, which in turn causes an increased respiratory effort so as to 'blow off' the excess gas. A fall in oxygen concentration in the blood (hypoxaemia) acts indirectly via chemoreceptors in the carotid body, but the net result is the same. These and other mechanisms permit a 10–20-fold increase in oxygen consumption during strenuous exercise.

The partial pressure of oxygen (pO_2) is about 95 mmHg in arterial blood but only 40 mmHg in venous blood because so much oxygen is extracted for use by cells during the passage of blood through the tissues. Nearly all *oxygen transport* occurs as oxyhaemoglobin, whereas carbon dioxide is much more soluble in blood and is carried largely as carbonic acid. The affinity of haemoglobin for oxygen is affected by both pH and temperature. Skeletal muscle contains a protein (myoglobin) that resembles haemoglobin but has a much lower affinity for oxygen; it can store some oxygen in muscle for release when the blood supply is reduced. Arterial blood is normally 97% saturated with oxygen; oxygen saturation can be measured fairly simply and is a guide to inadequate respiration (hypoxia). A more accurate assessment requires an arterial blood sample to be obtained for measurement of pO_2.

Nerves and muscles

A typical nerve cell or *neuron* has a star-shaped cell body with a fringe of short fibres (dendrites) and one long fibre (axon) which ends in little knobs or terminal buttons. One neuron communicates (synapses) with the next via the dendrites. Nerve cells are readily excited by electrical or other stimuli, and the resulting impulse is conducted along the axon to release a chemical messenger (neurotransmitter) which 'fires' the next neuron. The impulse generates an action potential, which is transmitted down the nerve and across the neuro-muscular junction, where the axon is expanded to form the motor end plate (Figure 1.2). Nerve fibres are of two main types: sensory (afferent) fibres convey feelings such as pain and touch to the brain, while motor (efferent) fibres stimulate muscles to contract. Sometimes the entire nerve is either motor or sensory; division results in loss of movement or sensation. Other nerves are mixed, e.g. the sciatic nerve, which innervates the skin and muscles of much of the leg. Both nerve conduction and muscle contraction are active processes that require energy expenditure.

Muscle cells are also excitable by electrical, chemical or physical stimuli. Their contraction is activated by the action potential conveyed down the relevant nerve. There are three different types of muscle. Striated muscle makes up the mass of musculature that moves the skeleton and is under voluntary control; its cross-striations give a characteristic striped appearance under

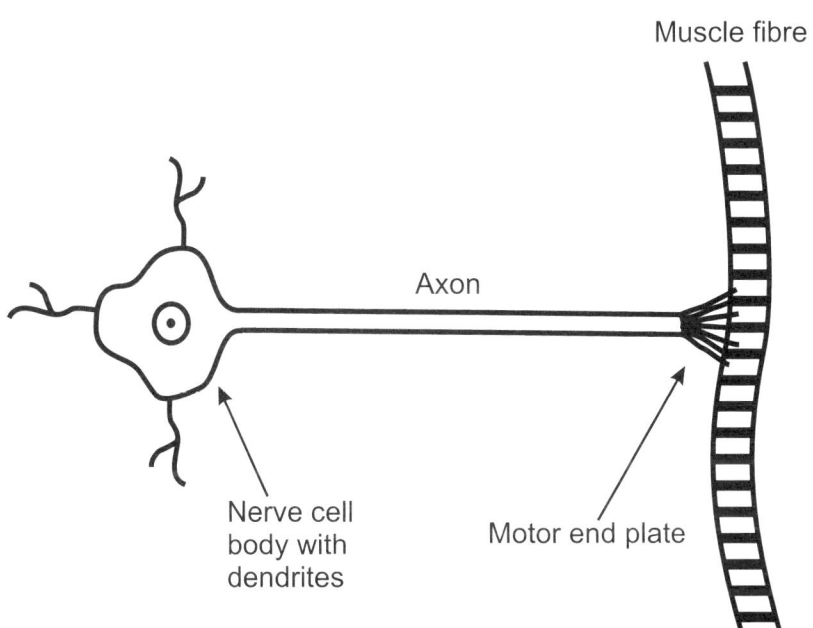

FIGURE 1.2 Effector neuron cell. An electrical impulse or action potential passing down the axon crosses the motor end plate and causes the muscle fibre to contract.

the microscope. Filaments of contractile proteins—actin and myosin—undergo shortening when the muscle is stimulated to contract. Smooth muscle lacks striations, and its contraction is involuntary. It is typically found in the wall of the gut where it undergoes spontaneous activity, but it is also under the control of the autonomic nervous system. Cardiac muscle is also striated; it is only found in the heart, where it contracts rhythmically without the need for external stimulation.

The basic unit of nervous activity is the *reflex arc*, which comprises an afferent neuron from the sensory organ (e.g. the skin), a central connection in the spinal cord, and an efferent neuron to the muscle. An example is the knee jerk response, where tapping on the patellar tendon causes the individual to kick. A lesion (disease focus) anywhere along this arc will lead to loss of this reflex. The brain exerts overall control over the spinal cord, however. Thus, interruption of the spinal cord higher up will lead to an uncontrolled or exaggerated reflex. Transection of the cord by injury produces paraplegia below that level, i.e. both paralysis and anaesthesia (lack of feeling). Internal organs have a different type of sensation similar to but different from the surface of the body. Thus, the bowel is not sensitive to pinprick but will cause pain if it is stretched or goes into spasm.

The external parts of the body (skin and muscles) are controlled mostly by the *somatic nervous system*. Somatic nerves, therefore, control movement of the trunk and limbs, as well as sensations such as touch, pain and temperature. By contrast, the viscera or internal organs of the body (heart, lungs, gut) are controlled by the *autonomic nervous system*. Autonomic nerves are either sympathetic or parasympathetic. Sympathetic nerves help the body to respond to sudden danger; they mediate the 'fright, flight or fight' response characterized by widening of the pupil, quickening of the heartbeat (tachycardia) and diversion of blood to the muscles. This process is assisted by liberation of the hormones adrenaline and noradrenaline into the bloodstream. The parasympathetic nervous system is concerned with vegetative processes such as swallowing and intestinal secretion, which are carried on during calmer times. Many viscera have a dual autonomic innervation, each with opposing functions. Thus, adrenaline makes the heart race, while stimulation of the vagus (parasympathetic) nerve causes the pulse to slow.

It is the size and complexity of the *brain* that distinguishes man from all other animals. The human brain is quicker and more versatile than any computer. Many unconscious activities, such as breathing and the response to changes in temperature, are controlled by centres in the brain stem. No thought needs to be given to breathing, but breathing can be stopped for a short time or be made faster by exercising conscious will. This conscious control is exerted by the cerebral cortex or grey matter of the brain (Agatha

Christie's character Hercule Poirot's 'little grey cells'), while the underlying white matter is concerned with the myriad of connections within the brain. Different parts of the brain control different activities, such as vision, speech, hearing, memory and behaviour. Thus, a stroke (cerebrovascular accident) that involves the speech centre will cause difficulty with talking or even a complete inability to speak (aphasia). Amnesia is quite a common outcome of head injury. Division of the frontal lobe of the brain (lobotomy) can turn an aggressive psychopath into a harmless individual but one with little or no proper cognitive function (thought and memory).

The gut

The functions of the gastrointestinal tract include transport, secretion of digestive juices, absorption of nutrients and clearance of waste. Besides the hollow tube of the alimentary canal (Figure 1.3), the gastrointestinal system comprises the biliary tract and pancreas, which are concerned with *digestion*, and the liver where much of the body's metabolism takes place—notably the biochemical processes by which nutrients are converted into energy and building blocks such as albumin (the main protein in the blood). Entry of food into the mouth stimulates the flow of saliva and gastric (stomach) juice; in fact, even the thought of food can induce salivation, as Pavlov showed in dogs. Swallowing, which starts as a voluntary exercise and continues involuntarily, transmits the bolus of food from the mouth to the stomach via the oesophagus (gullet). In the stomach food is physically mashed up by muscular contraction, and the process of digestion is begun by the proteolytic (protein-splitting) enzyme pepsin. Pepsin works at an acidic pH, and the strong hydrochloric acid secreted by the gastric lining also sterilizes the food; excess gastric acid contributes to duodenal ulcer disease.

It is during passage of food through the four metres or so of small intestine that virtually all the nutrients are extracted and absorbed into the veins and lymphatics that drain the gut. *Nutrient absorption* is an elaborate but highly efficient process that requires conversion of large molecules of carbohydrate, fat and protein into much smaller soluble particles for active uptake by the lining of the small bowel. The enzymes that split these three macromolecules are either contained in pancreatic juice or secreted by the mucosa of the small bowel itself. Digestion is a particular problem with fat, which is 'attacked' by the fat-splitting enzyme lipase and then solubilized by the detergent properties of bile salts. By interrupting this process, certain diseases of the bile duct and pancreas can result in the passage of very fatty stools (steatorrhoea).

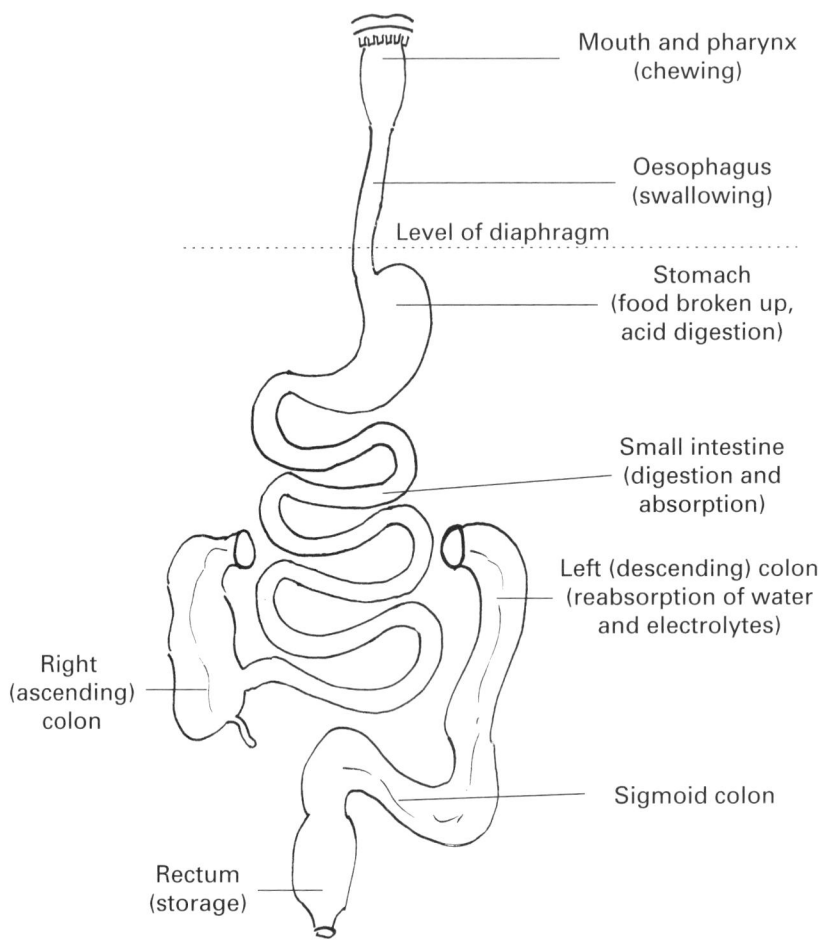

Mouth and pharynx
(chewing)

Oesophagus
(swallowing)

Level of diaphragm

Stomach
(food broken up,
acid digestion)

Small intestine
(digestion and
absorption)

Left (descending) colon
(reabsorption of water
and electrolytes)

Right
(ascending)
colon

Sigmoid colon

Rectum
(storage)

FIGURE 1.3 Alimentary canal and its functions. A single hollow tube leads from the mouth to the anus, but the different sections of this tube have widely differing functions.

The function of the large intestine is to reabsorb most of the water and electrolytes contained in the small bowel contents so that they are not lost in the faeces. Faecal matter is stored in the rectum and is evacuated by contraction of the muscles of the pelvic floor and relaxation of the efficient anal sphincter mechanism (defaecation).

Developmentally the liver, biliary tree and pancreas are part of the gut, and their functions complement those of the alimentary canal (Figure 1.4). As the largest gland in the body, the *liver* plays a major role in metabolism. It

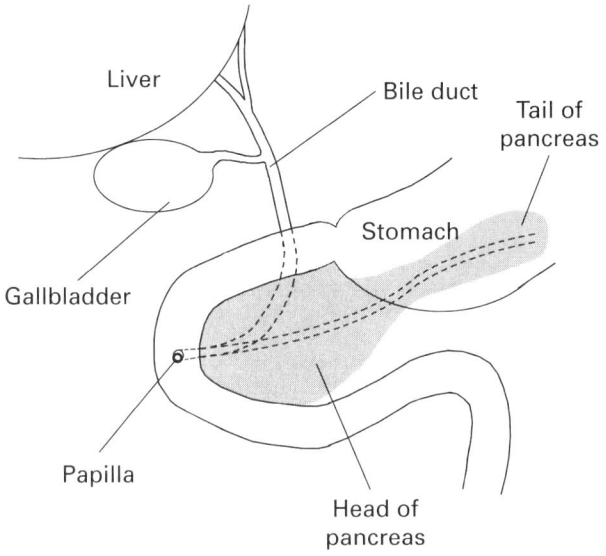

Liver

Bile duct

Tail of pancreas

Stomach

Gallbladder

Papilla

Head of pancreas

FIGURE 1.4 Biliary tract and pancreas. Bile is secreted by the liver, stored in the gallbladder, and delivered to the gut in response to a meal. The pancreatic duct joins the bile duct just as it enters the duodenum at the papilla. Both bile and pancreatic juice are needed for the proper digestion of food.

receives nearly all the nutrients from the gut via the portal vein. It is respon-sible for synthesis of albumin, several clotting factors, bile salts and choles-terol. The liver secretes bile, which contains bile pigments (degraded haemoglobin), bile salts, lecithin and cholesterol; imbalance in these constitu-ents leads to the formation of gallstones, which usually contain a mixture of cholesterol and bile pigment. The liver is also responsible for the detoxifica-tion of many drugs, including alcohol. Bile is secreted into the *biliary tree*, which conveys it to the upper small intestine (duodenum) where it assists in the digestion of fat. Liver disease and bile duct obstruction are the usual causes of jaundice, when retention of bile pigment in the blood provides the characteristic yellow pigmentation of the skin and eyes. The *gallbladder* is attached to the side of the bile duct and acts to concentrate and store bile until it is required at mealtimes. The *pancreas* has a double function: it elab-orates many of the enzymes needed for proper digestion of food and it syn-thesizes insulin (among other hormones), which is needed for the uptake of glucose into cells. Insufficiency of insulin leads to an increased blood sugar level or diabetes.

Renal function

The prime function of the *kidneys* is to rid the body of the nitrogenous waste products of metabolism, notably urea and creatinine. The renal reserve is such that about half of one kidney can preserve normal blood levels of these metabolites. By altering the secretion of water and electrolytes into the urine, the kidney plays a crucial role in maintaining the normal physiological balance of these compounds and also in regulating acid–base balance, i.e. the normal pH of the blood (about 7.4). Fluid depletion or dehydration is detected by osmotic receptors in the brain, giving rise to the sensation of thirst. Antidiuretic hormone (ADH or vasopressin) is secreted by the pituitary gland (see p. 13) and acts on the renal tubule to reabsorb water, thereby conserving body fluid and leading to a concentrated urine. After rehydration, any extra water in the bloodstream will switch off ADH secretion and allow the kidney to excrete the excess. This is an example of a process known as feedback inhibition, which helps to maintain a constant internal environment.

When the kidneys start to fail, blood levels of urea and creatinine begin to rise and the patient becomes acidotic; in fact, the first function to fail is the ability to reabsorb water from the renal tubules, so that patients may notice polyuria (increased passage of urine), especially at night. *Renal failure* is treated by restriction of dietary protein, because protein metabolism is the main source of blood urea. Thereafter, patients may require dialysis, a process by which the excess waste products are leached out of the blood or peritoneal fluid by some form of artificial kidney; renal transplantation is a more satisfactory measure in the long term.

The basic unit of renal function is the *nephron* (Figure 1.5), which is comprised of a filtering device (the glomerulus) and a complex system of tubules that serve to concentrate urea and creatinine in the urine. Each kidney contains over one million nephrons. Many useful substances, such as sodium, glucose and amino acids (the constituents of protein) enter the proximal renal tubule by diffusion across the glomerular membrane, but are then reabsorbed into the bloodstream. The efficiency of the kidneys is such that nearly 90% of water filtered through the glomerulus is normally reabsorbed, subject to the pituitary secretion of ADH.

Urine is collected into the renal pelvis on each side, which in turn is connected by means of a long tube (the ureter) to the bladder. The function of the bladder is to store urine until a convenient moment for *micturition* (voiding), and then to expel the urine via the urethra by contraction of the powerful muscle in its wall. As with defaecation, this process requires relaxation of the normal sphincter mechanism that guards against incontinence.

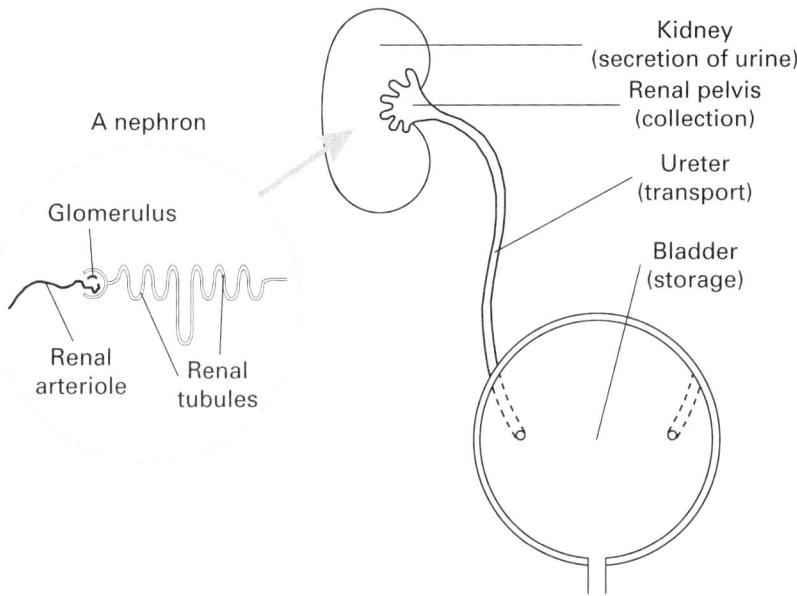

FIGURE 1.5 Urinary tract. Urine is secreted by the kidney and stored in the bladder. The inset depicts a nephron, which is the basic functional unit of the kidney.

Micturition is under the influence of the autonomic nervous system, with an over-riding control by the cerebral cortex.

Endocrine and reproductive systems

There are two main sorts of gland in the body. Exocrine glands, such as the salivary and sweat glands, secrete their juice into a duct, whereas endocrine or ductless glands secrete hormones directly into the bloodstream. Hormones are proteins that act as chemical messengers, travelling in the blood to modu-late the activity of a target organ that possesses the relevant hormone receptor. Endocrine tissue is found in many different organs, but it is concentrated in certain glands of which the *pituitary* is the most important. The pituitary gland is located inside the skull just below the brain and contains two main lobes. The anterior lobe secretes tropic hormones that control the activity of several other glands, including the thyroid, adrenal, breast, ovary and testis; it also secretes growth hormone, which affects the growth of many organs. The posterior pituitary secretes vasopressin and oxytocin, which act on the kidney and uterus, respectively. Pituitary insufficiency therefore has widespread effects. Pituitary secretion is controlled by a feedback system: rising blood levels of hormones secreted by the target organ in response to the pituitary hormone inhibit the secretion of that tropic hormone.

Situated at the front of the neck, the *thyroid* gland controls the level of tissue metabolism. Its principal hormone, thyroxine, is rich in iodine. If the dietary intake of iodine is low, the thyroid enlarges to trap all the available supply; the resultant swelling is called a goitre. An overactive thyroid causes an increased metabolic rate manifested by weight loss, tachycardia, and sweating. An underactive thyroid slows down many bodily functions, causing patients to gain weight and lose full mental faculties.

The *adrenal* glands are situated above the kidney on each side. They contain an outer cortex, which secretes corticoid hormones (steroids) as well as sex hormones, and an inner medulla, which secretes adrenaline and noradrenaline and can be considered as an extension of the sympathetic nervous system. There are several different steroid hormones and they have a wide range of activities in the body. Hydrocortisone causes breakdown of protein to release glucose and helps the body to cope with stress. Aldosterone prevents loss of sodium in the urine and other body fluids. Removal of both adrenal glands is fatal unless steroid replacement therapy is given. An excessive dose of steroids can lead to Cushing's syndrome, which is characterized by obesity and hypertension.

The *pancreas* contains both endocrine and exocrine tissue. Endocrine cells, which are found in clusters or islets, secrete the hormones insulin and glucagon, both of which affect glucose metabolism. Lack of insulin results in diabetes, a condition characterized by glycosuria (glucose in the urine), polyuria (excessive micturition) and weight loss. Pancreatic exocrine cells synthesize several different digestive enzymes.

The gonads comprise the *ovaries* in the female and the *testes* in the male. Each gonad has a dual function: to produce germ cells, i.e. ova and spermatozoa, and to secrete sex hormones. Pituitary hormones (gonadotropins) cause enlargement of the ovary and testis during childhood, and the resultant release of gonadal hormones brings about the changes of puberty, including the growth spurt and the secondary sexual characteristics of females and males. Oestrogens and progesterone secreted by the ovary cause girls to start their monthly cycle of ovulation and menstruation, while testicular androgens stimulate the production of fertile sperm and seminal fluid. If sexual intercourse takes place during the period following ovulation, when an ovum is shed from the ovary and passes down the female genital tract, then conception may take place as the sperm penetrates the ovum. The developing embryo implants into the wall of the uterus, leading to the formation of the placenta, and placental hormones then sustain the *pregnancy*. At birth, which occurs around 270 days later, pituitary oxytocin governs the onset of uterine contractions. The breasts have enlarged during pregnancy under the combined actions of oestrogen, progesterone and the pituitary hormone pro-lactin. After birth lactation is controlled by prolactin combined with oxytocin secreted as a reflex response to suckling by the infant.

If fertilization fails to occur during the menstrual cycle, then falling hormone levels cause the lining of the uterus (endometrium) to be shed at menstruation before the cycle starts anew.

Risk management in general practice

Frances Cranfield

In the context of the delivery of healthcare, risk management is the identification, analysis and control of potential adverse outcomes that threaten the proper delivery of healthcare to patients. An effective risk management programme will therefore be based on the following core elements:

Identity $\rightarrow$ Measurement $\rightarrow$ Control $\rightarrow$ Monitoring,[1] i.e.

- identifying each risk
- measuring the identified risk in terms of magnitude and frequency of occurrence
- controlling the risk
- constantly monitoring the effectiveness of the control measure.

Nearly one-third of all doctors in the NHS are general practitioners (GPs) and it is estimated that about 90% of all patient contacts are with GPs. Risk management is an essential component of modern professional life in general practice. Within a GP practice there is a tendency to think that risk management is someone else's responsibility but it should be regarded as everyone's responsibility.

Identification of risks in general practice

Doctors' claim history is a good indicator of where risks might be. Complaints can also form a useful way of measuring and forecasting risks and it is hoped that in future the recording and analysis of significant events will form a valuable source of information. Certainly, NHS Primary Care Organizations (PCOs) are now carefully analysing complaint profiles and are conducting 'Significant Event' analyses in general practice. Significant Events (or Critical

Incidents) include incidents and risks that could have led to harm to patients, i.e. near misses, and accidents that lead to actual harm.

The Medical Protection Society (MPS) statistics show that its GP claims have doubled since 1994 and there are currently around 500 a year. The MPS therefore anticipates that 36 out of every 1000 GP members (3.6%) will be sued as a result of medical work they have done in the previous 12 months.[2]

Some of the common pitfalls in general practice are:

- delayed diagnosis
- errors in prescribing
- failure in communication
- substandard regard of 'Health and Safety at Work' rules
- breach of confidentiality
- errors in certification and fees.

Delays in diagnosis

An analysis of 1000 consecutive general practice claims at the MPS showed that 63% of cases could be classed as due to delay in diagnosis (Figure 2.1).[3] In most cases more than one factor was identified. Looking at delays in diagnosis in general practice, 50% of the cases related to surgical conditions, 32% were medical and 18% related to obstetrics and gynaecology.

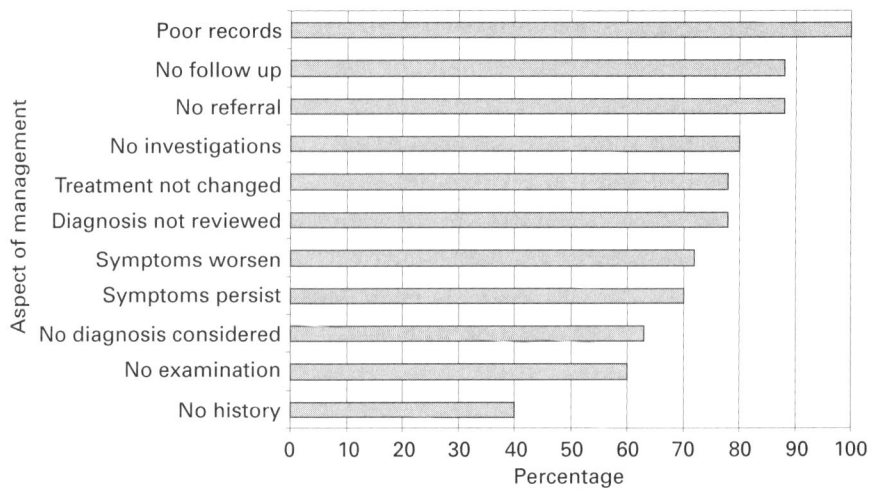

FIGURE 2.1   Analysis of a sample of settled MPS cases of delayed diagnosis in general practice.

Malignant neoplasms formed one of the largest category of claims where there was an alleged delay in diagnosis.[2] The problems appear to fall into clusters:

- failure to visit the patient at home or to see him or her in the GP's surgery
- failure to take an adequate history or to examine the patient at the initial consultation, leading to a wrong diagnosis or wrong treatment
- failure to refer the patient, arrange investigations or arrange for follow-up within an appropriate time and, if the symptoms persist or worsen, failure to consider a different diagnosis. In 23.4% of the MPS GP claims analysed it was alleged that GPs did not refer the patient correctly either for hospital admission or to a specialist for a second opinion.

Underpinning all of these problems is the need for high-quality contemporaneous records. These are vital for patient care as well as for a GP to defend his or her actions. All patient contacts should be recorded, including telephone consultations and visits.

In a study of past claims, the Medical Defence Union (MDU) looked at the common conditions that resulted in a delay in diagnosis as a percentage of total indemnity.[4] The MDU found that delay in diagnosis cases accounted for 55.5% of the total indemnity paid out for GP settled claims. These cases were broken down into specific conditions (see Figure 2.2).

Meningitis accounted for only 3% of delay in diagnosis claims but represented 17% of the indemnity payouts for delay in diagnosis, reflecting the fact that it can result in brain damage. By contrast, ectopic pregnancy was involved in 6% of the claims but only 2% of the indemnity paid. Other

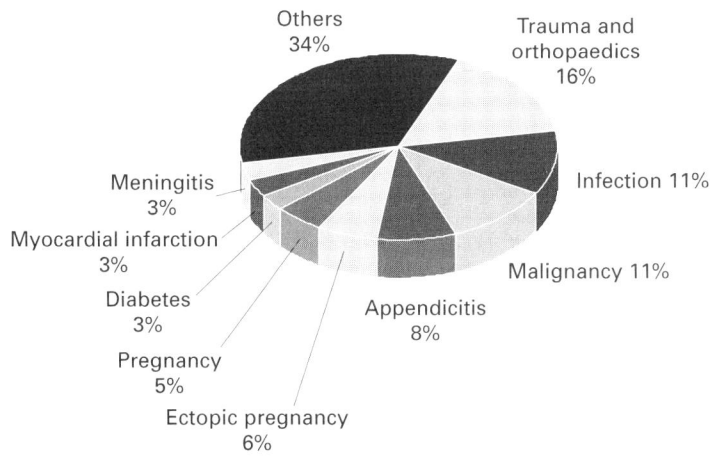

FIGURE 2.2 Analysis of delay in diagnosis claims.

conditions in general practice which are commonly involved in allegations of delayed diagnosis are pregnancy, appendicitis, myocardial infarction, diabetes, subacute bacterial endocarditis, subarachnoid haemorrhage, slipped epiphyses, fractures, significant inter-vertebral disc lesions, other serious infections and delay in the diagnosis of various cancers. Some examples of such cases are illustrated in *Clinical Negligence in General Practice*[5] and *MDDUS Case Studies in Medical Negligence*.[6]

Prescribing errors

Prescribing errors deserve special consideration.[7] On average a GP prescribes between 250–350 items every week. In an MDU analysis of 790 settled claims against UK GP members over a six-year period, 25% were directly related to errors in prescribing, monitoring or administration.[8] This is fairly similar to the figure of 19.3% identified in MPS settled claims. A number of problems have been identified including illegibility of prescriptions, incorrect or inappropriate dosage (particularly in children or with unfamiliar drugs), the wrong drug being prescribed, prescriptions given to patients known to be allergic or to have contraindications to certain drugs, inappropriate instructions for usage, administration errors and dispensing errors. Common groups of drugs involved in prescribing errors are:

- steroids
- non-steroidal anti-inflammatory drugs
- anticoagulants
- antibiotics
- opiates.

Failures in communication

- With patients:
  Effective communication is vital and forms the foundation of a good doctor–patient relationship. The doctor must be able to listen and respond to patients in a sensitive, caring and professional manner. The era of the authoritarian, paternalistic approach has passed and patients rightly expect to be informed and involved in decisions concerning their health. The issue of truly informed consent is contentious in all aspects of medical practice.

  With increasing pressure on their time, general practitioners are being actively encouraged to carry out telephone consultations. A doctor must put him- or herself in a position to be able to make an informed decision—

first whether or not to see a patient and then about the diagnosis. It is advisable to speak to the patient if possible or otherwise to someone who is well acquainted with the situation, e.g. a carer or family member. If there are several contacts it is wise to reassess the situation. Careful contemporaneous notes should be made.

It is appropriate to mention the use of *chaperones* at this point. Although allegations of indecent assault are small in number, they are very distressing to all involved. A survey published in the *BMJ* in 1993 showed that ~65% of male GPs never or rarely used chaperones and only 16% always used chaperones.[9] In November 1996, the General Medical Council (GMC) produced guidelines on intimate examinations. It is important to explain to a patient why an intimate examination needs to be carried out, what it involves and to offer a chaperone where possible. However, the protection organizations do acknowledge that there may be practical difficulties in providing a chaperone and it is not always appropriate.

- With general practice staff:
A doctor is responsible for the actions of his or her staff and must ensure that staff are adequately trained and supervised. There must be an effective channel of communication for messages and staff must always be able to contact a doctor to respond to urgent situations.

- With other health professionals:
This is most commonly a failure in communication between primary and secondary care, e.g. inadequate information about drugs or discharge arrangements. Another major area is in failure of communication of results, e.g. X-ray or pathology results, which do not arrive in general practice or, having arrived, are not acted upon. With increased use of co-operatives and deputizing services to cover out-of-hours work, a major challenge has been to ensure continuity of care (which requires good communication between all parties). In future, when general practitioners are able to opt out of providing out-of-hours care themselves, the duty may be shared between a number of different bodies, each with their own skills, and this will be an even greater challenge in the provision of effective communication.

Some failures of communication involve the failing of just one individual, but in many cases there is actually failure of a system.

Health and safety

The legal responsibility for health and safety lies with the GP as an employer and as someone occupying premises to which the public have access. A practice is legally required to assess and control health and safety risks and to carry out a risk assessment.[10] Some of the risks are common to all small businesses, others are specific to healthcare. The risks can broadly be categorized as relating to:

- people—stress and mental well-being, personal safety and protection against violence, staff health, manual handling procedures
- healthcare procedures—clinical procedures, clinical equipment, product liability, medication and other harmful substances, clinical waste
- the working environment—fire, electricity, asbestos, health, safety and comfort.[11]

Breach of confidentiality

Information acquired by a GP from or about a patient in the course of his or her professional work is confidential and must never be disclosed to others without either the consent of the patient or other proper justification. Any doctor who breaches confidentiality can be charged with serious professional misconduct. Guidance on this topic is issued by the GMC.[12]

It is important to remember that a GP is responsible for his staff and if they break confidentiality it is the doctor who will be called to answer. There are now also concerns about computer information—there are issues around the use of e-mails and the internet. Great care must be taken to ensure confidentiality and security, which is a complex area, and GPs must comply with the terms of the Data Protection Act.

Errors of certification and fees

A GP must exercise care when issuing certificates and signing documents and claim forms for fees. The doctor should not certify statements which he or she has not taken steps to verify. The GMC publishes guidance and, again, doctors who err may face GMC proceedings as well as rendering themselves liable to criminal sanctions.

Measuring the identified risk

Data collection and audit can be used to help measure the risk. However, once risks have been identified, consideration needs to be given to the consequences should the risk actually occur, e.g. a rating scale—insignificant, minor, moderate, major and catastrophic—could be used. Consideration then needs to be given to how likely it is that any particular risk will occur; a suggested rating is almost certain, likely, moderate, unlikely, rare. The use of the consequence and likelihood ratings can then be used to give a risk rating for each of the risks identified.[1] For example, if the lack of time and high number of patients attending the emergency surgery was identified as a high risk factor with potential catastrophic effects and an almost certain likelihood of problems occurring, then the overall risk rating would be very high and this would be identified as a high priority for review.[1]

Controlling the risk

Problems that increase the risk

Factors that currently get in the way of good health risk management are described below.

- Being human:
  It is the author's belief that the very humanity of the doctor of tomorrow will be the reason that the health professions will be needed more than ever but, unfortunately, being human means that inevitably mistakes will be made.
- Eight-minute consultations:
  An average GP consultation lasts just eight minutes. In this time a GP has to take an adequate history, obtain informed consent, undertake examinations, arrange investigations, provide treatment, discuss management plans and follow-up, and make adequate records. It is therefore not really surprising that there is potential for failure in communication and errors in management. The Royal College of General Practitioners is pressing for 15-minute consultations in its quality initiatives, but with current workforce problems, this would be unsustainable. However, the New General Practice Contract provides Quality Points with financial incentives if the length of routine booked appointments with the doctors in the practice is not less than 10 minutes, or in practices with only an open surgery, the average face-to-face time spent by the GP with the patient is at least eight minutes.
- Shortage of general practitioners:
  Although the total head count of NHS GPs has grown (27,523 in 1990 to 30,252 in 2000) the percentage of part-time GPs has also grown considerably (5% in 1990 to 18% in 2000). In addition, the range, complexity and amount of activity have changed dramatically. General practitioners have major roles and time commitment to NHS management through Primary Care Organizations (PCOs), there has been an increased shift of work from the hospitals to general practice, and there has been an increase in

TABLE 2.1 Increase in the number of consultations over the period
1991–2000

Patient age (years)	Increase in consultations (%)
45–64	24
65–74	47
75+	38

consultation rates. In July 2001 the RCGP Birmingham Research Unit showed a significant increase in workload over the period of 1991 to 2000 (Table 2.1).

In addition the Position Statement on GP workforce by the Royal College of General Practitioners and the General Practice Committee has shown that to achieve the targets of the NHS Plan 10,330 extra GPs are required—1200 specialist generalists, 3000 for clinical governance, 130 for appraisals, 3000 for national service frameworks and 3000 for intermediate care.

- Fatigue:
Fatigue and sleep loss are well known to result in errors.[13] General Practitioners who are self-employed are still exempt from the EC Working Time directives and many general practitioners have, in the past, had to work excessively long hours to fulfil their 24-hour responsibility to patients. However, this will improve significantly when GPs can opt out of providing out-of-hours care as they will then only have to provide care for 52.5 hours a week, although it is recognized that additional time may be required for administration. In addition, those GPs who are employed by practices or Primary Care Organizations will be governed by EC Working Time Directives and can only be required to work an average of 48 hours a week.

- Shortage of resources:
Waiting lists for surgery, lengthy waits for outpatient appointments and difficulties that general practitioners experience in obtaining adequate services for patients (such as counselling and physiotherapy) put both patients and general practitioners at risk. The new programmes for specialists in training, partly imposed in response to EU working hours directives, have added another complexity.

- Lack of trained personnel to whom to delegate:
One solution to the mismatch between General Practice workload and the number of GPs available would be for GPs to delegate some of their work – there appears to be a chronic shortage of trained health professionals in virtually every field of the NHS. General Practitioners also still retain the responsibility to ensure that those to whom they delegate are competent to undertake the task.

- Dangers of constant change:

  The biggest risk to an organization is during a period of change and the health service is no exception to this.[14] Such examples are in changes from Health Authorities to Strategic Health Authorities, Primary Care Groups to Primary Care Trusts to Primary Care Organizations, some practices changing from General Medical Services (GMS) to Personal Medical Services (PMS), and the latest and most dramatic change is the switch to the New GMS Contract. Personnel have not always been in place when changes are launched or they may not have received guidance and so do not know their role or do not have adequate resources to undertake their role. General practitioners and patients are then put at risk.

- Stress on doctors:

  Stress is a feature of living. Working in the health professions means constant exposure to stress. This stress can sometimes be enriching and motivating—positive stress. However, when it is negative it can produce a large number of problems (Figure 2.3). Issues, such as the potential for physical violence and complaints and litigation, can be high negative stressors.

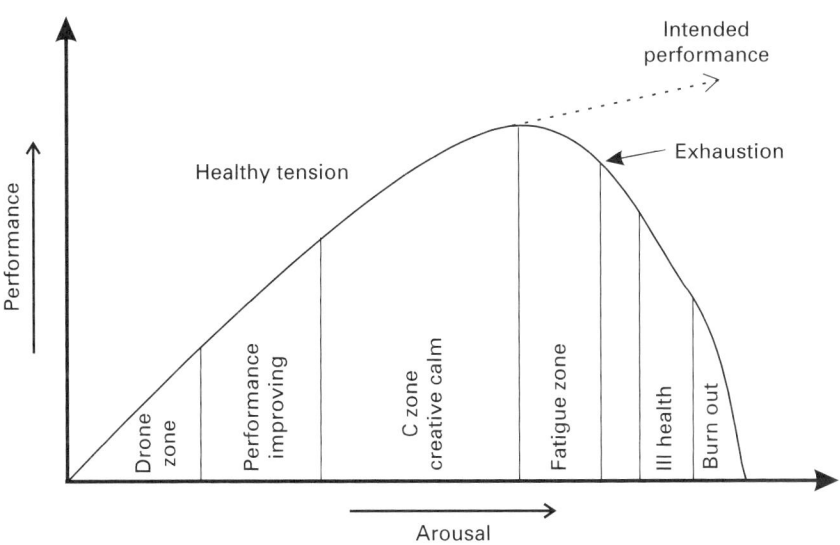

FIGURE 2.3 The 'human function curve'— the effect of pressure on performance at work.

'Burn out' usually manifests itself as:

- emotional exhaustion (tiredness, somatic symptoms, irritability, accident proneness, depression, excessive alcohol consumption)
- depersonalization (treating patients and other people as if they are objects)
- low productivity accompanied by feelings of low achievement.

It is well established that the medical profession has higher rates of depression, suicide, drug and alcohol abuse, and mental breakdown than most other professional groups.[15] Self-critical or perfectionist disposition are good markers in predicting stress and subsequent depression in doctors.

It should be remembered that complaints themselves are very high stressors for GPs. Part of this is the fact that, under the current system, general practitioners can face up to 11 separate investigations, with different bodies looking at the same facts again and again (Table 2.2).

TABLE 2.2 Investigations that could be instigated if a GP faces a single complaint over patient care

- Coroner's inquest
- Local resolution under the NHS patient complaint procedure
- Independent review panel for patient complaints that remain unresolved (This stage will be taken over by the Healthcare Commission—CHAI)[16]
- Ombudsman's investigation
- Medical Discipline Committee (Primary Care Organizations)
- Appeal to the Family Health Service Appeal Authority
- Civil litigation by patients seeking compensation
- Appearance before GMC's performance review panel
- Appearance before GMC's professional conduct committee
- Misuse-of-drugs tribunal
- Criminal investigation

- Inability to control workload:
  The workload of general practice is to a very large extent driven by 'patient demand'. Problems arise, however, when patients are led to have expectations that the service cannot necessarily always deliver, e.g. that the patient can choose whether to have a home visit or attend the surgery, and proposals such as access to a doctor within 48 hours on all occasions for routine matters. Sir Kenneth Calman described the deficit in the quality of life as the distance between a patient's hopes and aspirations (and often also the doctor's) and the reality of their situation (Figure 2.4). Whilst always striving to improve the quality of service offered, it is necessary for professionals and society to help patients reset their hopes and aspirations and improve their understanding and experience of practicalities and reality.

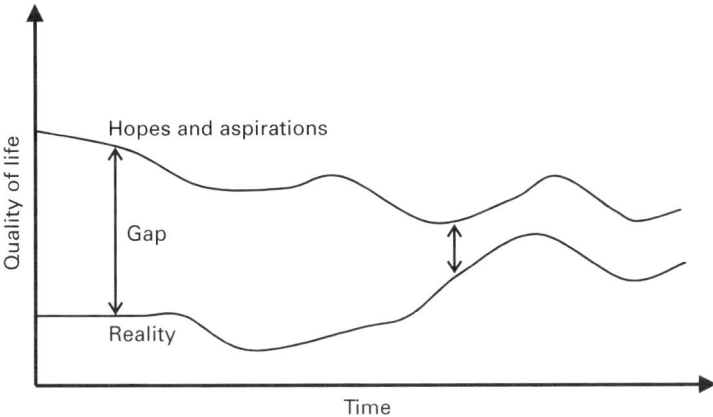

FIGURE 2.4 The 'Calman Gap'—quality of life deficit.

One of the signs of attempts to control workload to safe levels has been the tendency in the past for doctors to close their patient lists. A recent survey showed that in Hertfordshire 28% of practice lists were closed and in Bedfordshire 48% of practice lists were closed. However, despite this, Primary Care Organizations can compulsorily allocate new patients to these practices, and this is a risk factor under continuous debate.

It is said that the New GP Contract should bring some ability to control workload with the ability to opt out of some services. At present this is controversial with particular concern about open and closed lists and the amount of administration involved in data collection and auditing.

- Failures in systems for communication of patient information:
The small Lloyd George envelopes introduced at the instigation of the Health Service militate against clear, efficient record keeping in the 21st century. With recent changes in regulations allowing practices to go paperless, increasing numbers of GPs are taking this option. However, it is perceived that doctors are at increased risk whilst they have both paper and paperless systems simultaneously in operation. There is concern that some general practitioners do not have high levels of computer skills. In addition, a number of different computer systems operate in general practice and are not at present compatible with each other. There is no uniformity of methods of recording information and difficulties exist with the coding systems for diseases. Many trusts do not have computer systems that are compatible with each other or with general practice and their coding system for disease is different from that used in general practice. While there is such a diverse and uncoordinated system of recording and transferring data, it remains a risk factor for general practitioners and patient care.

- Super specialization:
  General practitioners are by definition generalists. It is the Government's wish that a large number of general practitioners will become specialists (GPs with a Special Interest), taking on work traditionally undertaken in hospitals, e.g. dermatology, endoscopy, anticoagulation, and minor injury treatment. In addition practices can bid to take responsibility for Enhanced Services that are essential, additional services delivered to a higher standard or extra specialized services, such as drug and alcohol misuse clinics, minor injury services and intrapartum care. All of this is quite possible but only with appropriate training, protected time, adequate resources and enough general practitioners to carry out this new work; otherwise, GPs and patients will be at increased risk. It is vital that general practitioners should recognize the limitation of their expertise and that they do not undertake work which is outside their competence.

Factors that assist in risk management

Clinical Governance

This is the cornerstone of good risk management. There are several definitions of clinical governance as applied to general medical practice:

'*A framework through which NHS organizations are accountable for continuously improving the quality of their services and safeguarding high standards of care by creating an environment in which excellence in clinical care will flourish.*' {*Gabriel Scally and Liam Donaldson—Department of Health*}.

'*A framework for the improvement of patient care through commitment to high standards, reflective practice, risk management and personal and team development.*' {*Royal College of General Practitioners*}.

Implementation requires effective change management and realistic resources, both financial and manpower. However, nothing will change unless clinical governance is understood and owned at grass roots level.[17] The first stage involves implementation of four key steps—leadership arrangements, baseline assessment, formulation of a plan and arrangements for monitoring.[18,19]

PCOs have a major role to play in implementing these steps in primary care and have a duty under the Health Care Act 1999. For the first time this Act introduced a statutory duty on Primary Care Trusts (and other NHS provider organizations) to assume and improve the quality of healthcare that they deliver and this must be regularly monitored. At a practical level attempts to meet this duty are by the implementation of clinical governance.

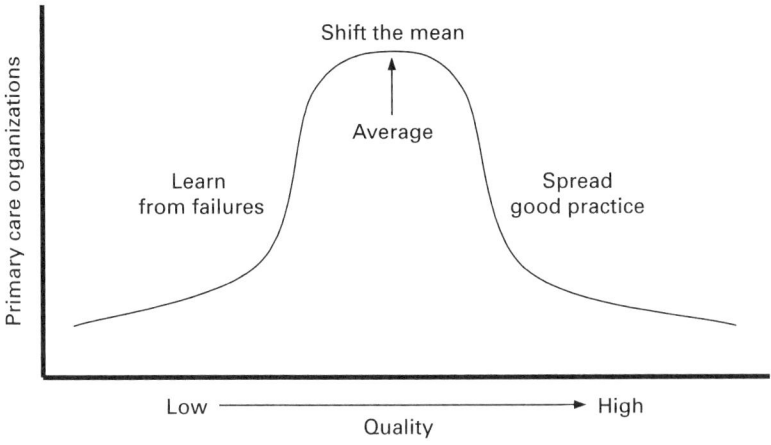

FIGURE 2.5 The 'quality curve'.

Clinical governance should act as a forum for clinical policy-setting, bringing together work from different parts of the organization and allowing individuals and practices to learn from and disseminate good practice.

The aim of clinical governance is to shift the quality curve (Figure 2.5) to the right. It should promote a spirit of openness about the care provided and, being externally accountable for care, it involves the whole of the primary care team.[17]

The quality and outcome (Q and O) framework of the New GP Contract[20] is designed to raise organizational and clinical standards in primary care, reducing morbidity and mortality as well as improving patient experience. It targets key areas:

- clinical
- organizational
- patient experience
- additional services.

Practices working under Personal Medical Services will also be expected to demonstrate such quality gains.

Targets—guidelines—protocols—audit

Targets are set by such bodies as:

- NICE—National Institute of Clinical Excellence
- NSF—National Service Framework
- HIMPs—Health Improvement Programmes

To a large extent these reflect national priorities and national standards but particularly in the case of HIMPs, there should be flexibility to reflect local needs. It is hoped that these will help to provide equity across the country. Proper practice should, wherever possible be based on evidence, i.e. determined by systematic methods based on literature review, critical appraisal, multidisciplinary consultation and grading of recommendation by strength of evidence. It is then possible to produce guidelines or protocols, which are statements about optimum performance. Such evidence-based guidelines improve the quality of clinical decisions, help replace outdated practices, provide a focus for audit of clinical practice and provide benchmarks for clinical governance.

Guidelines should be as they suggest, guidance and not commands. Clinical judgement should be used and they must be interpreted sensibly and applied with discretion. If a doctor follows the guidelines and his judgement is called into question he is likely to be on firm ground if there is a complaint. If, however, a doctor decides not to follow the guidelines and his judgement is called into question he will have to justify his actions.

The quality and outcome framework of the New GP Contract[20] should be a powerful tool for improving the services being delivered by general practice. The quality indicators are said to be based on the latest available research evidence and set out a range of clinical and organizational standards. Practices have targets to aspire to and PCOs will themselves have additional targets to meet.

Audit is the process of critically and systematically assessing professional activities with a commitment to improving personal performance and ultimately the quality and/or cost-effectiveness of patient care. It requires the setting of standards. In simple terms, it is the system by which doctors can measure the standard they have reached and compare it with the standards set by targets and guidelines, thus helping doctors to effect change.[21]

Computerization of records

This has a particularly important risk management effect in the area of prescribing. Errors as a result of illegibility are reduced and it is easier to check whether under- or over-prescribing of drugs has occurred. A fully developed prescribing system has the capacity to check the name of a drug against previous drug idiosyncrasies held in the patient record, against possible interactions with current medications, and against conditions in the patient record for which the drug is contraindicated. However, any system can only be as good as the information entered into it, but it should reduce the number of prescribing errors. Computerization will also greatly assist with auditing and monitoring of quality standards.

Personal learning plans, training, appraisal and revalidation

These involve every member of the primary care team and are a vital part of risk management. GPs are responsible and accountable for their clinical practice. To this end they must ensure that they have the appropriate skills to deliver care safely and therefore ensure that their continuous professional development programme is aimed at the maintenance or acquisition of new skills if these are required. This is the key to personal learning plans. General Practitioners are encouraged to look at their perceived strengths and weaknesses and produce personal learning plans, which identify learning needs that can be met with training. These are discussed with a trained appraiser who produces a report. It is expected that this will be an annual event. In future doctors who wish to stay on the full medical register held by the GMC will need to demonstrate, on a regular basis, their fitness to practise and to comply with the revalidation procedures. It is expected that *Good Medical Practice for General Practitioners* (2002)[22] will form the basis for standard setting for general practice. General Practitioners also have a duty to look at the training needs of their staff and carry out regular appraisals.

Greater openness

In the past decade there has been greater recognition about the problems surrounding error reporting and risk management, although there is still much work to be done. It is being recognized that with the rising complexity and greater reach of modern medicine comes an increased level of risk and harm to patients. It is recognized that one person alone is often not responsible for an error but that there may be 'system failures'. There is a slight move towards a 'no-blame culture' as it is known that blame reduces the reporting of incidents from which all practitioners can learn. Fear of litigation may lead GPs to over-investigate their patients and focus attention unduly on physical aspects of ill health. For medical audit of clinical mistakes to prosper, a climate has to be created in which 'uncomfortable' episodes can be freely discussed. Practices are now analysing their complaints and reported 'significant events', and under the New GP contract there are quality points with attached remuneration for carrying out these significant-event reviews. The document '*Building a Safer NHS for Patients*'[23] sets out the blueprint for the National Patient Safety Agency (NPSA) to provide a national centralized system for recording, classifying, analysing and providing feedback on adverse events.

Patients are increasingly being involved in monitoring and standard setting through patient participation groups in practices and through their role on PCOs and national bodies.

Procedures for underperformance and 'whistle-blowing'

General practitioners have a duty to inform others if they consider that a colleague is seriously underperforming, for whatever reason.

The GMC states 'You must protect patients from risk of harm posed by another doctor's or other healthcare professional's conduct, performance or health, including problems arising from alcohol or other substance abuse. The safety of patients must come first at all times. Where there are serious concerns about a colleague's performance, health or conduct, it is essential that steps are taken without delay to investigate the concerns, to establish whether they are well-founded and to protect patients'.[24]

Formal systems are now in place to investigate and help poorly performing GPs.

Monitoring

This is an essential component of risk management. Time, financial and manpower resources are required to enable regular audits to ensure that the standards set are being met and, if not, to instigate effective change. Primary Care Organizations are assessed by the Commission for Health Audit and Improvement (CHAI) on their adherence to guidelines produced by NICE and to standards set by the NHS. In addition it is expected that CHAI will instigate special measures if it has reason to suspect that, at a practice level, the healthcare is of an unacceptably poor quality or that there are significant failings in the way a practice is run. It is expected, however, that the vast majority of general practices will be able to demonstrate a very good standard of care for patients.

Conclusion

Medical errors continue to dominate newspaper headlines. Reports from the National Audit Office clearly show that huge sums of money are spent on clinical negligence, as do reports from the medical protection organizations. There is evidence of defensive medical practice in response to the threat of litigation and there is great human suffering. Human errors in general practice can never be completely removed but their number can be dramatically lowered and the seriousness of their outcome can be markedly reduced.

However, this cannot be done without continued investment in manpower, time and financial resources. Risk management must become a priority for general practice in the future.

References

1. *MPS Risk Management Package*. Leeds: Medical Protection Society, 2000.
2. Silk N. What went wrong in 1000 negligence claims. Part 1 and Part 2. *Health Care Risk Report* 2000; **7**: 13–15 and 2001; **7**: 14–16.
3. MPS Casebook 15th July 2001, pp 20–3 (www.mps.org.uk).
4. *Problems in General Practice – Delay in Diagnosis*. London: The Medical Defence Union, 1998.
5. Clinical Negligence. In: *General Practice*. Michael Drury (Ed). Oxford: Radcliffe Medical Press, 2000.
6. *Case Studies in Medical Negligence*. The Medical and Dental Defence Union of Scotland, 2002.
7. Alberti KG. Medical errors: a common problem. It is time to get serious about them. *BMJ* 2001: **322**: 501–2.
8. *Problems in General Practice – Medication Errors*. London: The Medical Defence Union, 2001.
9. Speelman A, Savage J, Verburgh M. Use of Chaperones by general practitioners. *BMJ* 2001; **307**: 986–7.
10. R. Moore, S. Moore. *Health and Safety at Work – Guidance for General Practitioners, Practice Organisation Series 1*. London: RCGP Publications, 1999.
11. NHS Executive. *Health and Safety in General Practice – a guide to risk assessment for GPs and practice managers*. London: Health Education Authority, 1998.
12. *Confidentiality; Protecting and Providing Information*. London: General Medical Council, 2004.
13. Vincent C. *Clinical Risk Management – Enhancing Patient Safety 2nd Edn*. London: BMJ Books, 2001.
14. Lilley R, Lambden P. *Making Sense of Risk Management. A workbook for primary care*. Oxford: Radcliffe Medical Press, 2000.
15. Brandon S, Oxley J. Getting help for sick doctors. *BMS* 1997; **316 (suppl)**: 52.
16. *Reforming the NHS complaints procedure – consultation on CHAI's proposals for the independent stage*. Commission for Healthcare Audit and Inspection, 2004 (http://wwwhealthcarecommission.org.uk).
17. van Zwanenberg T, Harrison J. *Clinical Governance in Primary Care*. Oxford: Radcliffe Medical Press, 1999.
18. *Clinical Governance Bulletin* 2001: **2**: 1–12.
19. *Managing the Risks in General Practice – Common Problems*. The Medical Protection Society, 2001. (www.mps.org)
20. *The New GMS Contract*. General Practitioners Committee, The NHS Confederation, 2003 (www.bma.org.uk).
21. Irvine D, Irvine S. *Making Sense of Audit*. Oxford: Radcliffe Medical Press, 1991.
22. Royal College of General Practitioners, General Practitioner Committee. *Good Medical Practice for General Practitioners*. London: RCGP Publications, 2002.

23. *Building a Safer NHS for Patients:* 2001. Department of Health. (www.dh.gov.uk/Publicationsandstatistics/Publications/fs/en)
24. *Good Medical Practice*. GMC, 2000. (www.gmc-uk.org)

3 Emergency medicine

Roger Evans

The discipline of emergency medicine arose in response to perceived deficiencies in the management of patients who arrived at hospital unexpectedly. Such patients generally fall into two groups. First, there are those who become seriously ill outside their home environment, e.g. at their work place, and well outside the boundary of the area served by their general practitioner (GP). Had they been taken ill at home, the appropriate response would have been to contact the GP. Second, there is the group of patients who sustain injuries of a severity sufficient to need hospital-based resources, e.g. X-rays.

What an emergency medicine department does not provide

The emergency medicine department is often confused with other hospital facilities, such as the outpatient clinic. In an emergency medicine department, due to the way it is staffed, a patient will not get a long consultation with a senior doctor in the same way that they might in an outpatient clinic. In general, emergency medicine department doctors are discouraged from making referrals direct to outpatient clinics in other specialties, as this may duplicate the work of the GP. Also, this would cut the GP out of the information loop and a major player in the provision of healthcare is left unaware of what is happening to their patient.

Emergency medicine departments neither provide services as an alternative to visiting the GP (patients who are on holiday can avail themselves of the temporary resident service from a local GP), nor do they offer second opinions regarding a diagnosis made by the patient's GP. Where a patient has a long-term problem it is best that they remain under the supervision of their GP in order to ensure continuity of care. It is much easier to be certain that the patient is receiving appropriate treatment if they are managed on a long-term basis, which then allows improvement or deterioration in their condition to be easily identified. During a single visit to an emergency medicine department, background knowledge of this type is usually unavailable and frequently leads to problems. Patients are indeed often unaware of what can and cannot be reasonably expected from a visit to an emergency unit

How do emergency medicine departments differ?

Emergency medicine departments may differ widely in the extent of the services they offer. Major units, usually based in large teaching hospitals, will see >100,000 patients per year and will be supported by a range of other disciplines, e.g. acute medicine, trauma/orthopaedics, paediatrics and neurosurgery. At the other extreme are the small 'cottage' hospitals. These are usually run by specially trained nurses, known as emergency nurse practitioners (ENPs), who are often supported by local GPs or by doctors from a nearby larger emergency medicine department, based at a district general hospital (DGH). Such a minor injuries unit (MIU) may see fewer than 1000 patients per year.

The majority of departments, however, are based in DGHs and these will be supported by major disciplines, such as acute medicine, surgery and paediatrics, but will often lack some of the more specialist units, such as neurosurgery or ophthalmology. This does mean that certain categories of patients, e.g. those with serious head injuries, may need to be referred to a nearby specialist hospital for treatment of complications (such as an extradural haematoma, see below).

Common mistakes

As a patient can present in an emergency medicine department with an illness or injury affecting any body system, it is impossible to cover all errors that might occur. This chapter therefore focuses on those areas that most frequently cause problems and the descriptions of the various conditions tend to be the classical ones. Unfortunately, life is not that simple and atypical presentations occur in many of the disorders outlined. This makes diagnosis a much more complex process and leaves it open to understandable errors.

Missed fractures

A common cause of a complaint made against an emergency medicine department for alleged substandard treatment is where a bony injury is missed. This may occur for one of four reasons:

- The doctor decides on the basis of an interview and examination that it is unlikely that a patient has sustained any underlying bony damage and hence it is pointless to request radiographic examination. This decision is usually made on the basis that when the injured part, e.g. an ankle, is examined, no bony tenderness is identified over the lateral or medial malleoli (the bumps on the inner and outer sides of the joint), the base of the fifth metatarsal, etc. Various bodies have drawn up guidelines to help make the decision as to whether or not to X-ray an ankle, e.g. the Ottawa Rules. These are often used, particularly in units run by ENPs.
- The doctor arranges an X-ray examination but fails to identify an abnormality on the films. Sometimes the abnormality is obvious and should have been picked up, but on other occasions the fracture may be extremely difficult to pick out or occasionally may not be identifiable. Many emergency medicine departments have arrangements in place to ensure that radiographs are subsequently reviewed by a specialist radiologist.
- X-ray films may be of inadequate quality, e.g. they may be under- or overexposed, thus obscuring the bony damage, or they may not cover the whole of the structure. An important mistake may occur when X-raying the cervical spine, i.e. the bones of the neck. X-rays of this area are normally taken from three directions (from the front, the side, and an open-mouth view). The side (lateral) view should include the whole of the cervical spine, from the base of the skull to its junction with the dorsal spine. Injuries to the neck often occur at the lower part of the cervical spine and failure to include good views of this area can result in significant injuries being missed, with catastrophic consequences.
- An X-ray of the wrong area is sometimes requested, e.g. an attempt may be made to exclude fractures to the facial bones on X-rays of the skull, whereas special facial views are necessary.

In an attempt to avoid or correct errors of interpretation two mechanisms have been instituted in many hospitals. First, the so-called 'red dot' whereby the radiographer who has taken the film, while inspecting it for quality, also seeks to identify any abnormalities on the basis that they will probably have many years of experience in reviewing films and hence their opinion is useful, if not definitive. Where an abnormality is identified a marker, such as a sticky red paper dot, is attached to the X-rays as an alert before they are returned to the emergency medicine department.

Second, most hospitals run an X-ray review system and in the 21st century there is no excuse for not having such a service. When the X-ray has been taken it is sent back to the emergency medicine department and interpreted by the doctor who requested it (who may be relatively junior and inexperienced).

The doctor writes their interpretation on the X-ray request form and when the patient has been discharged, the films are returned to the radiology department. Within 24 hours the films are reviewed by a consultant radiologist, who formally reports the radiographs and where there is a mismatch, i.e. the radiologist has identified a fracture missed by the emergency medicine department doctor, a recall procedure is set in motion. The patient is then asked to return to the department for further investigation and any treatment that is felt to be appropriate.

Scaphoid fractures

One of the most notorious missed fractures is that of the scaphoid. The scaphoid is a small bone in the wrist, the carpus, and it characteristically fractures in young men who sustain hyperextension injuries to their wrist, i.e. the wrist is forced backwards by, for instance, a fall onto the outstretched hand. The patient complains of pain in the wrist but there is often a paucity of physical signs, apart from the presence of tenderness in the 'anatomical snuff box' (in the wrist, near the base of the thumb).

Problems occur in diagnosing scaphoid fractures because of the relative normality of the injured wrist on examination and the fact that if an X-ray is taken within a short time of the fracture occurring, the damage to the bone may not be visible. The fracture only appears 10–14 days later as the repair progress is initiated.

Guidelines have evolved in order to minimize these difficulties. For most wrist injuries the usual two radiographic views are obtained, but to exclude a scaphoid fracture, four 'scaphoid views' are normally taken. If any doubt remains or pain continues, the radiographic examination should be repeated in 10–14 days, by which time the fracture may be more obvious on the radiographs.

Severed nerves and tendons

Wounds to certain areas, in particular the wrist/hand, may be complicated in that not only has the implement (broken glass, sharp metal) damaged the skin and subcutaneous blood vessels but it has penetrated deeply enough to damage nerves and tendons. Damage to such structures means that the patient can be left with a major impairment of their manual dexterity and nerves/tendons need to be repaired promptly in order to secure the best possible result. 'Best possible result' does not necessarily mean that the hand will regain 100% of its function but a primary repair (i.e. one undertaken soon after the accident has occurred) will, in general terms, be easier to perform and give a better final result than a secondary repair (i.e. where the repair has been delayed for weeks or even months).

Wounds must be carefully inspected and the examination should be meticulous in order to exclude such damage, which must be assumed to have occurred in injuries to the wrist, hand, ankle and foot.

Retained foreign bodies

Where a patient sustains a wound, e.g. when glass shatters in the hand, it is always possible that foreign bodies may be retained within the substance of the wound.

Foreign bodies fall into two categories:

- those which show up on X-ray, i.e. the radio-opaque ones, such as glass or metal
- those which are radiolucent and do not show up on X-rays, such as plastic or wood.

The most common foreign body to be left in a wound is a shard of broken glass and where there is any chance of fragments of glass being retained, then prior to the wound being sutured, the area should be X-rayed, so that any glass fragments can be identified and removed. Contrary to popular misconception, most glass is radio-opaque. Whilst X-rays will pick out metallic fragments, even large wooden splinters will not be demonstrated on radiographs and where there are suspicions that such a foreign body may be present, the investigation of choice is an ultrasound scan. Ultrasound scans, however, are not as easily or rapidly available as plain X-rays.

If a foreign body is not removed, then the wound may take longer to heal and indeed may not heal at all, as it persistently breaks down due to infection (even when this appears to have been adequately treated with an antibiotic). However, it is not always absolutely necessary to remove all inert foreign bodies, e.g. glass or metal, and indeed on some occasions if the foreign body is not causing any problems more harm than good may result from pointless interference.

Chest pain

There are very many causes of chest pain but the ones it is important to rule out and investigate/treat are those caused by ischaemic heart disease (IHD). Ischaemia means a lack of a satisfactory blood supply to an area, in this case the myocardium or heart muscle. In the vast majority of cases of IHD, this is due to narrowing of one or both of the coronary arteries. These conditions are grouped together under the term 'acute coronary syndrome', which includes myocardial infarction (heart attack, coronary thrombosis) and unstable angina.

Other major causes of chest pain include pulmonary embolism, dissecting aneurysm, spontaneous pneumothorax and pneumonia/pleurisy, although there are many others. Sometimes, especially in very young and elderly patients, chest pain may prove to be 'referred pain' from some intra-abdominal disease.

When a patient presents with chest pain, IHD needs to be ruled out and the most important facet of the consultation is the history, which must be comprehensive. Useful investigations include the electrocardiogram (ECG), chest X-ray and various tests to identify the presence of markers of myocardial damage, such as raised cardiac enzyme and muscle protein levels in the blood. Standard management of such patients would include taking a full history, identifying exacerbating and relieving factors for the chest pain, and those conditions that predispose to the development of IHD, such as a strong family history of the disease, heavy smoking and ongoing health problems [such as diabetes or hypertension (high blood pressure)]. Following this the patient should be examined, with particular attention being paid to the cardiovascular system, and then any investigations felt to be necessary should be requested.

Classically a patient with IHD presents complaining of a heavy/crushing central chest pain, which may radiate up to the shoulders, down the arms, through to the back or up into the neck and jaw. This may be associated with faintness/dizziness, nausea, vomiting and apprehension. However, there are considerable variations in the presentation and, especially in elderly patients, there may be no chest pain (a 'silent' heart attack).

Where there is a reasonable suspicion that a patient has IHD, then it is wise to retain them within the department for several hours, in order to repeat investigations, such as the ECG. It is useful to repeat the ECG because in a small percentage of cases, even in the face of a frank myocardial infarct, the initial ECG may appear normal.

Abdominal pain

As with chest pain, there are many causes of abdominal pain and it is often not possible precisely to identify the reason why a patient has presented with pain.

Common conditions which cause significant problems if left undiagnosed are:

- appendicitis
- a perforation of part of the bowel, e.g. a duodenal ulcer

- ectopic pregnancy
- pelvic inflammatory disease
- acute pancreatitis
- other causes, including aortic aneurysm, renal and biliary colic, intestinal obstruction.

Appendicitis classically presents with a history of gradually worsening abdominal pain which is originally central in situation but which migrates to the right iliac fossa, and which is associated with a mild fever, nausea/ vomiting and bowel disturbance, which could be either diarrhoea or constipation. On examination the patient is tender in the right iliac fossa, i.e. low down on the right side of the abdomen, and may be guarding the area, i.e. reflexly tensing the muscles of the anterior abdominal wall to prevent the examiner's hand exerting pressure on the inflamed contents. A rectal examination may be helpful in eliciting tenderness high up on the right side but unfortunately there is no diagnostic investigation, although the patient's white blood cell count may be elevated.

Unfortunately, as with IHD, while there is a classical presentation, a significant percentage (up to 50%) of patients (especially the very young and very old) with acute appendicitis may present atypically, e.g. with symptoms suggestive of a urinary tract infection.

A *perforated duodenal ulcer* should be suspected where the patient arrives with a history of sudden onset of severe abdominal pain and has board-like rigidity of the abdominal wall musculature when examined. The diagnostic investigation in this case is an upright chest X-ray, which, in a significant percentage of cases, reveals the presence of free air beneath the diaphragm.

Ectopic pregnancy must be considered in any sexually active female of child-bearing age, particularly if there is a history of a missed period.

Pelvic inflammatory disease again is a problem associated with young, sexually active females and tends to be linked with the presence of menstrual irregularity, vaginal discharge and grumbling lower-abdominal pain.

Pancreatitis can be associated with gallstones and excessive alcohol intake. The diagnostic investigation is the estimation of the level of the enzyme amylase in the blood, as this is released from the damaged pancreas.

Head injuries

When a patient sustains a head injury, damage to the brain may occur immediately, i.e. a primary brain injury, and such damage is usually irreparable.

Subsequent investigation and treatment is aimed at preventing secondary brain damage, which occurs when bleeding takes place inside the skull but outside the brain, producing either a subdural or extradural haematoma. This causes compression and hypoxia, i.e. a reduction in the level of oxygen reaching the brain, with the hypoxia exacerbating any primary brain damage that has occurred.

When a patient presents at an emergency medicine department with a head injury, management is usually aided by guidelines produced by bodies such as the Royal Colleges of Surgeons, which help the doctor to decide which patients need to be X-rayed, which need to be admitted to hospital for observation, etc. Those admitted are started on neurological observation charts and various parameters, such as their Glasgow Coma Scale, pupillary reaction and heart rate are measured at half-hourly or hourly intervals in order to detect any deterioration in their condition. If deterioration is noted, then other investigations are brought into play, such as computerized tomography (CT) scanning. Where the scan reveals a developing intracranial haematoma, arrangements are made to transfer the patient to a neurosurgical centre, where the haematoma will be evacuated.

The outcome for the patient depends upon the extent of the primary brain damage and any secondary damage that develops, e.g. due to delay in diagnosis and treatment.

Subarachnoid haemorrhage

This condition occurs when a small defect (an aneurysm) in the wall of one of the arteries in the base of the brain ruptures and blood is released into the fluid that surrounds and cushions the brain—the cerebrospinal fluid.

Subarachnoid haemorrhage (SAH) characteristically presents with a history of a very severe headache, often described as the most severe the patient has ever experienced, which comes on suddenly and which may be associated with nausea and vomiting.

The patient may collapse and be transiently unconscious, and over the course of the next few hours the patient may start to complain of neck stiffness. They may, for instance, be unable to touch their chest with their chin. The investigation of choice for the diagnosis of an SAH is a CT scan of the head and the treatment of choice is early coiling or clipping of the intracranial aneurysm.

Meningitis

Meningitis implies inflammation of the membranes surrounding the brain, i.e. inflammation of the meninges. Meningitis may be secondary to an infection with various types of organisms, such as bacteria or viruses, of which the most feared is the bacterium *Neisseria meningitidis.* This organism causes the so-called meningococcal meningitis, a disease that commonly afflicts the very young and that classically presents with fever, headache, nausea/vomiting and drowsiness. The most terrifying manifestation of a meningococcal infection, however, is septicaemia, which occurs when the organism gets into the blood and multiplies there. This condition can proceed with frightening rapidity, so that a patient who was able to go to school on one day can be dead the following morning. A diagnostic sign of this condition in an unwell, febrile child, is a petechial rash, i.e. spots that when pressed with a glass slide do not blanch (disappear).

Any delay in diagnosing this condition usually results in the patient's death or them being left with a major neurological disability. The problem in the diagnosis and management of meningococcal septicaemia is that its initial presentation is often non-specific. It is impossible to pick out the one irritable, febrile child who is going to develop meningococcal septicaemia, from the vast number of other children who present in exactly the same fashion, with nothing worse than a viral, upper respiratory tract infection.

Slipped upper femoral epiphysis

In children between the ages of about 11 and 14 years, when the skeleton is still immature, there is sometimes a disruption in the thigh bone or femur, at the point where the head/neck of the bone forms an angle with the shaft, to make up part of the hip joint. At the growing point (or physis) in the neck of the femur, there is a slippage of bone on bone, resulting in disruption of the normal anatomy, which if uncorrected will result in a major permanent disability.

Patients with this condition often present with a limp, which may have begun following an apparently minor mishap or even with no history of an injury to the leg. Patients complain of hip pain or occasionally of knee pain, as pain from the hip can be referred to the knee.

This condition always needs to be considered in a limping child, as failure to diagnose and correct a slipped upper femoral epiphysis early can leave the child with a major, life-long disability.

Spinal cord compression

The spinal cord is an extension of the brain and, like the brain, it tolerates compression and hypoxia badly. The most common remediable cause for such compression is a *central* prolapse of an intervertebral disc, usually in the lumbar region, where the bulging disc presses on a leash of nerves which supply the lower part of the body, the so-called cauda equina. Pressure on the cauda equina characteristically results in the patient complaining of low back pain which radiates down both buttocks and into the legs. This is subsequently associated with the development of lower limb weakness and an inability to initiate micturition, i.e. the passing of urine. Subsequently, difficulties with the bowel and sexual function occur, i.e. an inability to achieve and maintain an erection.

This is another condition that needs to be diagnosed early by a magnetic resonance imaging (MRI) scan, with decompressive surgery being performed swiftly. If the pressure is not removed from the cauda equina, the aforementioned problems may well become irreversible. However, many patients with low back pain do not have *central* disc prolapse, but have localized pressure on the nerves from other causes, with less serious sequelae. Like meningitis, the diagnostic challenge is distinguishing one from the other.

Conclusion

This chapter covers the classical descriptions of some of the more common conditions seen in a Department of Emergency Medicine. Unfortunately, atypical presentations occur in many of the disorders outlined. This makes diagnosis a complex process.

4 Intensive care medicine

John H Coakley and Charles J Hinds

Intensive care medicine (ICM) is a relatively new discipline. The first intensive care units (ICUs) were opened in the 1950s in the USA and Europe, and were developed in response to technological advances which allowed long-term respiratory support for patients with breathing difficulties. Such support was first shown to be effective during the polio epidemics of the 1950s; at around the same time, it was recognized that some patients could benefit from respiratory assistance after long or complex surgical procedures. Thus, it was the provision of respiratory support for patients with medical and surgical conditions that led to the evolution of present day intensive care. Initially, because of the requirement for expertise in mechanical ventilatory support, the specialty most involved in ICM, at least in the UK, was anaesthesia. The development of means of supporting other organs, and the need for investigation, diagnosis and treatment of the underlying condition, has led to increasing recognition that ICM is a multidisciplinary medical activity with input from anaesthetists, physicians and surgeons. This is most effective when directed and coordinated by a committed specialist in the field. In addition to the medical staff, there is a requirement for considerable support from nurses, physiotherapists, dieticians, pharmacists, radiographers and others. It can be appreciated, therefore, that running a modern ICU is a complex undertaking.

An intensive care specialist is difficult to define, but an 'intensivist' is recognized as a doctor who:

- has completed a recognized programme of ICM training and holds a qualification in ICM. This might include a certificate of completion of specialist training in ICM and the European or UK Diploma in ICM. More senior intensivists (such as the authors) may not hold these qualifications because their training predated such examinations
- devotes a substantial proportion of their clinical work to the practice of ICM
- recognizes the contribution of multidisciplinary teamwork to successful patient outcomes.

What does intensive care involve?

The ICU provides life-sustaining support for patients who have potentially reversible disease processes. It also provides support for patients after major elective or emergency surgical procedures. Traditionally, two levels of support have been defined for the critically ill patient: the intensive care patient generally has either two or more organ failures or severe respiratory failure and requires 1 : 1 nursing care; and the high dependency unit (HDU) patient does not have severe respiratory failure requiring prolonged mechanical ventilation and therefore requires less close nursing supervision with one nurse looking after two to four patients. These distinctions are artificial, and there is increasing recognition that both ICU and HDU patients are best managed in the same or adjacent units by the same medical and nursing teams. The management of these patients is complex and requires:

- a team of highly trained nurses, with many having an ICU nursing qualification
- treatment that is closely supervised by specifically-trained medical staff
- immediate availability of skilled medical staff at all times of day and night
- medical and nursing leadership
- input from other medical disciplines and professionals allied to medicine.

In addition to the staffing requirements of the ICU, there is the need for complex and expensive equipment, especially for continuous monitoring of vital functions, such as heart rate, blood pressure and breathing. This equipment is also often sensitive and therefore requires staff with expertise in managing it. Patients on an ICU may have complex illnesses, which requires the intensivist to pay great attention to detail when managing organ support. They should also be skilled in ensuring adequate communication, coordinating care and providing experienced input for any ethical dilemmas that may arise.

Organizational requirements

There are essentially two methods of organizing the delivery of medical care on the ICU, with units being 'open' or 'closed'. On both types of unit, nurses specifically trained in ICU deliver care, but medical input on an open unit is from the referring team and other specialists who may be asked for their advice. In other words, the team under whose care the patient was admitted continues to provide medical care on the ICU. The advantage of an open unit is that there is continuity of medical care from ward to ICU and back. The major difficulty, however, is that at any time there will be many medical teams with patients on the ICU, and thus many ward rounds all occurring at unpredictable times. In addition, some patients will be under the care of more than one referring medical team. This is a recipe for conflicting instructions, frequent changes in management decisions, mismanagement and poor communication.

In a closed unit, irrespective of the source of referral, the ICU medical team assumes overall responsibility for patient care, usually with continuing input from the referring team and other specialists as required ('shared care', 'semi-closed unit'). A closed unit has the added advantage of a dedicated team of intensive care specialists who keep up-to-date with recent developments in the field. There is persuasive evidence to suggest that patient outcomes are better on closed than on open units.

The role of the ICU doctors is complex and involves:

- recognition of the multidisciplinary nature of the job
- coordination of care with involvement of the referring team, and other supportive disciplines, such as radiology, microbiology and other laboratory services
- investigation and diagnosis both of the underlying condition and of the organ failures that develop as a result of it
- timely intervention to deal with the complications of the disease or its treatment
- management of the medical workforce
- ensuring that adequate facilities (equipment, storage space, drugs) are available to deliver the service
- evaluating new developments and instituting guidelines and protocols for treatment.

There are many difficulties in the safe provision of ICM. One of the major problems is the requirement for highly trained nurses. They are a scarce resource at present, and there are frequent examples of ICU beds being available, but not the nursing staff to provide the clinical care required. The authors calculated a few years ago that if all the physically available ICU beds in North East Thames could be staffed with nurses, the requirement to transfer patients for non-clinical reasons (see below) would be abolished.

There are also difficulties in the provision of medical trainees in ICU. Recent reductions in the duration of training for doctors, together with the progressive reduction in the working hours of trainees, has led to fewer man-hours being available than is required to provide a service. While many of these changes have been laudable and long overdue, they have occurred at a rate faster than the expansion of training and consultant grades.

The other major issue facing ICM is that the workload is variable; at times of peak demand the capacity to provide care may be compromized.

It is generally accepted that to cope with the peaks and troughs of demand, the ICU should operate with an average bed occupancy of 70%. Most ICUs in the UK, however, operate at >90% occupancy, and transfers from one hospital to another become inevitable. These events by definition occur with an ICU operating at maximum capacity, and usually lead to depletion of medical and nursing staff who must accompany a critically ill patient being transferred to another hospital.

There are obviously occasions when a patient will need to be transferred from one ICU to another for perfectly legitimate reasons (e.g. for specialist treatment). This is called a clinical transfer, as opposed to a non-clinical transfer, which occurs simply because there is no available ICU bed in the host hospital. The transfer of ICU patients, particularly for non-clinical reasons, poses an extreme clinical risk and there is a heightened risk of litigation. There is increasing recognition that the use of 'retrieval teams' may help in times of crisis. These are teams of specifically trained doctors, nurses and paramedical staff, who are available to transfer critically ill patients from one unit to another. Retrieval teams are most often used for the transfer of critically ill children, but it is likely that their use will spread to encompass adult transfers.

The other source of dissatisfaction, which potentially leads to complaints and litigation, is the timing of admission to and discharge from the ICU. Many intensivists will be familiar with the frequently expressed views of relatives that the 'patient should have been on the ICU yesterday' or that 'the patient needs another day on the ICU'. Often there is an element of truth in these views. There has been an appreciation for some time that care delivered on the wards may be inappropriate and lead to delayed admission to the ICU. This occurs both because of misunderstandings about the ability of ward staff to deliver care to the highly dependent patient, and also a failure to recognize impending deterioration and death.[1] In addition, it has recently been demonstrated that patients discharged from the ICU between 10 pm and 7 am have a higher mortality than those discharged during the working day. Those discharged between midnight and 5 am fare even worse.[2]

For the above reasons many hospitals, in part due to the document *Comprehensive Critical Care*,[3] have set up outreach teams and published referral criteria for ICU.

Dangers of intensive care medicine

Many of the life support techniques used on the ICU involve the insertion of sharp objects or tubes into various body parts and cavities. A fairly typical ICU patient will have the following devices *in situ*.

An *endotracheal tube* or *tracheostomy* (see Figure 5.1, page 58) secures the airway and allows mechanical ventilation of the lungs. They are inserted through the mouth or nose, or directly into the trachea, usually under general anaesthetic. They may be misplaced into the oesophagus or advanced too far (into the bronchi) or not far enough. A patient, relative or member of staff may unexpectedly remove them (not always accidentally). This may prove fatal.

Most ICU patients will have a *nasogastric tube* passed via the nose (or occasionally the mouth) directly into the stomach. This is used either to aspirate gastric contents, or more often as a route for the administration of nasogastric feed or drugs. These tubes are frequently misplaced and if this happens it is important that they are repositioned before being used to administer feed or drugs. Failure to recognize that such a tube is misplaced may lead to a catastrophic sudden failure of oxygenation and later severe pneumonia.

Arterial pressure monitoring devices may be inserted into an artery in the wrist, elbow or groin. *Central venous lines* are inserted into large veins in the neck, chest or groin. These lines are used to measure arterial and venous pressures continuously, while central venous lines are also used to administer irritant drugs. They may be inserted into the wrong vessel, they may rupture or otherwise damage the vessel, or lead to infection. Venous line insertion into the neck or chest may puncture the lung and lead to a pneumothorax (collapse of the lung due to the escape of air around it) or bleeding into the chest (haemothorax). Failure to recognize misplacement may lead to the administration of fluids into the pleural cavity. Any of these complications could prove fatal if not recognized and treated appropriately. The risk of central venous cannulation may be reduced by the use of ultrasound guidance to locate a large vein. The National Institute of Clinical Excellence has recently recommended that ultrasound guidance should be considered for difficult line insertion, but this has not yet been translated into routine clinical practice, in part because of the cost and training implications.

A *pulmonary artery flotation catheter (PAFC)* or *Swan-Ganz catheter* is usually inserted to monitor more accurately the performance of the heart and to allow precise dose adjustment of drugs designed to boost cardiac output or elevate blood pressure. The technique of insertion is initially the same as for a central venous pressure line, but the PAFC has an inflatable balloon at the tip, which allows it to be floated into the pulmonary artery. It is subject to the same complications as the central venous line, but in addition may cause infection of the valves on the right side of the heart, and may also knot in the heart or pulmonary artery and become difficult to remove. The PAFC is occasionally inserted under radiographic control.

The potent pharmacological agents used in the critically ill may also be associated with damage, especially when infusions are misplaced. Most ICU patients will receive a number of infusions (sedatives, pain killers, paralysing drugs, agents to raise or lower blood pressure, electrolytes) in addition to a large range of other drugs that are given by injection (such as anticoagulants, antibiotics and other antimicrobial agents). All of these may lead to adverse reactions and most have not been subjected to rigorous scientific evaluation in the critically ill patient population.

The devices used to secure continuous infusion at accurate rates may malfunction or even, very rarely, be deliberately interfered with.

In patients with failure of the kidneys it is usually necessary to provide artificial renal support. This requires the insertion of a large double lumen vascular device into a large vein. Blood is pumped out of one lumen, passed through the artificial kidney, and then returned to the patient via the other lumen. The risks of insertion of such a device are the same as for central venous line insertion, but perhaps magnified because the device is much larger than a conventional central venous line, and the patients tend to be much more ill (possibly having problems due to failure of adequate blood clotting).

Litigation

There are approximately 20 cases of intensive-care-related litigation per year in England and Wales (NHSLA, personal communication). Most litigation relating to ICM involves failure to make a correct diagnosis, failure to recognize complications or failure to observe postoperatively. These together account for >50% of the claims (National Health Service Litigation Authority [NHSLA], personal communication). Fewer than 10% of claims involve equipment failure, drug errors or problems with the airway or ventilation.

This illustrates the importance not just of immediate resuscitation and subsequently providing support to failing organs, but also of making a timely diagnosis so that the underlying disease precipitating ICU admission may be expeditiously dealt with. It is also vital to observe and monitor the patient closely so that complications may be corrected in a timely manner, or preferably prevented. The section above illustrated the considerable number of complications that may affect patients by virtue of the equipment used to treat them, and intensivists must act with vigilance at all times. It is likely that in future litigation surrounding transfers of patients from ICUs and failure to provide proper postoperative observation will increase as awareness of the appropriate standards of care among patients and their relatives increases.

Unrealistic expectations

It is important to recognize that expectation of what is possible in ICM sometimes exceeds the capacity of the ICU to deliver. This applies to patients and their relatives, and, to an extent, to medical and other hospital staff. These apparent shortcomings occasionally lead to serious disagreement between ICU staff and others, and have the potential to lead to complaints and litigation.

Changing outcomes

ICM, like many other specialties, has seen significant advances in recent years. It should be borne in mind that a condition that may have been unsurviveable only a few years ago may now be associated with a reasonable expectation of recovery. It is important to remember that care should be judged by the standards at the time it was delivered rather than those of the present.

Avoidance of litigation

The risk of litigation may be reduced by addressing the organizational factors which are likely to lead to litigation. High-quality ICM requires a properly trained, highly skilled cadre of nurses, with adequate provision of other essential staff, such as physiotherapists, dieticians, pharmacists and technical support staff.

It is likely that as the demands on medical staff increase there will be a tendency to employ medical staff with specific training in ICM and who devote an increasing proportion of their working week to ICM, rather than indulging in occasional ICM practice.

A number of other factors may reduce the risk of litigation. If litigation does occur the same factors may bring about a greater chance of a successful defence. These might include:

- guidelines for timely referral to the ICU, which may be activated by doctors and other healthcare professionals
- provision of follow-up services in the wards for patients discharged from the ICU
- regular multidisciplinary unit meetings
- analysis of critical incidents and serious adverse events

- written protocols and guidelines for ICU management, agreed, accepted and implemented by all medical and other staff
- 'evidence-based' approach
- recognition that the patient being transferred from one ICU to another or from an ICU to another facility (e.g. the operating theatre or radiology department) is at high risk, and the monitoring must be of an equivalent standard to that provided on the ICU.

References

1. McQuillan P, Pilkington S, Allan A, *et al.* Confidential inquiry into quality of care before admission to intensive care. *Br Med J* 1998; 316: 1853–8.
2. Goldfrad C, Rowan K. Consequences of discharges from intensive care at night. *Lancet* 2000; 355: 1138–42.
3. Department of Health. *Comprehensive Critical Care: A Review of Adult Critical Care Services.* London: Department of Health, 2000.

5 General anaesthesia

Tom EJ Healy

There have been many important advances in medicine, such as the introduction of penicillin, insulin and smallpox vaccination, but perhaps only the discovery of the anaesthetic effects of ether can be said to have 'divided mankind into those who came before it and those who came after it'. Anaesthesia has been the key which has opened the door to all the advances in surgery, to the developments in interventional radiology, to many advances in general medicine and, with the introduction of antibiotics, to many of the advances in obstetrics. Indeed without the skills of the anaesthetist some specialties, such as intensive care, would not exist. The discovery of anaesthesia was and will remain the single most important event in medical progress.

This chapter examines aspects of general anaesthesia, identifying some of the established failures in practice.

Preoperative information and assessment

Space does not allow an exhaustive account but the general principles are as follows: the patient and the intended operation must be identified and, if relevant, the correct side for surgery confirmed, e.g. amputation of the left leg. It must also be confirmed that the procedure and the risks associated with the anaesthetic and surgery have been explained to the patient. This must be done by the surgeon and/or the anaesthetist in a formal and agreed way, and not left to chance. For those patients who are not competent to take the decision because of age, mental health or unconsciousness, different considerations apply. Careful attention to issues about consent are essential. Many chronic medical diseases (e.g. diabetes, hypertension) increase the risks associated with anaesthesia and the anaesthetist must identify these and the question 'Do these conditions affect the patient's lifestyle?' must be answered.

A patient's physical status is usually assessed using the American Society of Anesthesiologists (ASA) classification:[1]

- ASA 1—the patient has no disease process other than that requiring surgery.
- ASA 2—mild to moderate systemic disease, e.g. diabetes, mild hypertension, obesity, mild respiratory or cardiac disease, mild anaemia.
- ASA 3—disease limits lifestyle. Severe systemic disease, e.g. cardiac disease, angina, severe diabetes.
- ASA 4—systemic disease which is a constant threat to life e.g. renal failure.
- ASA 5—moribund with little hope of success but surgery the only hope.

Certain investigations may be necessary and the results of these must be available before anaesthesia commences. Anaesthetists normally delay surgery when the patient's haemoglobin level is <10 g per 100 ml (the normal range being between $12-18$ g/ml), although in those with severe chronic renal disease, much lower haemoglobin levels are accepted. When surgical treatment is urgent or the patient is bleeding, the haemoglobin level can be raised quickly by blood transfusion.

Cardiorespiratory status must be considered when planning anaesthetic care. It is sensible to arrange an electrocardiograph for any patient with cardiac symptoms, such as an irregular pulse, angina or hypertension, but also for those aged over 55 years. Evidence of a previous but 'silent' myocardial infarction will indicate a need for careful monitoring and special caution to be taken in order to prevent variations in blood pressure and to ensure the maintenance of a stable cardiac output. The chest examination or a history of chronic respiratory disease, such as emphysema, chronic bronchitis or severe asthmatic disease, may indicate the need for a chest X-ray and pulmonary function studies.

It is essential to establish whether the patient has a history of epilepsy, as some agents used during general anaesthesia may cause or permit grand mal convulsions, while others are anticonvulsant. If a patient does have a history of epilepsy or convulsions it is wise to select those agents that are anticonvulsant.

The secretion of hydrocortisone by the adrenal cortex increases during stress, but when steroid therapy has been given, particularly over a prolonged period, the adrenocorticotrophic hormone (ACTH) secreted by the pituitary gland may be suppressed and the adrenal cortex atrophies and may not respond to stress by increasing hydrocortisone secretion. Profound hypotension may occur. It may be necessary to give booster doses of hydrocortisone.

The management of diabetes presents a special problem because of the need to fast before, during and following surgery. The safe management of these patients is now well described and requires intravenous insulin balanced with sugar solutions during and after surgery. Pre- and postoperative blood sugar levels must be measured, and intraoperative measurements should also be taken during prolonged surgery so that the anaesthetist can make appropriate adjustments.

Patients with thyroid disease, e.g. those with thyrotoxicosis (overactive thyroid) and an enlarged thyroid gland, may, if the gland is retrosternal, develop respiratory obstruction, so extra care is necessary. They may also show a tachycardia (fast heart rate) with atrial fibrillation (an abnormality in the rhythm of the heart). Those with a hypothyroid (underactive thyroid) function may exhibit a bradycardia (slow heart rate) and congestive cardiac (heart) failure. There are many other signs and symptoms associated with thyroid disease but the above are given as examples to reinforce the need to examine each patient fully.

Details of any physical handicaps must be noted. The back and neck are particularly common sites of pain. Arms and legs may not have a full range of movements. A failure to support the back or the neck, or to permit excessive movement of the arms, legs or hips may result in significant postoperative pain and even nerve and other damage.

Prisoners are a special group of patients. Security is essential but no patient may be anaesthetized if they are handcuffed or secured to the operating trolley. It is essential to be able to change a patient's position without delay in an emergency. Many prisoners have a real fear of the effects of anaesthesia and their human dignity must be protected at all times. Guards can be stationed outside the theatre doors.

The anaesthetist is required to question the patient about any previous experience with general anaesthesia, in particular adverse events. Serious allergic-like reactions to a drug can be prevented by avoiding the use of that drug and other closely related drugs. For example, a death occurred during an anaphylactic reaction following an injection of vecuronium. The patient had previously suffered a similar reaction following an injection of pancuronium. The chemical structures of pancuronium and vecuronium are almost identical. Anaphylactic and anaphylactoid reactions are clinically indistinguishable, but in the case of anaphylactoid reactions a previous experience with the drug or a closely related drug is unnecessary. The common presenting signs of these (the most frightening reactions seen in the anaesthetized patient) include:

- severe bronchospasm—laryngeal oedema and laryngospasm
- cardiovascular collapse—severe tachycardia, profound hypotension and hypoxia

- cutaneous signs—erythema (cherry red), urticaria, flushing and facial oedema
- level of consciousness—conscious patient rendered unconscious.

Such reactions present anaesthetic emergencies that require prompt recognition and appropriate, immediate treatment.

It is important to establish whether there has been a previous history of allergy and if there is a possibility of pregnancy. The anaesthetist should identify all drugs being taken, including the oral contraceptive. Alcohol intake is important as this may explain a resistance to some anaesthetic drugs, but may also, if cirrhosis is present, prolong recovery from drugs which are metabolized or excreted by the liver. Monoamine oxidase inhibitors (MAOIs) may lead to life-threatening reactions if patients taking them are given pethidine, morphine or fentanyl.

Clinical examination must include the heart, chest and lungs, but should also include assessment of the neck and other joint mobility. Examination of the patient's ability to open their mouth to allow tracheal intubation, even if intubation is not proposed, and the state of the teeth, including the presence of crowns and loose teeth, is essential. The patient should be asked to acknowledge the presence of any loose teeth and a note should be made in the clinical record. Loose teeth, if dislodged may be inhaled. If a tooth is 'lost' a chest X-ray may be necessary.

Certain blood tests are necessary, e.g. for patients of African or Mediterranean descent, a sickle test is necessary to exclude sickle-cell disease. This is a condition in which the round red blood cells become sickle-shaped when cold or in reduced oxygen situations. The sickle-shaped cells can cause thrombosis. Blood urea, electrolyte and creatinine measurements are essential for patients who are taking diuretic medication or who have renal impairment.

General anaesthesia

The periods of general anaesthesia may be considered under the headings induction, maintenance and recovery.

Induction

All monitors must be attached and pre-anaesthetic values recorded. In particular oxygen haemoglobin saturation, expired carbon dioxide concentration, pulse rate and an electrocardiograph must be displayed continuously.

Automatic blood pressure recordings must be recorded before and following induction and regularly (usually every five minutes) thereafter.

The induction of general anaesthesia describes the initial period during which anaesthetic drugs are introduced and the patient's level of consciousness is reduced until they are unresponsive to stimulation. Anaesthesia may be induced by the patient inhaling an anaesthetic drug or by intravenous injection of a drug such as propofol, thiopentone, etomidate or ketamine. Ketamine may also be given intramuscularly. Etomidate is frequently used for frail, debilitated patients, but propofol, introduced in 1981, is now a widely used induction drug. However, a fall in blood pressure may follow its use and therefore ketamine remains of value for those patients who are compensating for a reduced blood volume or who are hypotensive. Ketamine causes a rise in blood pressure but also has ganglion-blocking activity and may paradoxically cause a fall in blood pressure when combined with other drugs that interfere with ganglionic (at nerve endings) transmission. Ketamine may also cause hallucinations and very unpleasant dreams during recovery. Intramuscular injection of ketamine has, in some instances, found a special use in victims of severe accidents who are bleeding and require limb amputation to extricate them from the site. Although propofol has been reported to be an anticonvulsant, its use has been followed by convulsions and, therefore, thiopentone, which has been in use since 1934, is considered by many to be appropriate when the patient has a history of epilepsy or convulsions. Benzodiazepines, such as diazepam and midazolam, may also be used to induce anaesthesia and these drugs are anticonvulsants.

It must be remembered that in case an anaphylactic or anaphylactoid reaction occurs in response to one of the drugs given, an indwelling intravenous cannula is an absolute requirement before intravenous general anaesthesia is commenced. If no vein can be found, the induction of anaesthesia can be by inhalation and with the vasodilatation that then occurs, an intravenous cannula can, and must, be inserted.

Inhalation induction requires (for ease) a non-irritant vapour, such as sevoflurane or halothane, given with oxygen and nitrous oxide. Isoflurane, desflurane and enflurane have also been used for induction. Airway irritation limits their use but does not exclude it. Ether, the first anaesthetic drug, was very irritant to the airway but was only administered by inhalation. Anaphylaxis does not occur with inhalation anaesthetic drugs.

Once the patient is unconscious vital protective reflexes, e.g. the glottic protective reflex, are obtunded and therefore any regurgitated gastric contents may be inhaled into the lungs. Active vomiting may occur during an inhalation induction. Patients should therefore fast from food and liquid for at least

4 hours before induction of anaesthesia. However, in emergency situations anaesthesia must go ahead regardless (see cricoid pressure below).

Airway control

With induction of anaesthesia the tongue and pharyngeal muscles relax, fall back into the pharynx of the supine patient and cause respiratory obstruction. This can be avoided by the insertion of a Guedel airway or laryngeal mask, and by holding the jaw forward with the fingers behind the angles of the lower jaw. In patients who require controlled ventilation the trachea (windpipe) must be intubated. Some anaesthetists consider the use of a laryngeal mask safe for controlled ventilation, but it is the author's view that the airway cannot be as secure during controlled ventilation with a laryngeal mask as during endotracheal intubation.

Intubation of the trachea is a much more invasive procedure than using a Guedel airway or laryngeal mask. An endotracheal (ET) tube is inserted into the trachea with the aid of a laryngoscope used to visualize the glottic opening (Figure 5.1). A cuff close to the tip of the ET tube is usually inflated, except in babies, to achieve an air-tight fit. This enables anaesthetic gas mixtures to be forced into the lungs without escaping back into the mouth.

The oesophagus (gullet), which lies behind the trachea, is the organ through which food passes to the stomach, and conversely the route by which gastric contents may be passively regurgitated or vomited. Inhalation of gastric contents may occur before intubation and if this occurs severe pulmonary damage can result. If the anaesthetist fears the presence of a full stomach an assistant should apply pressure over the cricoid cartilage—the cartilage immediately below the thyroid cartilage (the Adam's apple) in the neck. Pressure over the cricoid squeezes the oesophagus during attempted intubation. This manoeuvre prevents passive regurgitation but does not prevent the escape

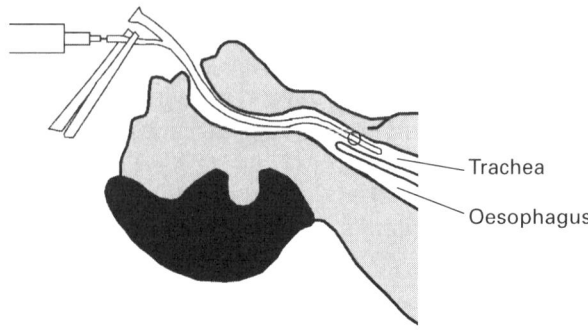

Trachea

Oesophagus

FIGURE 5.1 Lateral view of the endotracheal tube in position.

of gastric contents during active vomiting. An alternative technique, favoured by the author, is to carry out intubation with the patient lying on their side. This allows any gastric material to escape through the mouth and it also avoids the difficulty frequently met with intubation during incorrectly applied cricoid pressure.

Once intubated it is essential to confirm that the ET tube is in the trachea and not in the oesophagus. Of course, in most cases the tube can be seen to pass through the glottic opening during intubation. It may, however, have apparently passed correctly into the trachea, but has actually passed into the oesophagus. This will, if not quickly identified, lead to hypoxia and, if permitted to remain in the oesophagus, brain damage and death, a not infrequent cause of litigation.

The likelihood that intubation will be difficult can be assessed in the preoperative conscious patient.[2] The patient is asked to open their mouth as wide as possible. An easy intubation is likely if the uvula can be seen to hang clear of the tongue (stage 1). If the uvula is touching the tongue, intubation is also likely to be without difficulty (stage 2). However, if it is hidden behind the tongue but the soft palate can be seen, it can be assumed that intubation will be difficult (stage 3), and if only the hard palate can be seen, intubation is likely to be extremely difficult (stage 4). A senior anaesthetist experienced in fibreoptic laryngoscopy and other invasive techniques, including tracheotomy, designed to regain control of the airway if this is lost, must be present when a very difficult intubation is expected. The surgeon should also be present, scrubbed and ready to carry out an emergency tracheotomy if this becomes necessary.

No patient should be intubated, except in a life-saving emergency, without the use of a capnograph. This machine identifies and measures the concentration of expired carbon dioxide and confirms the correct position of the ET tube. The tube may be pushed too far into the trachea and in this case (if it passes into the right main bronchus leading to collapse of the left lung and sometimes of the upper lobe of the right lung) hypoxia results. Correct practice requires that the rebreathing bag is squeezed by the anaesthetist who listens over both sides of the chest to confirm that ventilation is equal over both lung fields. If there is impaired ventilation over one lung field, the ET tube may be withdrawn slowly until ventilation across the lung fields is equal.

Muscle relaxation

Intubation may be carried out following the sleep dose of the induction agent but it is very much more common to use a muscle relaxant drug.

The motor nerve impulse arrives at the distal end of the motor nerve close to the motor end plate and causes the release of a chemical agent, acetylcholine, which crosses the gap between the end of the motor nerve and the muscle. The electrical polarity of the muscle cell changes, i.e. it is depolarized, and the muscle contracts.

Muscle relaxant drugs are classified according to their mechanism of action as follows:

• *Depolarizing.* Suxamethonium, the only member of this group, has a rapid onset (60 seconds) but short duration (<5 minutes usually). Suxamethonium mimics the action of acetylcholine, i.e. depolarization of the muscle fibres occurs but repolarization is delayed. During this delay contraction of the muscles is prevented. This drug may lead to muscle pain postoperatively if the patient, usually female, is mobilized quickly. It is therefore not really suitable for day-case anaesthesia. Suxamethonium is broken down by the enzyme cholinesterase.

Some patients have an atypical cholinesterase and may remain paralysed for two or more hours and therefore require ventilatory support following short-duration surgery. It is not routine to test for the atypical enzyme before surgery.

Some patients may respond to suxamethonium and to halothane with a malignant hyperpyrexia (very high temperature). This condition may occur sporadically in the population but is generally inherited. Most of the families in the UK who carry the gene have been identified. These drugs must always be avoided in members of known families. When the condition occurs treatment includes oxygen and controlled ventilation, and cooling with ice packs and fans. The muscle relaxant dantrolene is required. Acidosis may be treated with sodium bicarbonate. Malignant hyperpyrexia, before the introduction of dantrolene, had a high mortality.

• *Non-depolarizing.* The first drug in this group (*d*-tubocurare) was developed from the arrow poison used by hunters in South America. The drugs in this group compete with acetylcholine, preventing its access to the motor end plate. Their action is prolonged, extending from 30 minutes (rocuronium) to two hours (pipercuronium). Other useful drugs in this group include vecuronium and atracurium.

Following the use of muscle relaxants the patient's breathing must be controlled until the paralysing effect has worn off (depolarizing) or been reversed (non-depolarizing). Reversal is effected by an anticholinesterase, a substance that blocks the action of cholinesterase. The effect is to allow acetylcholine concentration to increase, which can then compete successfully with the muscle relaxant. The actions of acetylcholine include unwanted effects, the prevention of which may require the concurrent administration of an anticholinergic drug.

Maintenance

Anaesthesia is continued with a vapour of which ether and chloroform were the forerunners. The agents used today are halothane, enflurane, isoflurane, sevoflurane and desflurane. The vapour is carried to the patient by oxygen and nitrous oxide. Sometimes air enriched with oxygen is used. Vapour concentration is adjusted to allow those patients who are breathing spontaneously to do so without movement and without respiratory depression. An additional muscle relaxant drug is given as required.

During anaesthesia and surgery a pulse oximeter must be used to measure oxygen haemoglobin saturation and this should be maintained between 96% and 100%. All changes must be recorded and the causes for change sought. Expired carbon dioxide must also be measured breath by breath. In addition to providing general information about the adequacy of breathing and an indication of the adequacy of the cardiac output, it also gives an immediate indication if the pipes taking anaesthetic and oxygen to the patient become disconnected.

The patient's blood pressure must be measured at regular intervals. A continuous recording of the pulse rate, by means of a continuous electrocardiographic display, is standard practice.

It is also important to monitor the inhaled and exhaled anaesthetic vapour concentrations. All values must be carefully recorded throughout the period of anaesthesia. Other important variables that are often measured include the patient's temperature and the degree of muscle paralysis.

A fluid input and output chart should be maintained throughout surgery, recording the volumes of blood, plasma expander and crystalloid solutions given, and recording an estimate of the volume of blood lost.

Careful positioning during surgery is essential. Patients placed in the lithotomy position (in which the patient's legs are raised and the feet placed in 'stirrups') may develop postoperative backache. These patients can benefit from a support placed in the small of the back. It is essential that patients undergoing prolonged surgery in the lithotomy position have their legs lowered every 3–4 hours to prevent the onset of ischaemia in the calf muscles, which may progress to compartment syndrome. If this occurs and is not treated quickly, leg function may be lost. This condition has also been reported following prolonged back surgery with the patient then placed in the knee–elbow position.

Recovery

Muscle paralysis, in patients given a muscle relaxant, must be reversed at the end of surgery unless there is clear evidence from the measured response to motor nerve stimulation that muscle function has fully recovered. The anaesthetic is then turned off and the patient is turned onto their left side and allowed to recover. The patient is extubated; a Guedel airway may be inserted provided the patient is unconscious and does not gag as this is positioned. Gagging may cause vomiting. The patient may inhale vomit material for up to two hours after the recovery of consciousness.[2]

Pain relief

The anaesthetist is responsible for the initial pain relief. Pain relief may be prescribed to be given by the nurse by intramuscular injection 4-hourly on the hour or 4-hourly but only if required (prn). The drugs commonly used are morphine, diamorphine or pethidine. Combinations of drugs, such as morphine or pethidine with nonsteroidal anti-inflammatory drugs, have proved useful. Pain relief may also be provided by a patient-controlled analgesia (PCA). The patient is instructed to press a button when their pain makes analgesia necessary. The machine will then inject into a vein a small dose of the analgesic drug; a lock-out mechanism prevents self overdosing. Some patients may have a spinal or epidural injection which may be topped up with local anaesthetic drugs or analgesic drugs, such as morphine or fentanyl, as required. All prescriptions for pain relief must be written clearly. The epidural injection (Figure 5.2) may of course have been the sole anaesthetic, as is frequently the case for lower limb surgery and Caesarean section. For spinal, epidural and caudal anaesthesia/analgesia an indwelling secure intravenous line must be set up before attempting one of these injections. Severe hypotension may occur and require rapid infusion of electrolyte or plasma expander solution in addition to a vasoconstrictor drug, such as ephedrine. In the case of a spinal injection the needle is passed through an interspinous ligament until cerebrospinal fluid (CSF) can be withdrawn. Sometimes, as the needle penetrates the dura, the patient jumps and describes a pain passing down a leg. The needle must then be withdrawn slightly and no injection made unless there is a free flow of clear fluid, i.e. the CSF. If blood is withdrawn, i.e. a bloody tap, the needle must be withdrawn and re-sited one space up or down the vertebral column to prevent an intravascular injection. The magnitude of the dose of local anaesthetic injected into the subarachnoid or epidural space may prove very toxic and lead to convulsions if injected directly into a blood vessel. Injection of a drug when the patient is complaining of pain, especially shooting pain in the leg, may result in nerve damage leading to loss of motor power and loss of sensation. The weakness and loss of sensation may be temporary or permanent and this form of damage has resulted in litigation.

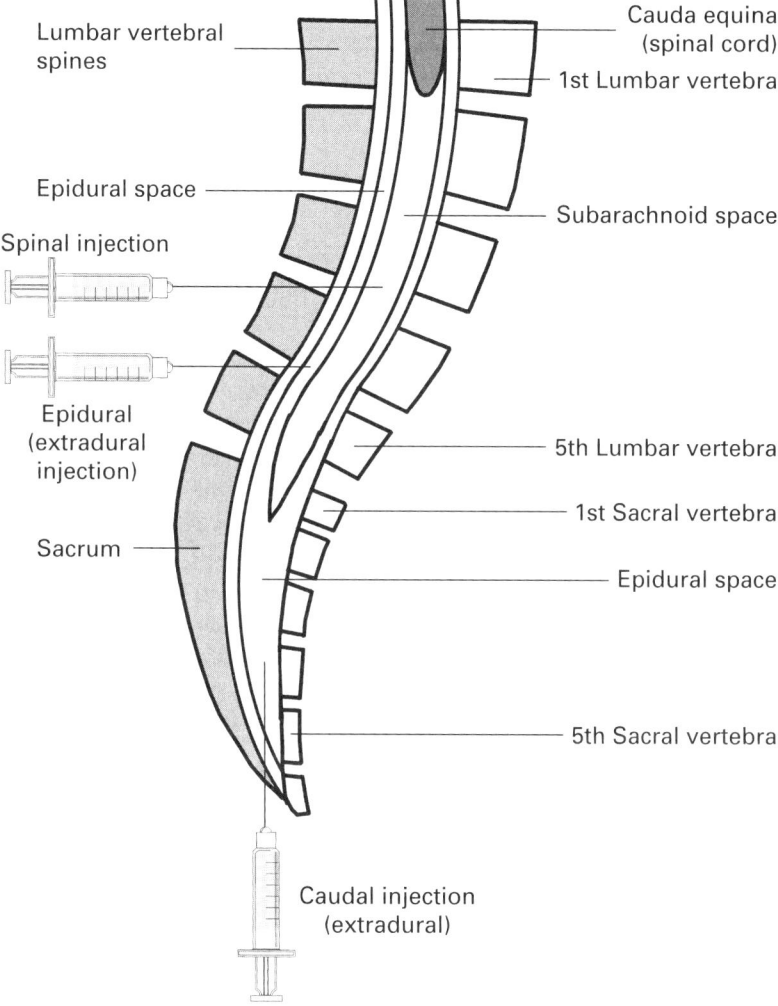

FIGURE 5.2 Lumbar and sacral region of spinal cord (showing correct positions for spinal, extradural and caudal injections).

Epidural and caudal anaesthesia/analgesia differ only in the spinal level at which the needle is inserted. In both, the needle is attached to a syringe containing saline. The needle is advanced while applying pressure to the saline. It is not possible to inject saline until the needle penetrates through the ligamentum flavum and the outer layer of dura mater in the case of an epidural. At this point the pressure in the 'space' is sub-atmospheric and the saline flows freely. Excess penetration will result in a CSF tap which may contain blood. The rules which apply to spinal injections with respect to a blood tap, or pain while inserting the needle or at the start of the drug injection, apply equally to epidural and caudal injections.

Conclusion

The practice of safe anaesthesia requires continuous attention to detail—attention which extends from the preoperative interview and examination of the patient into the recovery phase following surgery and anaesthesia. The anaesthetist must pay very careful attention to the patient's condition throughout the surgical operation. The continual charting of all measurement values ensures that any changes in the patient's condition are noticed as they occur. Generally, the practice of anaesthesia is without worrying incident but unexpected difficulties may occur and threaten the patient's life with a frightening suddenness. The motto of the Association of Anaesthetists of Great Britain and Ireland, '*In Somno Securitas*', must remain the principle supporting the practice of all anaesthetists.

References

1. American Society of Anesthesiologists: New Classification of Physical Status. *Anesthesiology* 1963; **24**: 111.
2. Malampati SR, Galt SP, Gugino LD, *et al.* A clinical sign to predict difficult intubation: a prospective study. *Can Anaesth Soc J* 1985; **32**: 429–34.

Cardiac surgery

Iain M Breckenridge

In recent years cardiac surgery has come increasingly under the public spotlight, even though this surgical specialty is far ahead of others in auditing its work. Since 1977 the Society of Cardiothoracic Surgeons of Great Britain and Ireland has produced an annual UK Cardiac Surgical Register that records the number of each type of operation and the hospital mortality from all NHS units. Private sector activity is not included and, although the data is unit-specific, it is presented in a pooled form with no attempt at 'risk stratification', so that its value for statistically valid outcome comparisons is limited. There seems to be no doubt that the climate of alleged 'transparency' in which surgeons now work will lead not only to the disclosure of this information to the general public, but also to pressure to publish the results of individual units and even surgeons, in response to demands for patients' freedom of choice. As has happened in the USA, this may deprive high-risk patients of the opportunity to undergo potentially life-saving surgery.

This chapter reviews some of the categories of cardiac operations, illustrating the most common pitfalls which might lead to litigation with examples from the author's own medico-legal experience. Table 6.1 provides a breakdown of the work carried out in the NHS cardiac surgical centres during the year from April 1999 to March 2000. A total of 38,509 operations were performed with a hospital mortality of 3.9%—a very reasonable figure considering that it comprises not only first-time elective procedures but also re-operations and emergency cases.

Before discussing the three marked categories, several aspects which are common to all cardiac operations must be mentioned.

The heart–lung machine

This device, one of the greatest inventions of the 20th century, was first used successfully in Philadelphia in September 1953. A British version was

TABLE 6.1 UK Cardiac Surgical Register Return for the year from April 1999 to March 2000

Procedure	Percentage
Coronary artery surgery	64
Valves—repair, replacement ± CABG	21
Congenital—paediatric	10
Transplantation—heart and/or lung	1
Miscellaneous, including aortic surgery	4
Mortality	3.9

CABG, coronary artery bypass graft

developed at Hammersmith Hospital in London by Dr Denis Melrose and first used clinically in 1954. Figure 6.1 shows the 'extracorporeal circulation' or 'cardiopulmonary bypass' (CPB) which is provided by the heart–lung machine (HLM).

After anticoagulation with heparin, venous blood is drained by cannulae in the right atrium through plastic tubing into a reservoir from which it is pumped into an oxygenator, where oxygen is absorbed and carbon dioxide is given off. The earliest oxygenators allowed direct contact between blood and gas, but this was shown to cause harmful changes to the blood and to the patient. Since the 1970s, oxygenators have imitated the human lung by separating blood from gas by a diffusible membrane. From the oxygenator the now oxygen-rich, arterialized blood passes through a heater/cooler and a micropore filter before returning to the patient through a cannula placed in the ascending aorta. Since the heart and lungs have now been bypassed, the

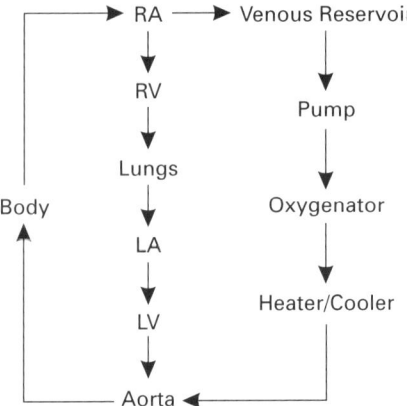

FIGURE 6.1 A cardiopulmonary bypass circuit. RA, right atrium; RV, right ventricle; LA, left atrium; LV, left ventricle.

heart can be excluded from the circulation by cross-clamping the ascending aorta below the cannula. The heart is then arrested and protected from the ischaemia produced by the cross-clamp by the infusion of a 'cardioplegic' solution of potassium-enriched arterial blood into the aortic root or directly into the coronary arteries through an incision in the aorta. The heart is thus rendered motionless, flaccid and empty of blood, providing the surgeon with ideal operating conditions.

The early cumbersome and dangerous HLMs have been replaced by smaller and safer models in which all components, except for the chassis and pumps, are disposable. They are no longer operated by doctors but by 'perfusionists' who are specially trained technicians examined and accredited by the College of Clinical Perfusion Sciences (affiliated to the University of London). During the period of CPB, responsibility for the patient's life is in the hands of the perfusionist rather than the surgeon or anaesthetist. In the NHS, perfusionists are indemnified by the employing Trust but in the private sector they require private indemnity arrangements, as do medical practitioners, e.g. from the medical defence organizations.

Informed consent to operation

Although Lord Scarman (in the *Sidaway* case) attempted to clarify the question of how much or how little a patient should be told with his idea of 'material risk', informed consent remains an issue which taxes both legal and medical minds. A recent joint paper stated that 'Courts in Australia and England have begun applying a tougher standard to the information that doctors should give their patients—that of what a reasonable patient might expect rather than of what a reasonable body of doctors might think.'[1]

Risk of death

In the early 1960s operative mortality rates were high, e.g. 30% for aortic valve replacement, so that death was a valid if crude outcome indicator. But now, with figures well below 5% for most procedures, it is not adequate and more refined markers are required, such as relief of symptoms, improvement in cardiac function and increase in life expectancy. Comparative assessment of the results of operations has been facilitated by risk stratification. Obviously some operations are intrinsically more dangerous than others, e.g. aortic arch replacement compared with routine coronary artery bypass grafts (CABG), while some patients are better candidates for the same procedure than others. Successful attempts to quantify patient- and procedure-related risk factors have resulted in the Parsonnet and Euroscore systems.[2,3] These are of great help not only in preoperative counselling but also in comparing the results from the various units which might have different 'case mixes'. For hospitals (including NHS hospitals) run on quasi-business lines, risk stratification also helps contract managers to quote suitable prices to purchasers of operations.

Common reasons for litigation

Sternotomy wound problems

The standard approach to the heart for all operations using CPB is a median sternotomy, involving a vertical skin incision through which the sternum ('breast bone') is divided longitudinally in the mid-line and the two halves retracted. This gives rapid and excellent access to the heart and great vessels with a risk of major complications of <2%. At the end of the operation the sternum is reunited by four to eight loops of strong stainless steel wire and absorbable sutures are used to close the superficial layers.

Complaints concerning the healing of this wound have accounted for 20% of the reports which this author has been asked to provide on cardiac surgical cases.[4] The incision is not ideal from the cosmetic aspect and sometimes the wide separation of the sternal halves can cause the clavicle ('collar bone') to compress the lowest nerves of the brachial plexus as they pass from the neck to the axilla. This can give rise to numbness and tingling on the ulnar side of one or both arms and hands, but fortunately this is nearly always temporary.

A more significant problem is partial or complete separation (dehiscence) of the two halves of the sternum, which can occur for various reasons—faulty surgical technique, poor quality bone (e.g. in elderly patients or those on steroid drugs), persistent coughing in smokers or those with obstructive airways disease and obesity. These mechanical factors account for 60% of cases of postoperative dehiscence but the remaining 40% are caused by deep sternal wound infection (DSWI), which is a much more serious problem. Sternotomy wound infection occurs in 2.5% of all cardiac operations, rising to 7.5% after CABG when transfer of bacteria may occur from the leg incisions used to excise a vein for grafting.[5] Fortunately, 85% of these infections are confined to the superficial wound layers and are easily treated, but in 15% the sternum itself and sometimes the underlying mediastinum (the structures in the centre of the chest, between the two lungs) are involved. DSWI is a very serious complication, with a mortality of at least 10%. Treatment often requires several reoperations to excise all infected and necrotic tissue, often including part or all of the sternum, so that assistance from a plastic surgeon may be necessary to hasten healing and to obtain a satisfactory cosmetic result. In DSWI, appropriate antibiotic treatment is no more than a valuable adjunct to surgical debridement, whereas the use of intravenous antibiotics given before operation and for 48 hours afterwards is essential to minimize the risk of wound infection.

Since sternal dehiscence and wound infection are not necessarily the results of negligent treatment, few legal actions are successful unless it can be shown that diagnosis and treatment were unduly delayed or that surgical debridement was insufficiently radical.

Stroke (cerebrovascular accident)

Stroke can occur during any type of cardiac operation but does not usually manifest itself until sedation has been withdrawn prior to the attempted discontinuation of ventilation. The main cause is embolization—the introduction into the cerebral circulation of air from the left-sided cardiac chambers; or of particulate matter, such as atheroma, in the ascending aorta in CABG; or fragments of calcification in valve replacement procedures. Global (as opposed to localized) cerebral damage can be produced by a period of profound hypotension during or after the operation, leading to coma or a persistent vegetative state. The best way to assess the extent of cerebral damage is by means of a CT scan.

Stroke occurs in 0.4–5.4% of cases,[6] and predisposing factors include a previous stroke or transient ischaemic attack (TIA), hypertension, atheromatous disease of the carotid arteries or ascending aorta, and old age. Clearly, failure to give specific warning to a patient with one or more of these factors would be unacceptable. Although no active treatment can be given for stroke, many patients, such as those with a hemiplegia, make a remarkable, if sometimes incomplete, recovery which can continue for at least 18 months. In the worst cases decisions about discontinuation of ventilation may have to be made after establishing that the criteria of brain-stem death have been met.

Since stroke is another recognized complication of cardiac surgery, few claimants succeed in proving liability, but the author believes that it might be possible to do so if a surgeon, confronted by an obviously atheromatous aorta, failed to modify their technique for CABG in order to reduce the risk of cerebral embolism by minimizing the amount of manipulation and clamping of the aorta.

Cardiac tamponade

The pericardial sac has to be opened to gain access to the heart, and at the end of the operation it is either left open or closed with sutures and drained. Unfortunately, neither method can totally prevent the collection of blood from various possible sources, which stops the ventricles from filling properly in the diastolic phase of the cardiac cycle and, therefore, also from ejecting a normal stroke volume during systole. This 'tamponade' creates a state of low cardiac output which is rapidly fatal unless the chest is urgently reopened to evacuate the blood and deal with its source. The clinical signs of tamponade are inconstant and even echocardiography is not always reliable, so the best diagnostic tool is a high index of suspicion. It is much better to reopen the chest in the Intensive Care Unit and find no tamponade than to have the diagnosis made at autopsy—there can be no greater tragedy in cardiac surgery.

Unexpected complications

Not surprisingly it is the unexpected and apparently unrelated complications after cardiac surgery that most often give rise to litigation. If a woman has a mitral valve replacement but then develops intestinal ischaemia due to a mesenteric artery embolism and dies following resection of several feet of gangrenous bowel, her family will say 'but doctor, she came in for her heart, there was nothing wrong with her stomach'. This outcome is too rare to constitute a material risk and to mention the remote possibility to the patient before operation would only cause needless anxiety. Such cases are difficult to deal with, but in the author's experience, a Coroner's inquest verdict of death from natural causes goes a long way to discourage claims.

Surgical operations

Specific aspects of the categories of operation listed in Table 6.1 are discussed below, with the exception of paediatric cardiac surgery and transplantation.

Coronary artery surgery

Atheroma is made of a fatty material which may become deposited underneath the intimal lining of all arteries in the body, producing narrowing (stenosis) and obstruction to blood flow. Its presence in the coronary arteries causes angina and myocardial infarction and can be demonstrated by coronary arteriography. Many cases can be effectively dealt with by the cardiologist, who uses a balloon catheter to dilate the stenoses and stents to keep them open. Unfortunately this has meant that the simpler cases are 'creamed off', leaving only the more complicated ones for the surgeon.

The purpose of CABG surgery is to bypass all stenoses of 70% or more in the major coronary arteries, using a conduit placed between the aorta and the artery distal to (on the 'far side of') the stenosis. This conduit can be either the long saphenous vein excised from the leg or the left internal mammary artery (LIMA). When the LIMA is used, it is dissected from the chest wall but left attached at its origin, so that no aortic anastomosis is required. After 10 years only 30–50% of saphenous vein grafts remain patent compared with >90% of LIMA grafts,[7] so that there is now a tendency to use as many arterial grafts as possible, e.g. right internal mammary artery (RIMA) or the radial artery from the forearm. Although most surgeons still prefer to make the tiny (1.5–2.5 mm) anastomoses on CPB with the heart arrested, a growing number are operating on the beating heart without CPB, using stabilizers to immobilize the area of the left ventricle being grafted.

The hospital mortality for CABG is <2% with nearly all patients experiencing immediate relief of angina, although after 10 years this figure falls to 60% because of graft failure and the progression of disease in ungrafted vessels.[8] There is convincing evidence that CABG also increases life expectancy, and this is naturally more obvious among patients with the most extensive disease.

Since CABG is essentially a palliative procedure which does nothing to modify the progression of coronary artery disease, it is difficult to see how a claimant could sue for return of angina unless they could prove that the wrong arteries had been grafted or that the anastomoses had been badly constructed (which would be virtually impossible to do). Unfortunately many NHS waiting lists for CABG are well over a year, so that unpredictable deaths during this time are not uncommon.

Valve operations

Of the four one-way valves in the heart, the two that most often require surgical attention are the mitral (between the left atrium and ventricle) and the aortic (between the left ventricle and aorta). Several disease processes, such as senile degeneration, rheumatic fever and infective endocarditis, can cause stenosis and/or incompetence of these valves, which often become calcified. Although 40% of diseased mitral valves can be repaired, for the remainder and for virtually all aortic valves excision and replacement are necessary.

The choice of replacement device lies between a man-made prosthetic valve and one composed of natural tissue—a human or a porcine aortic valve or a valve constructed from bovine pericardium. In 1999, 60% of valves implanted in the UK were prosthetic. Advantages of prosthetic valves include their durability and good haemodynamic performance even in small sizes, while the principal disadvantage is the need for permanent anticoagulation to prevent valve thrombosis and systemic embolism. On the other hand, although tissue valves are virtually free of the risk of thrombo-embolism so that most patients do not need to take potentially dangerous anticoagulants, they do not last for ever, making reoperation likely after 10–20 years. Obviously the patient should participate in a careful preoperative discussion of the choice of valve replacement device, although the surgeon should always reserve the right to the final decision depending upon the operative findings.

The most interesting litigation concerning heart valves was the class action brought in the last decade in the US against the manufacturer of the Björk-Shiley prosthetic valve. Although there was nothing wrong with it, in response to competition an attempt was made to increase the opening angle of the disc, which caused weakening of the joints between the metal struts and the housing of the valve. Subsequent fractures allowed the disc to escape and caused the death of many patients, although some survived emergency reoperation. The cost of compensating these patients together with those who underwent elective reoperation before anything happened was sufficient to drive the company out of business. The surgeons who implanted this modified valve in good faith were not held liable for its failure.

Aortic surgery

Operations on all portions of the thoracic aorta—ascending, arch and descending—used to be heroic procedures fraught with danger, particularly from bleeding, cerebral damage and paraplegia. But in recent years an increasing number of operations have been performed with better results—in 1999/2000 the hospital mortality, although still high, had fallen to 17%. Improvement has been due to the introduction of synthetic fabric grafts (which are impermeable to blood) and to drugs that maintain normal blood clotting, as well as to better understanding of the means to protect the brain and spinal cord.

Apart from aneurysms, emergency operation is needed to save the lives of the minority of patients who survive traumatic rupture of the aorta (the classical deceleration injury in air and car crashes) or acute dissection. In this interesting condition, which usually occurs in hypertensive patients, a localized tear occurs in the inner lining of the aorta, allowing blood under pressure to get between the layers of the aortic wall and 'dissect' in both directions. This usually causes rupture into the chest cavity or into the pericardium producing tamponade, both of which are rapidly fatal. As a rule of thumb, for every hour that passes without surgical treatment from the time of dissection, the mortality rises by 1%.[9]

Paraplegia is a recognized complication of aortic surgery, particularly when this involves the descending portion which provides the spinal cord with its blood supply. But paraplegia from less obvious causes may give rise to litigation. When a surgeon was performing a thoracotomy to remove a benign lung tumour he encountered bleeding from an inaccessible source at the posterior end of the wound, a not uncommon problem. He dealt with this in an accepted way by inserting packs, removing the retractor and waiting for 15 minutes. When he resumed, the bleeding had stopped and although the operation was completed uneventfully, when the patient woke up she could not move her legs and has been in a wheelchair ever since. The author believes that the packs had exerted lateral pressure on the spinal cord through an intervertebral foramen (window) which was sufficient to cause a transverse infarct of the cord producing paraplegia. The case came to trial 12 years after the event, and the judge found that the paraplegia was an unforeseeable consequence of a non-negligent act.

References

1. Skene L, Smallwood R. Informed consent: Lessons from Australia. *Br Med J* 2002; **324**: 39–41.
2. Parsonnet V, Dean D, Bernstein AD. A method of uniform stratification of risk for evaluating the results of surgery in acquired adult heart disease. *Circulation* 1989; **79(6 Suppl I)**: 3–12.
3. Roques F, Nashef SAM, Michel P *et al*. Risk factors and outcome in European cardiac surgery: Analysis of the Euroscore Multinational Database of 19030 patients. *Eur J Cardiothor Surg* 1999; **15**: 816–23.
4. Breckenridge IM. Problems with median sternotomy wounds. *Clin Risk* 2001; **7**: 132–5.
5. Wells FC, Newsom SWB, Rowlands C. Wound infection in cardiac surgery. *Lancet* 1983; **1**: 858–63.
6. Roach GW, Kanchuger M, Mangano CM, *et al*. Adverse cerebral outcomes after coronary bypass surgery. *N Engl J Med* 1996; **335**: 1857–63.
7. Kirklin JW, Barratt-Boyes BG. Stenotic arteriosclerotic coronary artery disease. In: *Cardiac Surgery*, 2nd edn. New York: Churchill Livingstone, 1993, pp 331–332.
8. *Cardiac Surgery*, 2nd edn. New York: Churchill Livingstone, 1993, p 318.
9. Stone C, Borst H. Dissecting aortic aneurysm In: Edmunds LH (ed). *Cardiac Surgery in the Adult*. New York: McGraw Hill, 1997, p 1137.

Abdominal surgery involves surgery on or in the abdominal cavity, including surgery on the gastrointestinal tract, oesophagus, stomach, small bowel and large bowel. Traditionally, abdominal surgery was carried out by general surgeons but more surgeons are becoming specialists within the field of general surgery. The liver, pancreas, bladder and kidneys all reside within the abdominal cavity (Figure 7.1) and as such form part of general surgery. There has been a complete surgical revolution (not unlike the industrial revolution in terms of its impact on society) during the past 10 years. Many traditional abdominal surgical procedures are now carried out using laparoscopic or non-invasive techniques and a patient's knowledge and expectations have increased dramatically. Surgery is not an exact science and even in the best hands the outcome is not totally predictable.

It must be remembered that antibiotics, blood transfusion and modern anaesthesia have all been introduced within the past 60 years. Much of what is done today in abdominal surgery depends as much on the support services available as it does on the skill of an individual surgeon. As surgery becomes more complex, surgeons become more specialized. Following a period of training surgeons are accredited by the Royal Colleges of Surgeons. The ultimate responsibility for surgery remains with the consultant in charge of the patient. It is the consultant's responsibility to assess and delegate cases, to assist trainee surgeons, and to ensure the standard of treatment provided conforms to that which is considered acceptable by his or her colleagues.

All doctors remain responsible for their actions but any consultant who permits a trainee to perform an elective surgical procedure for which the trainee is manifestly inadequately trained is at least irresponsible if not negligent and litigation can result.

Many unplanned emergency surgical admissions involve abdominal problems. A trainee doctor may initiate a surgical procedure in a life-saving situation. In most emergency situations concerning the abdomen, there is time to

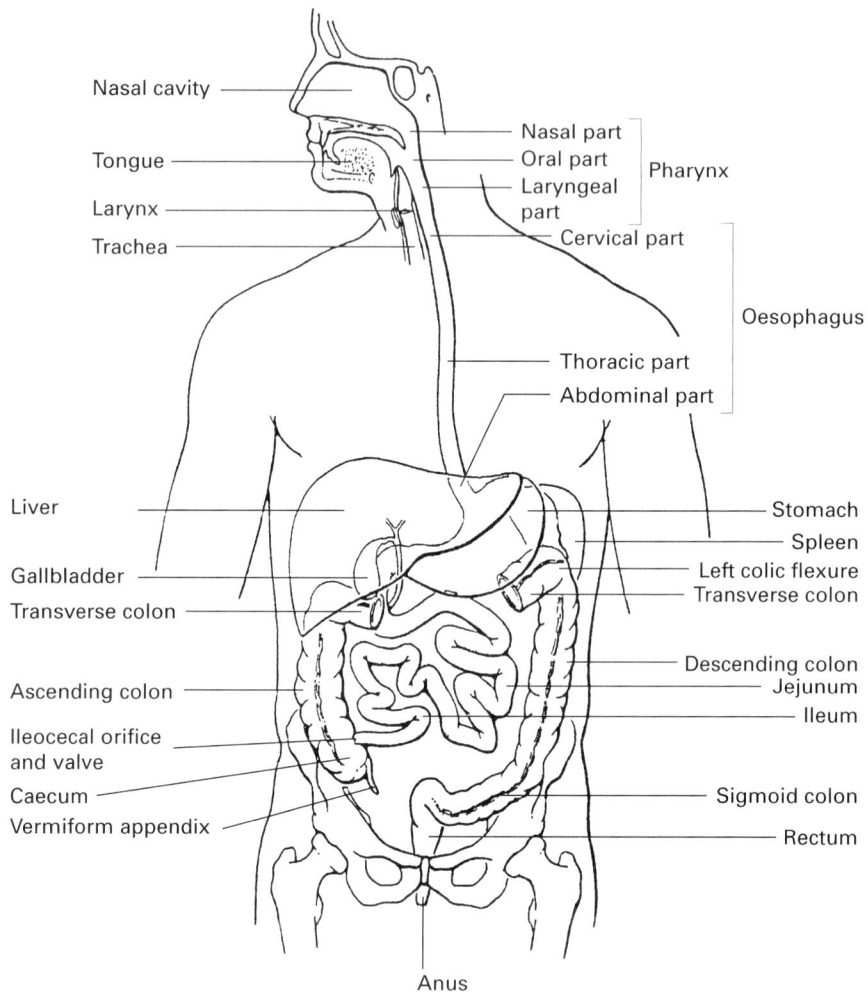

Nasal cavity

Tongue

Larynx

Trachea

Nasal part
Oral part
Laryngeal part
Cervical part

Pharynx

Oesophagus

Thoracic part
Abdominal part

Liver

Gallbladder

Transverse colon

Ascending colon

Ileocecal orifice and valve

Caecum

Vermiform appendix

Stomach
Spleen
Left colic flexure
Transverse colon

Descending colon
Jejunum
Ileum

Sigmoid colon

Rectum

Anus

FIGURE 7.1 Structures in the alimentary tract

take an adequate history, arrange appropriate investigations and prepare the patient properly. There should be an emphasis on preoperative resuscitation and appropriate surgical treatment performed by a surgeon competent to do this. An appropriate investigation is one that can be done without delaying the patient's management and that will significantly add to or may alter the course of treatment.

Before commencing any abdominal procedure adequate resuscitation, such that the patient is in a stable cardiovascular state able to withstand an anaesthetic, must be carried out. Anaesthetizing a shocked patient—a patient who has lost a considerable quantity of fluid and electrolytes—carries very significant risks.

All surgeons are now subject to audit and attempts to introduce outcome measures are likely to be introduced soon. Hospital league tables are a controversial area; they have done nothing to improve morale within surgery and provide very little useful information. League tables have little bearing on the outcome of a surgical procedure in most patients.

Anatomy

All surgeons require a good basic understanding of anatomy. Having mastered the anatomy, it is important to understand how the organs function and how this function may be modified by drugs or disease processes.

The abdomen may be thought of as a box. The roof of the box is the diaphragm separating the abdomen from the chest. The floor of the box is the pelvis containing the bladder and, in a woman, the uterus and ovaries. The side walls of the box include the anterior, lateral and posterior abdominal walls. Running through the abdominal cavity is the spinal column and in front of this the main blood vessel supplying the lower half of the body (aorta) and the main vein returning blood to the heart (inferior vena cava). The kidneys are situated on either side of the spinal column towards the back of the abdominal cavity. The liver is situated on the right-hand side of the abdominal cavity below the diaphragm. The spleen is on the left-hand side below the diaphragm. The pancreas lies across the abdominal cavity running from the left- to the right-hand side. The pancreas drains into the first part of the small bowel, the duodenum. The oesophagus takes food from the mouth, runs through the thoracic cavity, and enters the abdomen through the diaphragm.

The oesophagus enters the stomach, which is the reservoir for food prior to digestion. The stomach empties via the duodenum into the small bowel. The small bowel then empties into the large bowel. The first part of the large bowel is the caecum to which the appendix is attached. The caecum then empties into the colon. The colon is formed of the ascending colon, a transverse colon, a descending colon and a sigmoid colon. The sigmoid colon enters the rectum and the rectum is connected to the anal canal.

The stomach, liver and spleen are within the abdominal cavity, as are the small and large bowel. The kidneys are behind the abdominal cavity (extraperitoneal). In a female patient the uterus, ovaries and Fallopian tubes are also present within the abdominal cavity. Although these structures are present within the abdominal cavity they are usually treated by a gynaecologist. In an emergency a general surgeon operating on the abdomen may perform surgical procedures on the uterus, ovaries and Fallopian tubes.

In addition to understanding the structures within the abdominal cavity, an understanding of the abdominal wall is essential. One of the most common surgical procedures carried out is the repair of hernias. Hernias represent an abnormal protrusion, usually through the abdominal wall. The most common site for a hernia is the inguinal region (groin). Other sites include the femoral region, hernias protruding through the femoral canal (the canal that allows nerves, arteries, and veins to pass from the back of the abdominal cavity into the leg), umbilical hernias and incisional hernias.

Some understanding of the *function* of the abdominal organs is important. The oesophagus transmits food from the mouth to the stomach. It has no digestive function, although a number of medical conditions affect the oesophagus and make it difficult to swallow. The stomach acts as a reservoir; it produces dilute hydrochloric acid which initiates digestion. The liver is responsible for metabolizing digested food products. Bile, an emulsifying agent which aids digestion, is produced in the liver and concentrated in the gallbladder. When a particularly fatty meal is digested, the gallbladder contracts squeezing bile into the bile ducts and then into the duodenum, the first part of the small bowel. The food becomes emulsified with the bile and digestion is initiated. The pancreas produces enzymes that aid digestion. These enzymes are particularly caustic and if they escape from the pancreas can cause severe inflammation (pancreatitis). The pancreas also has one other function and that is sugar regulation; it produces insulin.

Digestion takes place in the small bowel and the products of digestion are absorbed from the small bowel into the portal venous circulation, which takes them to the liver for further metabolism. The contents of the first part of the large bowel, the caecum, are relatively liquid. By the time the contents reach the rectum they are relatively solid. The kidneys are responsible for filtering the blood and extracting waste products, which are then excreted in urine. The urine is stored in the bladder before excretion. In children the spleen is responsible for producing some of the red cells; in an adult it has immunological protective functions and is also involved in the regulation of platelets. Patients who have lost their spleen are more likely to suffer from pneumomococcal infections and for this reason the spleen is preserved if at all possible. If it is necessary to remove the spleen, then it is usual to start the patient on long-term penicillin prophylaxis or immunize the patient. The spleen is a particularly friable structure and can be damaged both during the course of surgery and as a result of external trauma, such as in a road traffic accident.

Abdominal wall surgery—hernia repair

Hernia repairs are one of the most common surgical procedures performed on the abdomen. A patient may present with a bulge in the groin, sometimes associated with an aching sensation. A hernia may arise as a result of a persisting congenital sac. During intrauterine life the testicle is situated behind the kidney. During the latter part of intrauterine life it descends through the posterior wall and groin to take up residence in the scrotum. As it descends it takes with it a covering of peritoneum which provides a potential sac running from inside the groin through the anterior abdominal wall to the scrotum. This sac is often obliterated by birth, but if it persists it provides a potential weakness for the development of an *indirect inguinal hernia* during later life. The second type of inguinal hernia is a *direct inguinal hernia*, which occurs as a result of progressive weakness of the anterior abdominal wall. As the wall becomes weaker and the muscle fibres part, intraabdominal contents can protrude. Direct inguinal hernias are often large, they occur over a long period of time and rarely give rise to severe symptoms.

An indirect hernia can be small, the contents can get stuck and the blood supply can be obstructed. The patient then presents with an *acute strangulated inguinal hernia* which represents a surgical emergency.

When a patient presents with a bulge or pain in the groin it is important to take a history and then to examine the patient. There are few appropriate investigations for the diagnosis of a hernia. Injections of dyes and ultrasound can be used in cases where the diagnosis may prove difficult. The treatment of hernias is usually surgical. A rare alternative method of treatment reserved for very elderly and infirm patients involves the application of a truss—a spring which holds the contents back inside the abdominal cavity. These are never very effective and are often associated with scarring, making the eventual hernia repair more difficult.

The principle of a hernia repair is to reduce the hernia, i.e. pushing it back into the abdominal cavity. If there is a sac of peritoneum this is removed, the hole through which the hernia appeared can be narrowed (not closed because important structures run through this hole). Some form of reinforcing mesh is inserted over which the tissues will then heal. These procedures can be carried out under general or local anaesthesia. Although the majority of hernias are still repaired using an open technique, laparoscopic repair of hernias is now an alternative method. There are pros and cons for using an open or laparoscopic technique for the repair of hernias.

Before carrying out a hernia repair, it is important to assess the patient's suitability to undergo, if necessary, full general anaesthesia. It is important to ensure that there are no potential complicating factors, such as:

- a bleeding tendency
- a tendency to develop urinary retention
- chest problems which may give rise to a cough and threaten the surgical repair
- concurrent medical conditions, including diabetes and cardiac conditions, which again may require specific management during the course of the surgical repair.

All patients should give full consent to the procedure. Consent involves explaining the nature of the condition, the reason why it is necessary to repair it and what is actually involved in terms that the patient can fully understand. It is now common practice to explain the potential complications. Patients must be given an opportunity to ask questions and their questions must be answered truthfully.

In obtaining consent it is important that patients appreciate exactly what the surgical procedure involves and whether they are going to have a full or local anaesthetic. The patient needs to know that all operations are painful but the pain is usually well controlled either by simple oral medication or by an injection. Bleeding and infection are the two most common complications associated with the repair of a hernia. The risk of infection can be reduced by giving prophylactic antibiotics. Given that most surgical repairs of hernias now involve the insertion of a mesh made of polypropylene, prophylactic antibiotics are almost routine. A certain amount of bruising will occur with any surgical procedure. Patients taking aspirin on a regular basis are more likely to bruise. Patients with a bleeding tendency are also likely to experience bruising and perhaps significant swelling of the scrotum. Patients must be warned that it takes up to six weeks for a hernia to become fully healed and that throughout this period of time there may be restrictions on what they can do. Although many people can go back to work within a day or two, some experience considerably more pain. Patients should be advised to take it easy during the immediate postoperative period.

Hernias in association with the umbilicus are common. They may be congenital (arising from birth) or may develop over a period of time. The principle of repairing an *umbilical hernia* is the same as an inguinal hernia—reduce the hernia and repair the defect. The defect is closed using a non-absorbable suture material, perhaps reinforced by a mesh. Antibiotic prophylaxis again may be appropriate.

Incisional hernias

Incisional hernias occur as a result of a previous surgical incision. Following a surgical incision in the abdominal wall the structures are approximated. Traditionally, this approximation has been with a non-absorbable suture material. Absorbable suture materials with a predictable rate of degradation, i.e. six weeks or more, are being used increasingly. An incisional hernia represents a failure of the initial repair. Following the surgical repair of an abdominal wound, healing takes place. The healing involves the laying down of fibroblasts, which then mature and organize, giving strength to the wound. This process can be inhibited by severe infection, uraemia or other conditions known to reduce the healing process. In a patient with a severe wound infection there is a very high incidence of incisional hernia occurring within the first year following surgery. An incisional hernia represents a delayed would dehiscence, i.e. the wound gives way slowly such that the skin remains intact but the underlying structures have given way.

The repair of an incisional hernia involves excising the scar, bringing the edges together and resewing the wound. With large incisional hernias the insertion of mesh may also be appropriate.

The same consideration should be given to consent, antibiotic prophylaxis and postoperative advice.

Biliary surgery

Gallstones remain a very common condition. Excesses of life are known to give rise to gallstones, their incidence increasing during peacetime and virtually being eliminated during periods of wartime when severe food restrictions were in place. Gallstones can be made of cholesterol (fat) or blood pigments, or can be mixed stones involving calcium, blood pigments and some cholesterol. They usually form within the gallbladder and may be symptom free. Many patients have gallstones without knowing about it. If a gallstone moves or blocks the cystic duct the gallbladder can expand and become painful. Although infection can supervene, the majority of cases of cholecystitis are simply inflammation of the gallbladder due to obstruction of the cystic duct.

If stones move from the gallbladder into the common bile duct the bile duct can become obstructed, giving rise to jaundice. Surgery to the gallbladder and bile duct is one of the most common intraabdominal surgical procedures performed.

Prior to 1990 all gallbladders were removed using an open surgical incision. This involved making an incision in the upper right-hand corner of the abdomen. The gallbladder was exposed and dissected free from the liver. The cystic duct (draining bile from the gallbladder into the bile ducts) and the cystic artery (the artery supplying the gallbladder) were divided. Having removed the gallbladder it was common practice to leave a drain to the gallbladder bed, the abdominal wound was closed and the patient recovered over a period of 3–5 days.

In 1990 laparoscopic surgical techniques were introduced in the UK and now the majority of gallbladders are removed using this technique. Although laparoscopy had been used for a much longer period of time, it was the development of instruments that could be used in association with the laparoscope that allowed the advances in laparoscopic surgery. With these advances came a number of problems. The first was that in 1990 the majority of practising consultant surgeons had no experience with laparoscopic surgical procedures. It took several years before training programmes were fully established and sufficient experience was gained to make this a routine surgical procedure.

Damage to the bile duct has always been a concern. During the early days of laparoscopic cholecystectomy a significant increase in the number of bile duct injuries was seen.

The laparoscopic removal of a gallbladder involves the same basic principles as removing it with an open surgical procedure. A laparoscopic procedure involves injecting gas into the abdominal cavity. This creates a space between the lining of the abdomen and the guts allowing visualization of the gallbladder and its surrounding structures. After identifying the gallbladder dissection of the cystic duct and cystic artery takes place. Once these have been positively identified the cystic duct and cystic artery are ligated. Many surgeons apply clips to these structures, dividing between the first and second clip leaving two clips on the cystic artery and two clips on the cystic duct within the abdominal cavity. This reduces the risk of the clips dislodging and either bile leaking into the abdominal cavity or bleeding. Once the cystic duct and cystic artery are ligated the gallbladder can be detached from the liver bed by blunt dissection, often using diathermy.

It is important to get good visualization and to ensure that the anatomy is clearly demonstrated. Anatomical abnormalities, excessive amounts of fat, and bleeding can make visualization difficult.

As part of the consent procedure, in addition to informing the patient of the indications for surgery and how the surgery will be carried out, patients should be warned that there is a risk that if the procedure becomes difficult or visualization is obscured, then it will be necessary to convert to an open surgical procedure. Conversion rates range from 2–15%. No surgeon should be criticized for opening an abdomen before he or she has caused damage to an important structure, i.e. for adopting a cautious approach.

Laparoscopic cholecystectomy involves very little damage to the anterior abdominal wall and as a result very little postoperative pain. Patients typically go home within 24 hours of the surgical procedure and have often fully recovered within a week.

A modification of the old open surgical technique using a very small incision is again associated with rapid recovery and early hospital discharge. One of the advantages of using the small open procedure is that in difficult cases the incision can be extended quite readily and the gallbladder removed safely.

Hepatic (liver) surgery

Hepatic surgery is usually carried out in specialized units. The majority of hepatic surgery involves resection of metastases, repair of the liver following trauma and liver transplantation. Liver transplantation is becoming increasingly common and more successful. A number of conditions, notably alcoholism, give rise to cirrhosis of the liver, where the liver contracts, becomes scarred and fails to function. The liver has an enormous spare capacity and transplanting part of the liver is often adequate to restore normal liver function.

When carrying out a liver transplant tissue matching is important to avoid rejection. Liver transplantation involves joining up the blood supply and the venous drainage to the liver and connecting the bile duct. This surgery is carried out in a specialist unit as there are significant problems associated with it. The risks need to be explained in full but it should be remembered that when this surgery is successful the outcomes can be highly successful, restoring an almost normal quality of life.

Splenic surgery

Splenic surgery is almost solely reserved for major trauma, with just a few haematological indications. The spleen can be removed as part of the staging process for a number of lymphomatous conditions. A number of haematological conditions, including idiopathic thrombocytopenic purpura, improve following splenectomy.

If the spleen can be preserved in trauma then it should be. Removing the spleen involves simply dividing the splenic artery and splenic veins. The spleen is extremely vascular and very profuse amounts of blood loss can occur with relatively minor damage.

Gastric surgery

In the past 30 years there has been quite a reduction in the number of gastric surgical procedures carried out. Peptic ulceration involving the stomach and the first part of the duodenum is now routinely treated with medication. It is only the complications of peptic ulceration, including perforation and bleeding, that are treated surgically. Removal of part of the stomach to control acid secretion is now virtually never performed. Surgery on the stomach is now restricted to surgery of hiatus hernia and removal of the stomach in cases of gastric cancer.

Hiatus hernia

Hiatus hernia is a condition where part of the stomach extrudes into the chest. As a person's weight increases there is even less room for the stomach within the abdominal cavity and the stomach gets squeezed into the chest. As it does so, the entrance of the oesophagus into the stomach becomes distorted and acid contents from the stomach can reflux into the oesophagus, giving rise to indigestion-type symptoms—particularly severe restrosternal chest pain.

The management of hiatus hernia is usually medical initially. All patients are advised to lose weight and control the symptoms with antacids and a variety of other medical compounds. If patients fail to respond to medication then surgery can be carried out. A number of surgical procedures have been described to repair hiatus hernias. The most commonly practised surgical repair is the Nissen fundoplication. This operation involves mobilizing the upper portion of the stomach, having reduced it back into the abdominal cavity. The stomach is then wrapped around the lower end of the oesophagus creating a non-spill inkwell effect. This procedure, originally carried out via an open abdominal incision or occasionally via thoraco-abdominal incision, is now routinely carried out endoscopically using the laparoscope and instruments to mobilize and control the lower end of the oesophagus.

Although these operations can be successful, patients need to be informed that there is a potential failure rate. Again, consent before carrying out these procedures is essential. Patients must understand the reason for the operation, they must be given an opportunity to try conservative measures before undergoing surgery, and they must fully understand the potential complications that can arise. These complications include:

- a failure to control the symptoms
- thoracic complications with pneumothoraces, bleeding complications and infective complications.

There is a risk that the oesophagus can be perforated during the course of mobilization and this may require a separate surgical intervention.

Stomach cancer

Early diagnosis of stomach cancer via endoscopy has improved the results of stomach cancer surgery. The overall five-year survival rate, however, remains low. A combination of surgical treatment followed by chemotherapy now forms the basis of standard treatment. Surgical treatment of gastric cancer involves removing the stomach and re-anastomozing the oesophagus to the small bowel. The patient then no longer has a stomach and is only able to eat small, frequent meals. By looping the small bowel and joining it side to side, a small stomach can be created.

Before carrying out stomach surgery it is important to 'stage' the cancer correctly and this can involve computed tomography and magnetic resonance imaging, and looking for spread of the cancer outside the stomach to lymph nodes or to the liver. Patients who have metastatic disease are unlikely to do well and may be better treated conservatively.

Those patients who have stomach cancer involving the last part of the stomach can present with obstructive symptoms, including profuse vomiting. This is extremely unpleasant and in many instances these patients are better treated with a bypass procedure. Although the procedure does not prolong life, it improves quality of life.

Pancreatic surgery

This form of surgery is again carried out in specialist units. Surgery for the pancreas is carried out for inflammatory conditions (pancreatitis) and for malignant conditions (carcinoma of the pancreas). Pancreatitis can be a very severe condition with a very significant mortality. Following recurrent attacks of pancreatitis some patients are left with severe chronic pain. A pancreatectomy can be carried out under these circumstances but, having removed the pancreas, the patients then require insulin and digestive enzyme supplements. Pancreatic surgery is major surgery, again with a very high mortality rate. There are few long-term survivors among patients who develop cancer of the pancreas. Some justification for operating on the pancreas may be that it improves the severe pancreatic pain that these patients experience in the later stages of their illness.

Small bowel surgery

There are few conditions which affect the small bowel. Tumours of the small bowel are extremely rare, although the small bowel can be involved with lymphatic spread.

Crohn's disease

Inflammatory bowel disease (Crohn's disease) is perhaps the most common inflammatory condition affecting the small bowel. The small bowel wall thickens, adhesions form and abnormal communications between loops of bowel occur. This can give rise to abnormalities of digestion, severe pain and profound weight loss. Although the principal treatment of Crohn's disease remains medical, there are occasions when surgical intervention is appropriate. Surgery may involve small bowel resection and re-anastomoses, or it may involve creating a temporary opening—an ileostomy. The small bowel may get stuck in hernias causing obstruction. If this is not recognized immediately when the obstruction is relieved, it may be necessary to resect segments of small bowel. Patients often have intraabdominal adhesions which have been present since birth. Any patient who has undergone surgery is likely to have an increased number of intraabdominal adhesions. Intraabdominal adhesions can cause the small bowel to twist and to obstruct. If the obstruction does not settle with conservative treatment, i.e. intravenous fluids, then it will involve opening the abdominal cavity, untwisting the bowel, dividing the adhesions, and if the bowel is in any way damaged, resecting it and rejoining it.

Intussusception

This is a relatively rare condition, more commonly seen in young children, where the small bowel intussuscepts (see Figure 12.1). It is thought that the lining of the bowel (lymphoid tissue) enlarges, perhaps as a result of infection, and is passed down the bowel, taking the bowel with it such that it turns itself inside out. This condition can sometimes be treated by passing fluid through the rectum but may involve an open surgical procedure to reduce it. If the bowel has been damaged, a resection is inevitable.

Meckel's diverticulum

This condition occurs in up to 2% of the population and involves the formation of a pouch in the small bowel, usually about 2 inches from the ileo-caecal valve. It may present in a very similar manner to appendicitis. The pouch often contains gastric lining and therefore gastric-type symptoms of indigestion can occur. It is one of the obscure causes of unexplained abdominal pain. Diagnosis is often difficult, with a Meckel's diverticulum often only being found by chance.

Appendicitis

Appendicitis is perhaps the most common surgical emergency. The appendix is situated on the end of the caecum and consists of a collection of lymphoid tissue. One of its functions is to control local infection and swelling of the appendix is probably quite common and will usually resolve. If the lumen of the appendix becomes obstructed, the appendix can swell and burst, giving rise to abdominal pain which then localizes towards the right lower side of the abdomen as the inflammation affects the outer part of the appendix. If the appendix is left *in situ* it may rupture giving rise to generalized peritonitis.

Appendicitis is often preceded by an upper respiratory tract infection or other vague symptoms. Diagnosis of appendicitis is made on the history and clinical findings. If a patient presents to a general practitioner and is given antibiotics, the symptoms may settle and the diagnosis becomes even more difficult. Unfortunately, no test definitively confirms or refutes the diagnosis of appendicitis. Although a surgeon is reluctant to remove a normal appendix, it is often safer to do that than risk an appendix rupturing. Rupture of the appendix in a young female patient may result in infection of the Fallopian tubes and may compromise fertility in later life.

An appendicectomy involves making a small incision in the lower right-hand corner of the abdomen. The appendix is usually easily identified and brought to the surface. The appendix is then removed and the small hole in the caecum following removal of the appendix is closed with a purse string suture. If the diagnosis is delayed, then the appendix may be surrounded by loops of bowel and fat (appendix mass). If the appendix mass is well established it may be impossible to locate the appendix. Sometimes there is an abscess within the middle of the mass which can be drained by blunt dissection using a finger.

The administration of antibiotics during the course of an appendicectomy has reduced the risk of local infection dramatically. In 1972, the risk of wound infection in appendicectomy was $>50\%$. Now the risk of infection following an appendicectomy is well under 10% and probably nearer 2%. Clearly, early diagnosis and removal of the appendix will reduce the risks further. Patients who present with appendicitis and established peritonitis have a significant risk of wound infection.

Colonic surgery

This involves surgery to the colon. Operations on the colon are largely determined by the blood supply to the colon. To remove the caecum it is usually necessary to remove part of the terminal ileum and the ascending colon. This is because the whole of the caecum and right side of the colon are supplied by one artery. This operation is a right hemicolectomy.

Operations on the colon are carried out for inflammatory bowel conditions, including ulcerative colitis, diverticulitis (pouches occurring in the colon), more common on the left side of the colon than the right, and cancer. A number of other rare indications, including ischaemic colitis and infective conditions, may also warrant surgery. The majority of colorectal surgery is carried out via an abdominal incision, although it is increasingly more common to see laparoscopically-assisted colonic resection being carried out. This involves mobilizing the colon laparoscopically, bringing out the diseased segment through a very small incision, and carrying out the anastomosis on the surface before returning the colon to the abdominal cavity.

The principal surgical procedures carried out on the colon include:

- right hemicolectomy
- transverse colectomy
- left hemicolectomy
- sigmoid colectomy
- anterior resection
- abdomino-perineal excision of the rectum.

The first three operations involve removing that segment of the colon and performing a simple end-to-end anastomosis. The anastomosis must be performed without tension and ensuring that there is a good blood supply to the colon at the site of the anastomosis. Where the anastomosis may be compromised a temporary defunctioning ileostomy or colostomy can be performed to protect the anastomosis.

A sigmoid colectomy involves resecting the sigmoid colon. This operation may be performed for early cancer but is usually reserved for diverticular disease. Mobilization of the descending colon before carrying out an anastomosis with the rectum is important.

An anterior resection involves resecting the proximal portion of the rectum, but leaving sufficient rectum to carry out an anastomosis with the descending colon. An abdomino-perineal excision of the rectum is usually carried out for cancer of the rectum where it is not possible to leave sufficient rectum to create the anastomosis.

Following anterior resection it is important that the anal sphincters continue to function. If anal sphincters do not function then it is extremely difficult to manage this condition and patients are often better off having the whole rectum excised and a permanent colostomy.

Perianal abscess

Infective conditions around the anus are common. Small glands can become infected and patients can present with extremely painful abscesses. Superficial abscesses (perianal abscesses) are easy to treat by simple surgical excision. Given that these glands arise in the anal canal they may leave a false tract from the anal canal to the surface giving rise to a fistula. A fistula is an abnormal communication between two epithelial surfaces, the lining of the bowel and the skin. These can result in persistent infection and require specialist treatment. A deeper abscess may point into the ischio-rectal space (the space alongside the rectum). These abscesses are much deeper and will eventually point to the surface. Their drainage will inevitably lead to the development of a fistula, which again requires specialist treatment. When a patient presents with an abscess it is important to take a history and to examine and drain the abscess. There is no place for the management of abscesses by antibiotics alone.

Haemorrhoids (piles)

Piles (haemorrhoids) are extremely common. At a recent meeting, surgeons estimated that 50% of the population had piles and the other 50% were liars! Piles represent a protrusion of the lining of the anus. With defecation and straining the lining gets stretched such that it can hang out. There is an extremely good blood supply to the lining and it is often scraped and therefore bleeds. If a significant portion protrudes it may become strangulated and patients present as an emergency. When a patient presents with piles, they may have perianal pain, which is more commonly associated with a small fissure and bleeding, although a more serious bowel disease must be excluded, or simply with discomfort and a protrusion. All patients presenting with pile-like symptoms should be investigated, initially by taking a history and then by a full examination. A full examination should involve a digital examination of the rectum, proctoscopy and sigmoidoscopy. In the absence of other pathology, piles can be treated by injections, banding (applying an elastic band to the pile), freezing or surgical excision. Surgical excision of piles is usually reserved for the most severe cases. In most cases injection of early haemorrhoids is a very effective form of treatment.

It is difficult to cure piles, as this is a condition which can recur and may require treatment at intervals.

Summary

The principles of abdominal surgery include taking a proper history, proper examination, appropriate explanation and consent, appropriate surgical procedures, and careful follow-up. The introduction of endoscopic techniques, laparoscopic techniques, and minimally invasive procedures for the treatment of many conditions has changed the practice of abdominal surgery. The introduction of medication for the treatment of peptic ulcers is one example of how a whole section of abdominal surgery has disappeared. The introduction of drugs to treat gallstones could affect the treatment of gallbladder disease in the future, although removal of the gallbladder and the treatment of stones remains the most effective form of treatment. Medicine, like many other 'high-tech' subjects, changes rapidly. Educating surgeons and the public remains an important function. Patients must have realistic expectations and should fully understand the principles of the surgical procedure and the expected outcome. Complications can occur even when the most experienced surgeons are operating and they do not by themselves represent negligence. All surgeons experience complications but it is the recognition of the complication and the appropriate management of that complication which differentiates the negligent surgeon from the surgeon who is carrying out his practice in accordance with standard clinical practice.

8 Oncology

Margaret F Spittle

Cancer is an extremely emotive word for the general public who may be aware that one in three people in this country die of cancer. Since cancer is a disease of the elderly, as the population ages, it will account for a higher proportion of deaths. Although there has been a downturn in some smoking-related cancers, such as lung cancer in males and stomach cancer, others (such as cancer of the pancreas, malignant melanoma, and prostate and breast cancer) are increasing in prevalence.

Radiotherapy and chemotherapy are the major non-surgical fields of management for patients with cancer. The popular concept is that such treatment is unpleasant. Although the two treatment methods are often confused, the implications regarding the induction of sickness and vomiting, hair loss and general fatigue, as well as redness and soreness of the skin during a course of radiotherapy, are well perceived. As cancer is seen as a life-threatening disease, many patients are prepared to undergo unpleasant treatment and to accept both short- and long-term side-effects if there is a chance of cure or long-term survival. Indeed, many papers have described the fact that the medical profession is, in general, more conservative about what patients will want to tolerate in the way of side-effects for what may be a very small increase in survival. Much of the management of patients with cancer is palliative, i.e. designed to improve symptom control rather than to increase longevity. However, happily, an increasing percentage of treated patients are being cured. Cure is defined as having been achieved when a cohort of patients with the disease in question reaches the same rate of death as the normal population.

It is relatively rare that patients with cancer have only one form of treatment during the course of their disease. Radiotherapy and chemotherapy may be combined with each other or with surgery as part of the management of the patient. Informed consent for treatment is a major concern and the many side-effects that can occur with radiotherapy and chemotherapy must be adequately discussed.

With attempted curative treatment it is very unusual for patients to refuse such treatment on the grounds of side-effects. However, when treatment is palliative then clearly informed consent must be asked for since the patient may be exchanging one set of problems for another, and any treatment will take up time and entail visits to hospital in what will be a limited lifespan.

Oncology is the management of patients with cancers using, either singly or in combination, radiotherapy, chemotherapy, hormone treatment or biological response modifiers. Oncologists have a broad training. Trainees in oncology will elect to become either medical or clinical oncologists. Clinical oncologists are trained to give both radiotherapy and chemotherapy. Medical oncologists give chemotherapy but as yet their licence does not extend to giving radiotherapy, although this is under discussion. Certain cancers, such as leukaemias and lymphomas, may be under the care of medical oncologists or haematologists specializing in malignant disease.

Screening

An increasing number of cancers are detected by screening. The UK has the only national programme of breast screening for women between the ages of 50 and 65 years. This screening programme, which followed the cervical cancer screening programme, has taken on, as part of its remit, a great deal of education and research so that the general public can understand the screening process. Clearly, screening is an attempt to discover the disease earlier in its history, when curative treatment may be possible. It is, of course, neither completely accurate nor preventive and the general public must be encouraged to understand the population screening procedure and relative risk. A screening procedure is not a diagnostic test.

Screening procedures must be meticulous and confidentiality must be observed. There should be a good chance of appropriate treatment if the disease is discovered early and the screening process should not be deleterious to the health of the population. It is vital that all consent documents state that the screening programme cannot detect all cancers and that if serious symptoms occur related to that organ after screening they should not be ignored. Breast screening, for example, will find only nine out of 10 breast cancers in the population screened.

Radiotherapy

Among the general public radiotherapy is the least understood modality for the management of cancers. Although the taking of X-rays is understood for diagnosis, treatment with radiation conjures up similes with the atomic bomb, nuclear war and the induction of leukaemia. Radiotherapy has been used to treat cancer almost since the discovery of X-rays by Roentgen in 1895 and there have been large numbers of technical and innovative advances during the course of the development of current standards. Radiotherapy treatment is prescribed and planned by the clinical oncologist with the help of a team of medical physicists and the treatment is given daily by radiographers. The most frequently prescribed type of radiotherapy is external beam radiotherapy given by linear accelerators. These large and expensive machines are present in all cancer centres in the UK and therefore access to state of the art machinery should not be denied to anyone.

A patient may be prescribed radiotherapy following incomplete excision of the tumour. At this stage the clinical oncologist will be required to designate, with the help of computed tomography scans or magnetic resonance images and the surgeon's operative notes, the area at greatest risk of recurrence of disease. Areas that include any particularly radiosensitive structures, which would be irreparably damaged by the radiotherapy dose, need to be avoided. A balance must be struck between the amount of damage that normal tissues can tolerate in exchange for eradicating the cancer. The dilemma of radiotherapy is when structures such as the optic nerves, large areas of the lungs, brain or spinal cord, are intimately related with a risk of recurrence of tumour.

Computer planning allows the X-ray beam to be directed in a non-uniform manner in all dimensions so as to most closely conform to the minimum area that the clinical oncologist has designated. A 'standard' cancer could be treated with 50–60 Gy (Gy = Gray, the unit of dose) for a period of 4–6 weeks in doses given daily, Monday to Friday. The treatment is given by X-rays produced by a linear accelerator. The treatment itself takes less than 5 minutes. However, the calculation of the dose, which is tailored to each individual patient, and the technique of delivery may involve the skills of the hospital physicist.

Radiographers are skilled in helping the patient into the identical position for each treatment and this may take a further 10 minutes. The positioning is done not only by laser lights attached to the machines, but also with the use of plastic masks or moulds to immobilize moveable areas, such as the head and neck or limbs, in the same position. This immobilization is vital when irradiating radiosensitive structures. It also prevents unacceptably high or low doses in areas of overlap of the several radiation fields, which may be necessary to give the required treatment plan.

Diseases such as lymphoma or seminoma will in the main be treated in three or four weeks as a lower dose is required. Skin tumours, where the area of radiation is very small, can be treated with a smaller number of higher-dose fractions. Treatment that is radiobiologically equivalent, and therefore equivalent in damage to the tumour, can be given in a large number of small fractions, which spares the normal tissues, or a small number of larger fractions for the convenience of the patient.

Palliative treatment is often given for metastases (spread of disease). If the outlook is poor and symptom control is attempted, radiotherapy will be given in a very small number of treatments, possibly one or two, so as not to make increasing demands on a limited lifespan.

Radiotherapy treatment is painless but prolonged exposure to achieve a radical dose will certainly cause symptoms in the area irradiated. If the pelvis is treated, urinary frequency and diarrhoea may result; treating the stomach will result in nausea and vomiting. Breast radiotherapy, which includes treating the breast skin, will cause considerable soreness to the skin, which is maximal at the end of the treatment and for one week afterwards. In the head and neck area, not only will skin soreness occur, but the patient will develop a painful mouth and throat, difficulty in swallowing and dryness. These are all short-term effects of radiotherapy and should subside in 4–6 weeks following completion of treatment. Few side-effects would be expected following radiotherapy for palliation. The patient would of course be monitored regularly during the course of the treatment so as to try to alleviate any symptoms from which the patient is suffering.

Electron beam therapy

This radiation is also produced by the linear accelerator and is used for treating some skin tumours and to prevent damage to vital organs, such as the spinal cord. The beam can be of limited penetration.

Brachytherapy

This is the implantation of a radioactive or X-ray source into the patient, e.g. by implanting seeds, pellets or needles. Examples of intracavitary brachytherapy are:

- the implantation of a radioactive source into the uterine cavity and vagina to treat cancer of the cervix
- irradiation given via a radioactive pellet down a tube introduced either into the bronchus or the hepatic duct.

Brachytherapy can also be given in the form of radioactive needles or implants inserted into the tumour. This can be done in the mouth or prostate and the implant may be either temporary (removed after 4–5 days) or left in place to gradually decay over years. The advantage of brachytherapy is that by placing the source of the radiation very close to the tumour bed, a much higher proportion of the radiation will be given to the tumour than to the surrounding tissues. When radiation is given from a linear accelerator, which is at a distance from the patient, it is more difficult to irradiate just the tumour bed without also involving surrounding structures in the radiotherapy dose.

Chemotherapy

Chemotherapy is the administration of cytotoxic drugs in an attempt to cure or palliate cancer. Most chemotherapy is given intravenously, although some oral agents are now being used. Chemotherapy may be given by an intravenous injection of one or, more frequently, several agents. It is usually given in courses, normally 2–4 weeks apart, and the patient may need to have six or more courses. A combination of several chemotherapy agents may also be combined with other drugs, such as steroids, in the treatment regime.

The chemotherapy regime and doses will be prescribed by a medical or clinical oncologist and will be administered by nurses who have a specialist training in oncology, with the help of dedicated oncology pharmacists. Most chemotherapy is given as an outpatient but some regimes entail admission to hospital for treatment.

Chemotherapy may produce nausea and vomiting and a general feeling of malaise, accompanied by a decrease in the elements that form blood, most notably white blood cells, which are used to combat infection. Thus, from about 10 days after a chemotherapy injection, when the white cells arc at their nadir, patients will need to be monitored to ensure that they are not at any greater risk of infection, and if they are, prevention or treatment must begin. An overwhelming infection can occur at this point and is, unfortunately one of the most serious side-effects of chemotherapy. In addition, each specific chemotherapy agent has its own special range of side-effects, e.g. some drugs may be toxic to the heart and some to the kidneys.

Patients need to have a blood count prior to each course of chemotherapy to ensure that the fall in blood count which has resulted from the previous course has recovered sufficiently to administer the next. Most courses of chemotherapy are given by intermittent intravenous injections but for some tumours, notably tumours of the bowel, infusional chemotherapy over several days can be given as an outpatient by the insertion of a venous access line, or port, through which the chemotherapy may be pumped. There are different regimes of chemotherapy and different agents are used for different tumours.

The chemotherapy and radiotherapy that is usually given to patients with cancer is a standard regime which has shown its superiority in controlled clinical trials. The evidence base for regimes must be clear as this improves accountability and uniformity of treatment, and ensures the standard of care.

Chemotherapy may be given on its own as curative treatment for those patients with chemosensitive diseases such as leukaemia, some lymphomas and testicular cancers.

Combined treatment is given when radiotherapy and chemotherapy are prescribed at the same time. Clearly the side-effects of the treatment may be more difficult for the patient to tolerate when this is the case. However, in cancers arising in several sites, especially in the head and neck, combined treatment has been shown to improve survival.

Chemotherapy may be given as an *adjuvant treatment*, i.e. when no evidence of disease is clinically detectable in the patient and yet there is a high risk that somewhere there are enough malignant cells left to enable the disease to regrow. In such cases chemotherapy can be directed to all parts of the patient's body and will hopefully 'mop up' any residual cells.

Chemotherapy can be given in *advanced disease* in a palliative manner. In some chemosensitive disease, such as carcinoma of the ovary, chemotherapy may be given even when long-term palliation of symptoms and improved survival may be possible.

Chemotherapy is considered an expensive form of treatment. However, much less is spent on it in the UK than on laxatives. Clearly, it is important to consider cost and effectiveness, particularly as far as patients with palliative needs are concerned. The decision must be made with the patient in full knowledge of what benefit is likely to be expected from the treatment.

Breast cancer

The management process is illustrated by describing a typical treatment regime for a patient who has breast cancer.

This patient may have been invited for a standard screening and then had a recall letter for a further assessment if the mammogram was in any way suspicious. If a subsequent radiological and cytological assessment proves that this is cancer, the patient will be seen by a breast surgeon and discussed at a multidisciplinary meeting. Ideally, this meeting involves the breast care specialist nurse, oncologist, pathologist, radiologist and any other interested research groups. Many patients with cancers are managed by such a combined approach.

Chemotherapy for breast cancer can sometimes be given prior to surgery if the lump is considered too big for the patient to be offered excision and radio-therapy. Six courses of chemotherapy given prior to surgery may make the lump small enough for a lumpectomy and for radiotherapy to be the treatment of choice. This is called *neo-adjuvant treatment*.

If it is the patient's preference and the lump is small, the tumour may be removed by a local excision and sampling or removal of the glands under the arm, which are likely to be the first station of spread of the disease. If the patient has decided to conserve the breast rather than have a mastectomy, she will need a full course of radiotherapy to the residual breast area to prevent local recurrence.

The site of the original primary growth is the most common site of recur-rence in the small percentage of patients who do have a recurrence following lumpectomy, and thus, following a full course of radiotherapy, an extra dose is given to this area. If there are no involved glands under the arm then tradition-ally no radiotherapy will be given there or to the area above the clavicle. In the past radical radiotherapy would frequently be prescribed after surgery if there were any cancerous glands under the arm, but this practice is now more selective. The addition of radiotherapy to try to cure any disease in the armpit following radical surgery in this area means that the patient will have a higher chance of having a residual swollen arm due to increased difficulty with lymphatic drainage.

The historical problem of brachial plexus neuropathy, which is induced by over-treatment of the nerve branches and is associated with loss of function and pain in the whole arm, is now rarely seen. This was an infrequent but very severe complication of previous treatments and was the subject of a series of medico-legal concerns culminating in a report by the Royal College of Radiologists.

If the patient is young and has high-risk disease with spread to glands under the arm, then she will be offered adjuvant chemotherapy in the absence of any known residual disease. If chemotherapy is suggested it will usually be given before the radiotherapy course to the breast.

Several chemotherapy agents will be given in a pulsed manner over six courses at three-weekly intervals. Depending on the agents used, patients may or may not lose their hair during the treatment. Alopecia will not usually be permanent.

If on pathology analysis the breast cancer is considered to be hormone-sensitive, the patient will be offered a hormone drug (such as tamoxifen) in an attempt to reduce the number of viable cells which have remained in the body. Adjuvant chemotherapy and adjuvant hormone therapy in specifically indicated cases have an extensive evidence base of effectiveness.

Following surgery, chemotherapy, radiotherapy and hormone therapy, if appropriate, the patient will be seen regularly in outpatient clinics for at least five years with yearly mammographic monitoring and examination for any locally recurrent or widespread disease.

In the unfortunate circumstance of the disease recurring in a metastatic site such as the lung, liver, bone or brain, local radiotherapy for pain or to reduce brain swelling, and chemotherapy to reduce the extent of the disease in the lungs and liver, will be offered in an attempt to improve the quality of life. A close relationship with the palliative care team, general practitioner and hospice in continuing care will be maintained at all times.

Happily, patients with cancers are increasingly involved with their treatment and informed where there are choices to be made. They may be asked to be part of a clinical research trial if there is genuine doubt as to which of two treatments is appropriate and when they are considered to be equally effective.

In most cases, patients with cancers are managed by multidisciplinary teams so that the many specialists involved in diagnosing and treating cancer can offer the patient the benefit of combined opinion. The specialist nurse will help to steer the patient through the bewildering variety of personnel. The patient must always feel that there is every opportunity and facility to discuss the treatment and her anxieties or concerns, and her relatives must be welcomed into the discussion throughout the process.

Gynaecology

Roger V Clements

More than a decade ago the Harvard Study demonstrated poor correlation between adverse outcome and litigation.[1] In that study over 30,000 sets of notes were reviewed and 14 times as many adverse events were discovered as there were paid claims. Similar results have been found in other parts of the world, including a pilot study in the UK.[2] One factor which influences this relationship is the nature of the patient's original complaint or condition. Throughout medicine there is an inverse relationship between pathology and the risk of litigation. The more ill the patient, the less likely they are to sue in the event of a bad result. Nowhere is this better illustrated than in gynaecology. The gynaecologist (cancer apart) treats very few ill patients; most interventions are social or for relatively minor symptoms, such as menorrhagia. The patient who enters hospital well for a social intervention does not expect to be harmed; expectations of health are high and litigation is common when those expectations are not met.

Anatomy

The non-pregnant uterus is a thick-walled, muscular, hollow organ the shape and size of a small pear; its overall length is about 8–9 cm and at its widest it measures 6 cm. The uterus lies entirely within the pelvis and separates the bladder in front from the bowel behind (Figure 9.1). The anterior and posterior surfaces of the uterus are covered in peritoneum; in front a small vesico-uterine pouch separates it from the bladder but posteriorly there is a cul-de-sac (the pouch of Douglas). Any free fluid in the peritoneal cavity will tend to collect in the pouch (Figure 9.2). Most commonly, the uterus leans forward over the empty bladder (Figure 9.2) in a position of anteversion and anteflexion, but other positions are common and normal. The uterus tapers downwards towards the neck or cervix, which protrudes into the vagina (Figure 9.2).

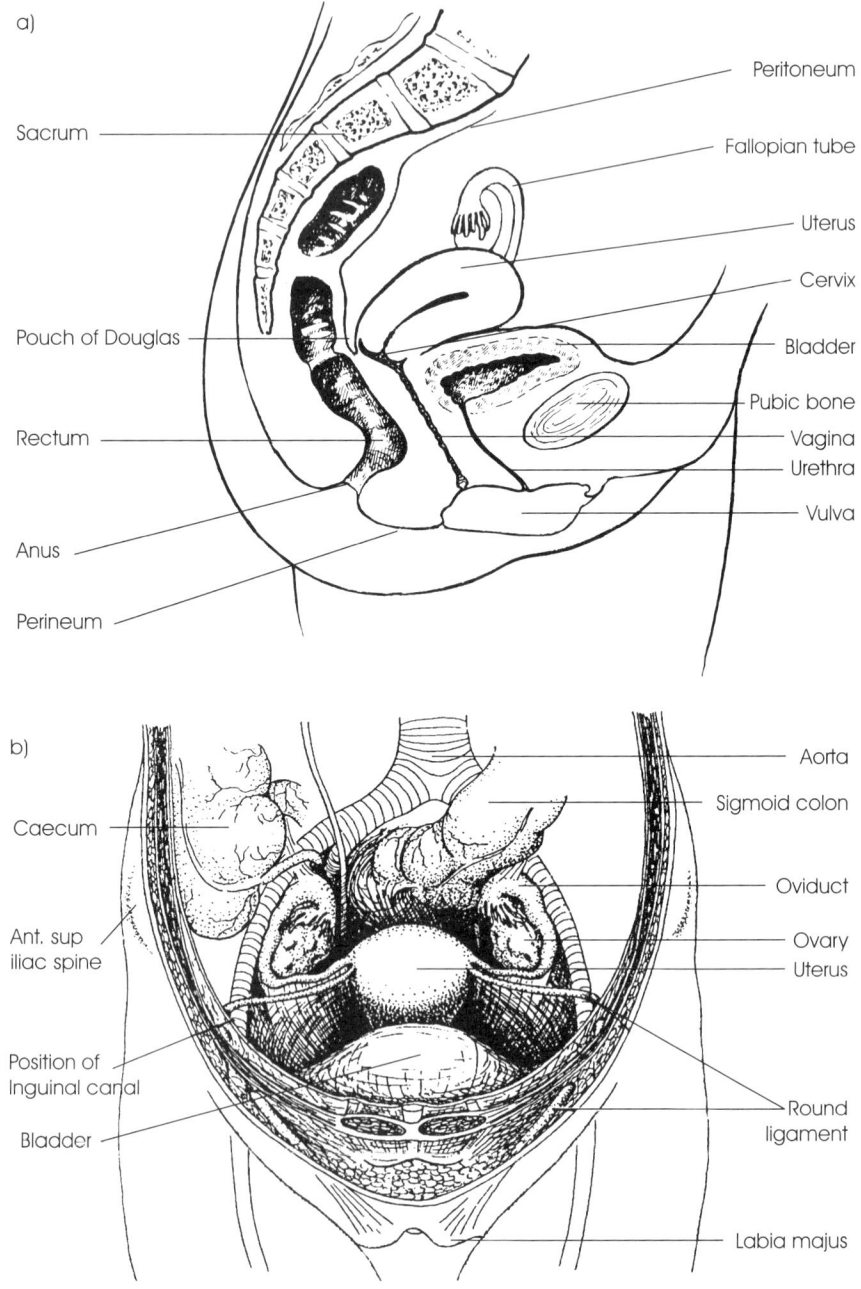

FIGURE 9.1 a) Female pelvic organs viewed from the side. b) Female pelvic organs viewed from the front. Adapted from Llewelyn-Jones D. *Fundamentals of Obstetrics and Gynaecology: volume 2, 4th edition*. Faber and Faber: London, 1986.

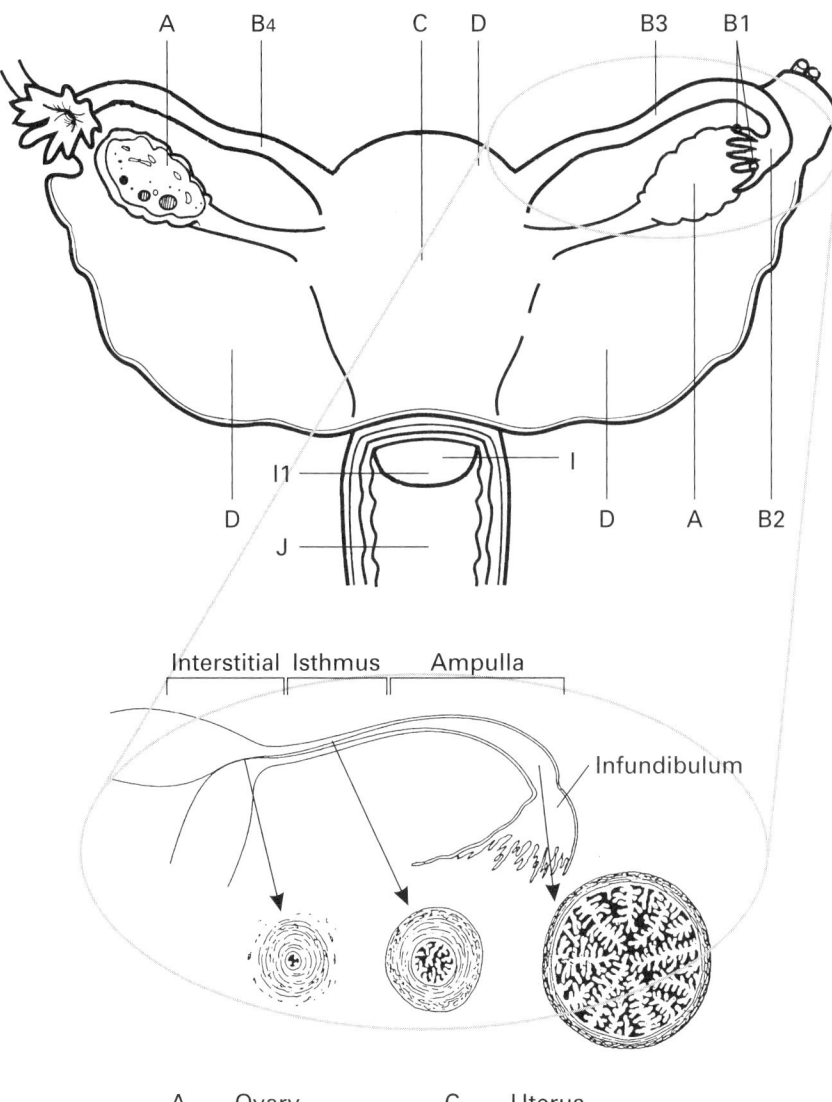

A	-	Ovary
B1	-	Fimbriae
B2	-	Infundibulum
B3	-	Ampulla
B4	-	Isthmus

C	-	Uterus
D	-	Broad ligament
I	-	Cervix
I1	-	Cervical os
J	-	Vagina

FIGURE 9.2 The Fallopian tube and its relations.

The peritoneum, which covers the anterior and posterior walls of the uterus, joins at the lateral margin to form a curtain that extends to the pelvic side wall. From the posterior surface of the curtain hangs the ovary—the only structure in the peritoneal cavity not covered by peritoneum. Along the top of the curtain, like a rod, runs the Fallopian tube. The cavity of the uterus is triangular, narrowing to an isthmus, which joins the cavity of the corpus uteri to the cervical canal. The lower end of the canal opens into the vagina at the external os.

Procedures most often leading to litigation

In common with all surgical procedures, gynaecological operations may be complicated by haemorrhage, anaesthetic mishap, thromboembolism and retained swabs. Litigation in gynaecological surgery is dealt with at length elsewhere.[3] Gynaecologists, perhaps more often than most surgeons, are accused of operating unnecessarily and beyond consent. The operations most commonly alleged to be unnecessary are hysterectomy and oophorectomy. The procedures which give rise most often to litigation are considered under six headings:

- dilatation and curettage (D&C), and vaginal termination of pregnancy
- intrauterine contraceptive devices (IUCD)
- laparoscopy
- sterilization procedures
- hysterectomy and related operations
- cervical cytology and surveillance for cancer.

Dilatation and curettage (D&C)

Access to the uterine cavity, whether for biopsy (curettage), examination (hysteroscopy), or operative intervention, such as termination of pregnancy or endometrial ablation, requires dilatation of the cervix. The steps involved in a simple 'D&C' operation are:

1. A vaginal speculum is inserted to expose the cervix and the anterior lip is grasped with a vulsellum (grasping forceps), drawing the cervix downwards into the vagina and straightening the endocervical canal, so as to make the passage of instruments safer.
2. A uterine sound is passed to measure the length of the cavity. Great care must be taken not to create a false passage or to perforate the fundus of the uterus with this relatively sharp instrument. This step is

strictly contraindicated in pregnancy; when terminating a pregnancy the size of the uterus is estimated by bimanual palpation, not by a metal sound.

3. The cervix is then dilated by the passage of graduated metal rods (Hegar dilators), each 0.5 mm greater in diameter than its predecessor. The operator must never pass the dilator further than the known length of the cavity. The extent of dilatation depends on the operation to be performed. For diagnostic procedures it is seldom necessary to dilate the cervix >7 or 8 mm, but for termination of pregnancy the extent of dilatation depends on the size of the fetus to be evacuated. If the cervix is to be dilated >10 mm, some preoperative preparation, either with prostaglandins or a hygroscopic dilator, is essential to prevent damage.

4. Examination of the uterine cavity may indicate minor pathology, such as a polyp, which can be simply avulsed.

5. For diagnostic purposes, a blunt spoon (curette) is used to scrape off the outer lining of the endometrium.

Hysteroscopy and operative procedures on the non-pregnant uterus require its prior distension with a suitable fluid medium.

All of these procedures have in common the following risks:

- damage to the cervix by laceration or over-distension
- haemorrhage
- perforation of the uterus
- infection.

Termination of pregnancy

Termination of pregnancy involves special risks; a detailed examination of them is outside the scope of this short chapter and is dealt with at length elsewhere.[4] When terminating a pregnancy in the first trimester (3 months) the operator, instead of a curette, inserts a plastic cannula and evacuates the pregnancy by suction. After about 14 weeks the pregnancy cannot be terminated solely by suction and if the vaginal operation is to be used at this gestation the fetus must be broken up by destructive instruments before it can be extracted. The two most common complications of vaginal termination of pregnancy are incomplete evacuation and trauma to the uterus.

Incomplete abortion

In all large series of vaginal terminations, at whatever gestation, there is a small incidence of retained placental and membrane fragments. In this sense incomplete termination of the pregnancy seems occasionally to be unavoidable and is not necessarily evidence of lack of skill or care. Where, however, significant parts of the fetus are retained there can be no excuse for the surgeon. It is mandatory that when terminating a pregnancy beyond about 10 weeks (when fetal parts can readily be distinguished), the operator should make sure that the complete fetus has been evacuated. The passage of a significant part of the fetus later by the patient at home is a distressing event and one likely to lead to litigation.

Skilled operators can safely terminate a pregnancy vaginally up to 24 weeks and this operation is readily available in the private sector. In the NHS the delegation of the task to junior doctors means that the skills are not available and, in practice, NHS terminations are usually not performed by this method after about 12–14 weeks. The alternative is 'medical termination' where 'labour' is induced by prostaglandins and the patient experiences the 'birth' of the fetus. At the other extreme, in very early pregnancy, the fetus may be missed altogether either because it has not yet arrived in the uterine cavity or because it is so small that it is easily missed by the suction curettage. For this reason most surgeons prefer not to attempt termination of pregnancy before about six weeks' gestation. Before the fetus is recognizable the operator relies on their judgement of the volume of tissue removed, to assess completeness. If the volume of tissue appears inadequate then the operator *must* investigate further by histological examination of the evacuated material and by ultrasound. A pregnancy test is unhelpful because, even if the pregnancy has been effectively terminated, the test will remain positive for several weeks afterwards.

Damage to the uterus

If the cervix is not adequately prepared, dilatation beyond Hegar 10 may cause deep tears in the cervix, perhaps even penetration into the broad ligament. Superficial damage to the cervix by a vulsellum is seldom important in the long term but deep tears may cause both short- and long-term problems. Haemorrhage into the deeper tissues may prove difficult to control, leading occasionally to hysterectomy, and in the long term the cervix may be incompetent in future pregnancy. Perforation of the uterus carries special risks when the suction cannula is being used—the cannula, free in the peritoneal cavity, may draw into its orifice a portion of bowel, which with further traction may be damaged. Perforation is not necessarily indicative of lack of skill or care but the operator should know when an instrument has passed beyond the confines of the uterus, and damage caused thereafter may be difficult to defend.

Intrauterine contraceptive devices

Like any other instrument passed blind into the uterus, an intrauterine contra-ceptive device has the potential to perforate the uterus at the time of insertion. There are seldom serious sequelae but the device then 'goes missing' and usually requires laparoscopy or laparotomy for its retrieval. Most such perfor-ations are silent and present as a pregnancy with no sign of the device at the cervix. The rate of perforation is commonly quoted as about 1 in 1000; it is usually difficult to establish that the perforation arises from a lack of skill or care, except when the operator has clearly mistaken the position of the uterus and inserted the device in the wrong direction. It is essential that the operator establishes the position of the uterus before the device is inserted.

Although the levonorgestrel-containing (hormone impregnated) intrauter-ine system (Mirena) has proved immeasurably superior to old-fashioned devices, both in terms of efficiency and unwanted side-effects, large numbers of the older devices are still being inserted on the grounds of economy.

Laparoscopy

Gynaecologists have had the diagnostic facility for examining pelvic and abdominal contents with a telescope since the middle of the last century. In the past 20 years the instrument has been developed as an operative tool. While these complicated procedures, relying on the virtual image, are a fertile ground for litigation, there is no space in this short chapter to deal with them. Diagnostic laparoscopy still generates the majority of complaints.

In order to introduce a telescope safely into the peritoneal cavity (Figure 9.3) the operator must first pass a needle blind, so as to introduce gas (a pneumoperitoneum); the gas separates the pelvic and abdominal viscera, allowing a view. The uterus is held steady (Figure 9.3) and a uterine cannula is inserted, through which dye can, if necessary, be injected to test the patency of the Fallopian tube.

It is this passage of the blind needle which is most likely to give rise to inad-vertent injury. The needle, designed by Janos Veress (for drainage of a hydro-thorax), has an ingenious mechanism which prevents the perforation of mobile structures.

Bowel is ubiquitous within the abdomen but because it is usually mobile, it escapes injury with the Veress needle. Fixed loops of bowel, adherent to pre-vious surgical incisions, may however be vulnerable and the operator should avoid insertion of the needle close to a previous abdominal incision. The main hazard is injury to a major blood vessel either on the abdominal wall (the

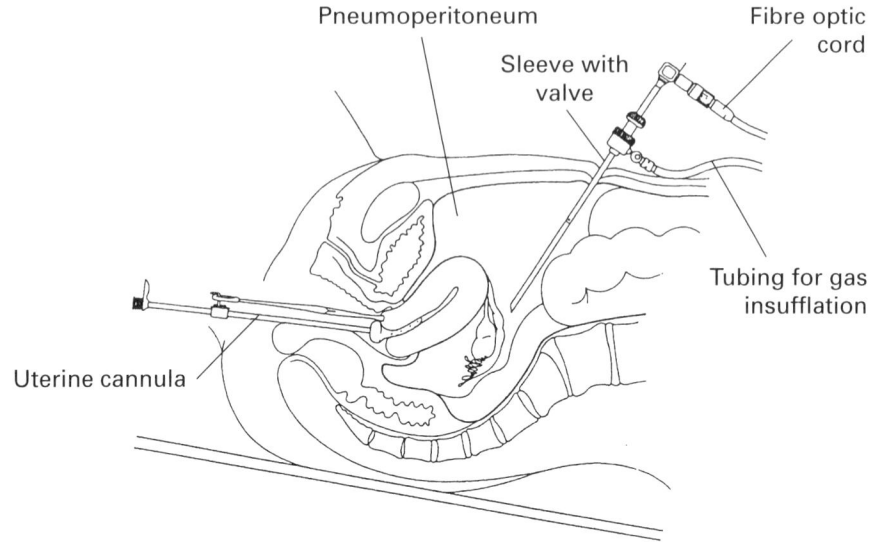

FIGURE 9.3 Laparoscopic visualization of the pelvis. From McKay EV, Beisher NA, Pepperell RJ, Wood C. *Illustrated Textbook of Gynaecology*, 2nd edn. W B Saunders, Bailliere Tindall, 1992, p 195.

inferior epigastric artery) or more importantly the posterior abdominal wall where the aorta and vena cava lie close to the thoracic spine. The avoidance of injury to these structures has been dealt with at length elsewhere.[5]

Sterilization

Traditionally there have been two causes for litigation in relation to female sterilization:

- defective consent
- defective surgery.

Defective consent is now diminishing as a topic for litigation. Since the early 1980s there has been a universally acknowledged duty to warn of failure in respect of both male and female sterilization. The cases of Eyre *v* Measday,[6] Gold *v* Haringey,[7] and Kean *v* Plymouth Health Authority[8] all mark this watershed. Mrs Eyre was sterilized in 1978, Mrs Gold in 1979 and Mrs Kean in 1980. To the author's knowledge the argument that there was a responsible body of medical opinion which would not have warned the patient has not succeeded since Kean. The message seems to have got through and it is now rare to find the accusation by a potential claimant that she was not warned. The breach is in any event usually without causation for it is the universal experience of gynaecologists that women who are properly warned accept the operation and take no additional precautions. The Court of Appeal in Lybert[9] held that it was 'in normal circumstances' intrinsically improbable that a couple would use contraception as well as sterilization.[10] Surgery may fail for innocent reasons or because of incompetence. It follows therefore that the existence of a pregnancy after sterilization proves nothing. The claimant needs to prove that in her particular case the restoration of fertility has not occurred by natural means. The key to the understanding of this problem is the anatomy of the Fallopian tube.

There are numerous methods of sterilization, some requiring open laparotomy, others performed through the laparoscope. They all have as their object the creation of a gap in the Fallopian tube (see Figure 9.2). It is not the application of stitches, clips or rings which effects the sterilization but rather the gap created by the absence of part of the tube. Even though that gap is effectively created, natural healing may achieve closure of the gap but there are always tell-tale pathological traces of the process. The Fallopian tube is composed mainly of muscle whose thickness varies throughout its length, and is lined on the inside (endosalpinx) and outside (serosa) by epithelium. While epithelium is capable of regeneration, muscle is not. When destroyed, muscle is replaced by scar tissue (collagen). The histopathologist can therefore *always* recognize the section of tube which has undergone recanalization. If the Fallopian tube, following whatever method of sterilization, is found to have an intact muscle layer throughout its length, it is a safe conclusion that that tube has not been subjected to a proper sterilization procedure.

The principal errors leading to failure are:

- operation on the wrong structure
- use of poor materials
- improper application.

From Figure 9.1 it will be apparent that the round ligament, a fibrous structure leading from the upper border of the uterus into the inguinal canal through the groin and into the labium majus (outer vulval lip) on each side, may be mistaken for the Fallopian tube. It should not of course be mistaken; its lateral anatomy is quite different. Equally, the inexperienced surgeon may mistake the ovarian ligament for the Fallopian tube.

Permanent suture materials, such as thread and silk, should not be used in open laparotomy methods, as they prevent the formation of a gap; being permanent, the continuous presence of a suture encourages fistula formation between the two cut ends. When clips and rings are applied it is important that the operator applies them to the correct part of the Fallopian tube. The Filshie clip is intended to be applied to the isthmus—if and when applied to the ampulla it will frequently fail to occlude the whole of the Fallopian tube lumen.

There is, at present, little agreement on the true failure rate of female sterilization; there is even less on the failure rate for vasectomy. It is inherently improbable that the failure rate for vasectomy could ever be known. Although Schiemann J in Gold v Haringey[7] 'found' that vasectomy was less likely to fail than female sterilization, the expert evidence on which he based that statement was flawed and never challenged. It used to be said that tubal interruption (by whatever method) had a failure rate of three or four per 1000, but that figure no longer looks credible in the light of the large US collaborative review, which prospectively followed 1685 women who were sterilized by a variety of methods. The cumulative risk of pregnancy was highest among women sterilized at a young age by bipolar coagulation (55.3 per 1000) and clip application (52.1 per 1000) and postpartum partial salpingectomy came out best at 7.5 per 1000, exploding another myth.[11] It is fair to point out, however, that the clips used in that review were mostly Hulka clips, a previous generation whose results are less good than with Filshie clips.

With the introduction of the hormone-containing Mirena in 1994 it is now increasingly difficult to justify sterilization as a first-choice method when it requires a separate operation; the failure rate for Mirena is strictly comparable and it is a virtually 'no risk' method with additional benefits to the woman.

Hysterectomy

The uterus may be removed either abdominally or vaginally; the vaginal operation has significant advantages for the patient with much less postoperative pain and a reduced hospital stay. It does however require a greater degree of skill on the part of the surgeon, skills which are no longer easily acquired because of the truncated training programmes now available to most specialists in training.

The principal complications of hysterectomy are:

- unnecessary surgery
- associated unwarranted castration
- haemorrhage
- accidental injury to bowel, bladder or ureter.

Many women who present to their gynaecologist with pelvic pain undergo hysterectomy without any measurable benefit. More than 50 years ago Jeffcoate condemned the practice:[12]

"Hysterectomy is a relatively easy operation to perform and it is often easiest when least necessary.... The surgeon lacking in conscience or care to make an accurate diagnosis.... resorts to hysterectomy on the slightest pretext and for indications such as 'chronic pelvic pain' of unknown aetiology."

Whilst unnecessary hysterectomy seldom leads (so far) to litigation in the UK, there have been several celebrated cases in which doctors have been disciplined for the removal of ovaries without consent. The most contentious complication of hysterectomy is damage to the urinary tract. This is dealt with in full elsewhere.[13–16]

There seems to be a consensus that in circumstances of normal anatomy it is not permissible for the surgeon to injure the ureter, as the steps required to protect the ureter are set out clearly in the textbooks and should be followed. Where the pelvic anatomy is distorted by disease, such as endometriosis, chronic infection or cancer, the surgeon may be excused for accidentally injuring a deviant ureter. But even in those circumstances the surgeon has a duty, before leaving the operative field (except in circumstances of grave emergency), to check that the ureter is intact.

"The venial sin is injury to the ureter, but the mortal sin is failure of recognition."[16]

Cervical cytology

Unlike most other cancers, the most common form of cervical cancer can be prevented by the surveillance of cervical cytology. Because the tumour goes through a 'preinvasive' phase it can, if detected, be removed before it becomes dangerous. There are three common complaints:

- failure to test
- failure to recall
- failure to diagnose.

While the first two are in the hands of the clinician, the third depends upon the skill of the cytological screener and cytopathologist. Dyskaryosis describes the appearances of isolated individual cells, whereas dysplasia describes abnormalities in the direction of cancer within the context of cell architecture, and is possible only with tissue biopsy. Colposcopy allows the examiner to determine which area of the cervix should be sampled, so as to examine for dysplasia. If colposcopy cannot identify the source of the abnormal cells the whole cancer-bearing area should be sampled in a cone biopsy. Cervical screening and recent litigation arising from it has been fully discussed elsewhere.[17–20]

References

1. Brennan TA, Leape LL, Laird NM *et al.* Incidence of adverse events and negligence in hospitalized patients. *N Engl J Med* 1991; **324**; 370–6.
2. Department of Health. *An Organization with a Memory*. Report of an Expert Group on Learning from Adverse Events in the NHS. London: HMSO, 2000.
3. Soutter P. Gynaecological surgery and oncology. In: Clements RV, ed. *Risk Management and Litigation in Obstetrics and Gynaecology*. London: RSM Press, 2001, Chapter 15.
4. Paintin D. Induced abortion. In: Clements RV, ed. *Risk Management and Litigation in Obstetrics and Gynaecology*. London: RSM Press, 2001, Chapter 18.
5. Clements RV. Major vessel injury. *Clin Risk* 1995; **1(2)**: 112–15.
6. Eyre *v* Measday [1986] 1All ER 488–97.
7. Gold *v* Haringey [1987] 2All ER 888.
8. Kean *v* Plymouth Health Authority—Unreported.
9. Lybert *v* Warrington Health Authority [1996] 7 Med LR 71.
10. Jones MA. Failed sterilization and omission to warn: the causation problem. *Clin Risk* 1998; **4(1)**: 12–16.
11. Peterson HB, Xia Z, Hughes JM *et al.* The risk of pregnancy after tubal sterilization: findings from the US Collaborative Review of Sterilization. *Am J Obstet Gynecol* 1996; **174**: 1161–70.
12. Jeffcoate TNA. Hysterectomy and its aftermath. In: *Principles of Gynaecology*. London: Butterworth, 1st edn, 1957, Chapter 46.
13. Clements RV. Urinary tract injury in gynaecology. *Clin Risk* 2000; **6(3)**: 89–93.
14. Stanton SL, Shah J. Recognition and management of urological complications of gynaecological surgery. *Clin Risk* 2000; **6**: 94–101.
15. Gumbel EA. Damage to the urinary tract at hysterectomy: A review of reported and unreported cases and discussion of the quantum of general damages. *Clin Risk* 2000; **6(3)**: 102–5.
16. Higgins CC. Uretral injury. *JAMA* 1962; **182**: 225–9.
17. Hudson EA. Cervical screening. *Clin Risk* 2000; **6(5)**: 177–81.
18. Wells W. Medico-legal aspects of histopathological reporting of cervical pre-cancer and cancer. *Clin Risk* 2000; **6(5)**: 182–5.
19. Soutter P. Diagnostic errors, surgical complications and causation in cervical cancer and pre-cancer. *Clin Risk* 2000; **6(5)**: 186–90.
20. Denton AS, Lambert H. Late complications arising from radiotherapy for carcinoma of the cervix. *Clin Risk* 2000; **6(5)**: 191–8.

10 Midwifery and obstetrics

Beverley Gordon and Gareth Thomas

There is no line of distinction between midwifery and obstetrics. In practice, a midwife will assist a woman through normal pregnancy and childbirth while an obstetrician is trained to manage any abnormalities encountered during that time. Midwives must know how to prevent or detect those abnormalities in a skilled and timely manner.[1] Equally they have a duty to inform and acknowledge patient choice. Sometimes the balance can be very difficult to achieve.

Midwifery: balancing risks with choices for childbirth

Modern midwifery practice works within a statutory framework set by the United Kingdom Central Council (UKCC—now the Nurses and Midwives Council since April 2002). At the same time it is subject to Department of Health (DoH) initiatives and to guidance from the Royal College of Midwives (RCM). Further influences come from the consumers whose rising expectations have been spurred on by initiatives, such as the government-sponsored Changing Childbirth project.[2]

The requirement to provide a flexible, responsive service while avoiding unnecessary risk is an everyday challenge for midwives and managers of maternity services.

Risk avoidance

The midwife who, as part of the initial antenatal booking process, records the medical and obstetric history of the pregnant woman can identify factors that might indicate whether the woman is at risk of complications in pregnancy and childbirth. The midwife should be able to use her knowledge to assess that risk and to provide evidence-based information for the woman and her partner. This will enable them to make informed choices about their care. Involvement of clients in clinical decision-making generally promotes trust both in the maternity service and in the individual professionals involved.

All advice and information taken from and given to the woman should be documented so that everybody involved in her care is aware of potential risks and misunderstandings. This documentation should be readily accessible to all the professionals giving care to the woman through her pregnancy. This is best achieved by asking each pregnant woman to carry her own notes with her at all times.

Risk reduction

Midwives must possess the knowledge necessary to provide women with up-to-date and accurate information and also the skills to ensure safe care. All practising midwives have to be registered through the NMC. They have to fulfil strict Post Registration Education and Practice (PREP) standards in order to maintain their registration. These self-declared standards may be audited at random. The practice of midwives is also monitored through a statutory system of supervision; each midwife has a named Supervisor of Midwives whose duty it is to review the individual's practice by audit and discussion.

This system of supervision is central to the protection of the public. It also offers support to midwives, to help them achieve high standards of care and to maintain their role in being 'minders' of normality.[3] Consequently, it has an important role to play in all aspects of clinical governance.

Clinical governance

Clinical governance is a collective term which encompasses risk management, the training and professional development of staff, the use of evidence-based guidelines and protocols, the setting of standards and the auditing of practice.

Risk management and the recording of adverse incidents are effective ways of protecting patients by improving standards. Analysis of adverse incidents highlights risk issues and helps prevent recurrence.

Adequate training of all maternity staff must be a high priority. Training needs may be identified through both the risk management process and the Supervision of Midwives.

Evidence-based guidelines for midwifery and obstetric practice also form part of the clinical governance initiative. These may originate locally, regionally or nationally. The National Institute for Clinical Excellence (NICE) has published two guidelines relating to childbirth and more are planned.[4,5]

Standard setting and clinical audit can lead to changes in practice and an improvement in the quality of care. Each midwife is expected to audit her own practice and to keep statistics relating to her work. Supervisors of Midwives are also involved in monitoring standards of maternity care.

All NHS trusts with obstetric units should have a Maternity Services Liaison Committee which has both professional and lay representation. This group is in a position to examine all aspects of the local maternity services with a view to effecting improvement.

The challenge of midwifery

The requirement to provide a flexible, responsive service while avoiding unnecessary risk is an everyday midwifery challenge in which a balance is sometimes very difficult to achieve. The more common examples of such challenges are given in Table 10.1, and the means of achieving the balance are listed in Table 10.2.

TABLE 10.1   Balancing risk with choice in maternity care

- *Prolonged labour*. Some women choose not to have their labour augmented. Maternal exhaustion and fetal distress may develop. Risks of morbidity and mortality are raised, both maternal and fetal.
- *Induction of labour for post-term dates*. NICE recommends that a pregnancy should not be left to pass beyond 41 weeks' gestation,[8] but some women choose to let nature take its course. Placental function may become impaired and in the worst case scenario the fetus may die.
- *Home birth* is sometimes requested when there has been a previous obstetric complication, e.g. Caesarean section. The community midwife cannot insist that the woman goes to hospital. She will be unable to monitor the fetal heart continuously at home. NICE recommends continuous monitoring[4] in patients with previous sections as it gives relatively early signs of uterine rupture of which there is a small but significant risk.
- *Caesarean section refused* by a woman when clinically indicated. Most women choose what is best for their baby but occasionally a woman will express her absolute objection to such intervention. In the past Court orders have been obtained to allow a Caesarean section to proceed[7,8] but only as a result of misrepresentation. The competent mother's decision is final. The fetus has no rights.
- *Screening tests*. (1) For abnormalities of the fetus. These should be carried out only at the request of the mother, but the choice must be offered. (2) For blood-borne viruses (HIV and Hepatitis B, most commonly). This screening has far reaching implications for the baby, family and health professionals giving care. There are treatments available which reduce transmission. Nevertheless, whether or not to screen remains an opt-in choice; it is the patient's decision. Universal precautions by midwives and other health professionals can reduce the risk of most infections being transmitted and should be in place for all situations where blood and body fluids are shed.

TABLE 10.2 Good practice guide to achieving the balance

* Assess the risks with care
* Give accurate information and realistic choice
* Involve the mother in the decision-making process
* Gain the mother's trust by keeping her informed at all times
* Agree the limitations of midwifery practice and when to refer
* Avoid falling out with the patient
* Consult the Supervisor of Midwives if choice entails excess risk
* Maintain good records and documentation

Obstetrics: managing divergence from the norm in maternity care

Having examined the principles that guide the management of a normal pregnancy, it is now important to study those areas in which clinical management may go wrong, particularly those instances where adverse outcomes frequently lead to litigation. Areas of care where expertise additional to that of an obstetrician is necessary are highlighted. The text includes a brief outline of the anatomy and physiology of labour.

Obstetric/midwifery care may be divided into four parts:

1. advice and counselling before conception
2. antenatal care and diagnosis
3. intrapartum care and delivery
4. postpartum care.

Advice and counselling before conception

This is commonly referred to as prenatal counselling. Many general practices and hospitals make specific provision for prenatal advice. However, the facility is not universally available despite there being several examples in which specific advice before pregnancy is likely to reduce the risk of a suboptimal outcome. These include:

* cessation of oral contraception three months before conception as there is a tenuous link between the 'pill' and subsequent fetal abnormality
* use of a folic acid supplement for three months prior to conception as there is strong evidence that it reduces the risk of neural tube defects, such as spina bifida
* provision of specific advice for epileptic patients who are particularly prone to folic acid deficiency. Some antiepileptic drugs are known to raise the risk

of teratogenesis. The care of epileptic patients should include prenatal discussions and a possible change of therapy under the supervision of a neurologist

- provision of specific care for diabetic and hypertensive patients in whom clinical control should be optimized by the relevant physicians before pregnancy is considered
- cessation of smoking, as nicotine is known to impair placental circulation.

Clinical genetics is a fast-moving specialty and it is now possible to screen individuals with relevant family histories for some disorders, such as cystic fibrosis and the muscular dystrophies, well in advance of conception.

In multiparous women (those who have given birth before) prenatal care starts with completion of the management of the previous pregnancy. Any diversion from the norm should be assessed and its relevance determined in order to help with the management of any subsequent pregnancies. Many requests for elective lower segment Caesarean section (ELSCS) come from women who have had a previous long-haul labour followed either by a difficult vaginal operative delivery or by an emergency lower segment Caesarean section (EmLSCS). For many there are symptoms which suggest the possibility of post-traumatic stress disorder. These women remain very frightened of having another similar experience, but this is often not raised in discussion until the last 2–3 months of pregnancy.

Antenatal care

Once a woman becomes aware of her pregnancy she should make contact with her general practitioner's surgery where appropriate healthcare professionals

TABLE 10.3 Antenatal care

- Booking at GP surgery
- Choices or options of care discussed
- Identification of lead professional
- Ultrasound scan at 10–12 weeks to confirm gestational age
- Hospital booking clinic if lead professional is an obstetrician or hospital-based midwife. Risk assessment
- Screening for chromosomal abnormalities, e.g. Down's syndrome. Other screening blood tests if not already carried out
- Mid-trimester fetal anomaly scan for physical abnormalities, such as spina bifida. Repeat risk assessment and planning of antenatal care
- Series of follow-up examinations usually shared between lead professional and other disciplines, e.g. midwife, GP and obstetrician
- Repeat risk assessment about term. Delivery management discussed

will arrange a series of screening processes which are known collectively as antenatal care. The basic plan of care is shown in Table 10.3.

Antenatal care should be a constant process of screening for fetal and maternal problems—an ongoing process of risk assessment. Where there is any doubt the patient should be referred to an obstetrician if the lead clinician is not one.

Table 10.4 shows the more common problems which may be identified. This list is not exhaustive but it represents the areas of antenatal care in which obstetric medico-legal activity occurs most frequently. Macrosomia is more likely to be associated with mechanical problems in labour or with maternal diabetes. Intrauterine growth impairment is more likely to be associated with intrauterine or intrapartum fetal death as it may be caused by poor placental function.

Multiple pregnancy carries its own specific problems. There is an increased risk of maternal complications of pregnancy, and a risk of twin-to-twin transfusion *in utero* when the pregnancy has arisen from one egg cell, as well as a series of added risks to the second twin during labour and delivery.

The risks of breech presentation in labour are so great and well-known that a recent multinational study comparing primigravid vaginal breech delivery with delivery by ELSCS had to be abandoned, first because of poor recruitment and second because of an early obvious difference in outcomes.[9]

'Grand multips' (sometimes defined as women with >4 previous viable pregnancies) are, like mothers with twin pregnancies, more prone to maternal complications of pregnancy, particularly anaemia and haemorrhage. The combination of grand multiparity and previous Caesarean section carries the risk of uterine rupture and the consequences may include litigation.

The risk of a ruptured uterus following a previous Caesarean section appears to be related to the inappropriate use of drugs to stimulate uterine contractions in a subsequent pregnancy.

TABLE 10.4 Antenatal risk assessment

Large fetus—macrosomia (birthweight >4 kg)
Small for dates fetus—intrauterine growth impairment
Multiple pregnancy
Malpresentation, e.g. breech
Grand multiparity (>4 previous viable pregnancies)
Previous Caesarean section
Maternal medical conditions, e.g. anaemia, diabetes mellitus
Maternal medical complications specific to pregnancy

Pregnancy-specific medical complications

Maternal medical conditions require the clinical expertise of appropriate physicians. Just as there are occasions when midwives fail to refer to obstetricians in a timely manner, so too are obstetricians sometimes slow in appropriate referral. During the past two decades there have been considerable improvements in the outcomes of pregnancies in diabetic mothers, thanks to the provision by most obstetric units of a combined antenatal/diabetic clinic. A similar approach to the management of hypertensive (raised blood pressure) pregnancies has been slower to take off, mainly due to a lack of local resource and the impracticality of managing such pregnancies at a distance on a regional referral basis. Repeated maternal mortality reports[1,10] have shown that the complications of poor management of hypertension in pregnancy continue to be lethal. These and other medical complications of pregnancy are also frequent subjects of obstetric medico-legal activity (see Table 10.5).

TABLE 10.5 Pregnancy-specific maternal complications

- *Pre-eclampsia and eclampsia.* In pre-eclampsia there is poor fluid balance, raised blood pressure, and protein in the urine, but not necessarily all three. It occurs in 20% of first pregnancies to a partnership. Poor clinical management may lead to eclampsia in which epileptiform fits present considerable risk to both mother and fetus.
- *Abruption*—retroplacental antepartum bleeding leading to placental separation, intrauterine fetal asphyxia and death, serious bleeding disorders in the mother (disseminated intravascular coagulation [DIC]) and HELLP syndrome (see below). There is a significantly greater risk of this in hypertensive and pre-eclamptic pregnancies.
- *HELLP syndrome*—this syndrome consists of the breakdown of red blood cells (Haemolysis), Elevated Liver enzymes and Low Platelets. Liver enzymes tend to rise and platelets tend to fall in worsening pre-eclampsia. The end result of HELLP syndrome is DIC, liver degeneration and other organ failure.
- *Cholestasis of pregnancy.* The flow of bile from the liver becomes static. The pregnant woman will present with intense generalized itching (pruritus). Liver enzymes, bilirubin and bile salts in the blood will be disordered. The condition is associated with increased risk of intrauterine death and fetal distress in labour. Pruritus of pregnancy is often dismissed as a 'minor' symptom of pregnancy.

Antenatal diagnosis

Various screening tests are available for fetal chromosomal abnormalities such as Down's syndrome. When screening suggests a risk of >1 in 250 the patient is offered either an amniocentesis (the withdrawal of liquor amnii via a needle through the abdominal wall at 15–18 weeks) or, if screening has taken place earlier by measuring the nuchal fold (the skin at the back of the neck), a chorionic villus biopsy, the taking of a small sample of placental tissue. There are strict Royal College of Obstetricians and Gynaecologists (RCOG) guidelines regarding the experience required for these two procedures. Regrettably the most common complication of each procedure is miscarriage. In the case of amniocentesis this occurs usually within 7–10 days of the procedure. It is usually due to the introduction of infection at the time of the procedure. Injuries to the fetus may occur, albeit rarely and despite the use of simultaneous ultrasound scanning. Not unnaturally such cases may give rise to litigation. Generally the discussion centres around issues of experience, failure to warn the patient and failure to notify the midwife or obstetrician of results of the screening tests.

Intrapartum care

Induction of labour: the dangers of Syntocinon

In a normal pregnancy labour should start spontaneously somewhere between 37 and 42 weeks from the date of the first day of the last menstrual period (LMP), assuming a 28-day menstrual cycle. The expected date of delivery (EDD) is the date exactly 40 weeks from the first day of the LMP. In a significant number of pregnancies the EDD will have been reassessed and changed following ultrasonographic measurements of the fetus and consideration of all the evidence. If a pregnancy passes beyond the EDD it becomes 'post-dates'. When it remains intact beyond 42 weeks it becomes 'post-mature' in which case there is a higher risk of poor placental function, fetal distress and the need for an EmLSCS in labour. In such pregnancies the fetal head has often remained fixed in the brim of the bony pelvis but is not engaged (Figure 10.1).

It is usual to offer induction prior to 42 weeks. This involves either artificial rupture of the membranes (ARM) and stimulating uterine contractions with an

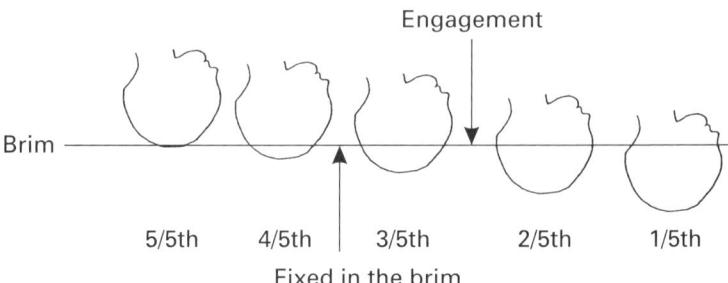

FIGURE 10.1 Diagram showing relationship between the fetal head and the brim of the pelvis and how engagement takes place between 3/5 above and 2/5 above the brim.

intravenous preparation of an oxytocic drug (known as Syntocinon) or inserting a vaginal preparation of a drug known as Prostin (prostaglandin E2). The decision depends on the state of preparedness of the cervix which should be assessed by vaginal examination and a scoring system known as the Bishop score. It is not uncommon to have to encourage cervical preparation with prostaglandin and then to move on to ARM and Syntocinon. Syntocinon should never be used unless the membranes are ruptured.

Measurement of the strength of contractions may be achieved using an intrauterine catheter but the method is rarely used, mainly for reasons of practicality. Instead, assessment of contraction strength continues to depend on clinical palpation by midwives and obstetricians. Unfortunately overdosage with Syntocinon or use of Syntocinon too soon after prostaglandin may result in contractions which are too strong or too frequent, or a resting tone which does not return to normal between contractions. In these circumstances there is a high risk of fetal distress because the placental blood flow is reduced by approximately 30% at the height of a normal strength contraction and more in the presence of excessively strong contractions (hypertonia).

Until 2001 each obstetric unit had its own guideline on induction of labour and the use of Syntocinon but a universal guideline from NICE, based on the best available evidence, is now available.[6]

Preterm labour: preterm rupture of membranes

A pregnancy becomes legally viable at 24 weeks. Labour occurring between this time and 37 weeks may be classed as preterm. Sometimes it may be preceded by spontaneous rupture of the membranes or bleeding. Provided there is no bleeding, attempts may be made to stop the labour by administering tocolytic agents but these are rarely successful if the cervix is >3 cm dilated or if the membranes are ruptured. There is strong evidence that two doses of steroids administered to the mother at least 24 hours prior to delivery will improve the survival rate of the preterm infant by reducing the risk of respiratory distress syndrome. Every effort should be made to administer these steroids. Simultaneous administration of tocolytics and steroids can present medical risks to the mother so that close monitoring is required. Preterm delivery, particularly in the 24–28 week period, is associated with a high risk of cerebral palsy (as high as 50% at 24 weeks).

Litigious activity in this area is usually associated with assessment of risk and issues of prevention rather than the management of labour. Expert opinion from appropriate specialists (e.g. obstetricians and paediatric neurologists) is essential in cases where there are questions about the standards of neonatal care and causation.

TABLE 10.6 Stages of normal labour

First stage—from onset of labour to full dilatation at 10 cm
- Latent phase: slow dilatation of cervix and descent of head may take days
- Active phase: rate of cervical dilatation varies with parity but average rate in a primigravid patient is 1 cm/hour

Second stage
- Inactive phase: from the detection of full dilatation to the onset of pushing
- Active pushing: from the onset of pushing to the completion of the delivery of the neonate. Should not exceed 1 hour

Third stage—from completion of delivery of the neonate to completion of delivery of the placenta and membranes

Failure to progress in labour

It is important to understand the features of normal labour (Table 10.6). Labour is divided into three stages. The first stage consists first of a slow latent phase followed by a faster, more predictable active phase. The second stage, associated with expulsion of the fetus, sometimes consists of a preliminary inactive phase prior to pushing. It seems to be the length of the pushing phase which is all important in the well-being of the neonate.

Progress in labour is not just a matter of cervical dilatation. It must be assessed also in terms of descent and rotation of the fetal head as it is pushed through the pelvis, first by uterine action and later, during the second stage, by maternal expulsive effort also. Matters are aided by the ability of the fetal head to mould, a process whereby the bones of the fetal skull are able to overlap, thus reducing the diameter of the skull. Moulding is graded from + to ++. If there is any more than one plus of moulding and still no progress, then there is likely to be cephalo-pelvic disproportion, in which case delivery should be completed by EmLSCS.

Labour is managed actively by means of four-hourly vaginal examinations. If progress appears to be slow then corrective measures are taken, such as the provision of better pain relief or the administration of oxytocic drugs. Re-examination is then brought forward by two hours. Further failure to progress in the first stage then necessitates an EmLSCS. Difficulties arise when progress does not actually stop but slows considerably in the later stages of the active phase or in the second stage. The fetus is at risk of becoming hypoxic and acidotic (fetal distress) and there comes a point where continuation of the labour runs the risk of fetal asphyxia. Under such circumstances fetal well-being is monitored by cardiotocography (CTG), which consists of a continuous print-out of fetal heart rate and a qualitative assessment of uterine activity (see page 123). The technique is inexact. Often there is no obvious time to intervene and a small number of neonates are born in a poor physiological state.

Cerebral palsy is a subject for paediatric neurological expertise. It is said that only one in 10 cases of cerebral palsy are associated with circumstances as described above. However, the aetiology of the condition is not well understood and its causation is the subject of scientific as well as legal debate. Subsequence must not be confused with consequence. It is very unlikely that cerebral palsy will be the result of intrapartum asphyxia if the following conditions are not met:

- low Apgar score
- evidence of hypoxic ischaemic encephalopathy (HIE)
- evidence of appropriate changes on magnetic resonance imaging (MRI).

Operative deliveries

Vaginal breech deliveries are increasingly uncommon. It is deemed unwise to attempt such a delivery in a primigravid patient. It is suggested that when there is a persistent breech presentation in later pregnancy some effort should be made to turn the fetus, using tocolysis if necessary. The more experienced the obstetrician in carrying out external cephalic version, the better will be their rate of success. However, there is no guarantee that the fetus will remain in the turned position—some will revert spontaneously to a breech presentation.

When labour fails to progress in the first stage there is no option but to deliver by EmLSCS. When there is failure to progress in the second stage and the presentation is by the head (cephalic) it is possible to effect most deliveries by operative vaginal delivery using mid-cavity forceps or, more commonly, the Ventouse vacuum extractor. The choice will depend mainly on the experience of the operator. Efforts are made to assist the uterine contractions and maternal effort in order to effect delivery. Guidelines suggest that it is unwise to persist through more than three contractions unless there is evidence of obvious progress.

A failure to deliver necessitates an EmLSCS. Caesarean sections at or near full dilatation can be very difficult. There is greater risk of not being able to extract the fetal head from the pelvis and of tearing in the region of the uterine blood vessels with the potential for serious sequelae, such as hysterectomy or disseminated intravascular coagulation (DIC). The outcome of litigation in such cases usually centres around the degree of experience of the operating surgeon.

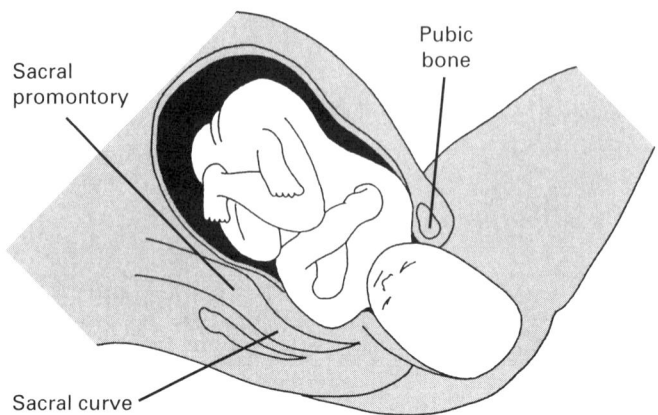

FIGURE 10.2 Shoulder dystocia. The fetal shoulders may become obstructed by the brim of the maternal pelvis. Note that the anterior shoulder is being pushed against the pubic bone. The posterior shoulder is in the sacral curve of the bony pelvis. The shoulder dystocia is more severe, with risk of greater consequences, if the posterior shoulder is also obstructed, i.e. above the sacral promontory.

Risk does not cease with delivery of the head. All obstetricians and midwives must be prepared to contend with the nightmare situation of shoulder dystocia. There are strict guidelines on the management of this obstetric crisis in which one or both shoulders fail to enter the maternal pelvis following delivery of the fetal head (Figure 10.2). The situation is likely to occur when the diameter of the fetal shoulder girdle exceeds the diameter of the head. In 50% of cases the baby will weigh in excess of 4 kg (macrosomic), and in 50% there will be injury to the ipsilateral brachial plexus (the complex of nerve roots which leave the spinal cord on each side in the region of the neck). The injury is known as brachial plexus palsy. This may resolve if the injury is limited to bruising but may not resolve if there is actual tearing of the brachial nerve roots. Shoulder dystocia, albeit rare, presents particular difficulties when litigation arises as expert opinion is divided over the diagnosis and management of the condition.

Cardiotocography

No commentary on intrapartum care would be complete without specific reference to CTGs. A cardiotocograph (CTG) is a simultaneous recording of uterine activity and fetal heart rate (Figure 10.3). The uterine activity is usually detected by means of a pressure transducer, which is strapped to the maternal abdomen. Sometimes the record is obtained by means of an intra-

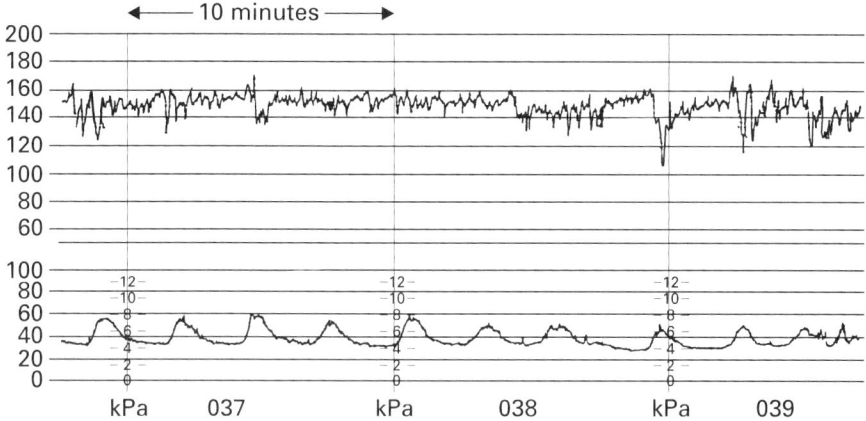

FIGURE 10.3 Cardiotocographic record. The trace was taken in the active phase of the first stage of labour. There are no accelerations of fetal heart rate (FHR) of note and there are some early decelerations that are within normal limits. The rate and baseline variability are normal. There are regular contractions on this record. The figures on the left side (60–200) represent FHR in beats per minute. The figures 0–100 are measures of uterine pressure, expressed as mmHg. The smaller figures (0–12) on the vertical lines represent kPa–a modern measurement of uterine pressure.

uterine pressure catheter. The fetal heart rate is derived using an ultrasound transducer, which again is strapped to the maternal abdomen. Sometimes the record will be obtained by means of an electrode attached to the fetal scalp (fetal scalp electrode). The trace paper runs at 1 cm per minute unless specifically indicated otherwise.

Some lawyers appear to believe that CTGs represent an exact record of the timing of events through labour. However, for obstetricians and midwives they represent an inexact and poorly developed science.

Space does not allow an in-depth description of CTGs. Suffice it to say that in a search for intensive monitoring of the fetal ECG in the 1960s, it was discovered in the USA that the fetal heart *rate* (FHR) changed predictably in certain physiological situations in the labouring rhesus monkey. Similar predictable changes occur in the human. If a fetus is short of oxygen the fetal heart rate will decelerate following a delay (late deceleration). The heart rate will recover only slowly when oxygen levels are corrected. All fetuses experience a certain degree of hypoxia during labour, usually at the time of strong contractions. Whether or not it has an adverse effect depends on the fetal reserves of energy and the frequency or duration of the hypoxia.

If the head of the fetus is squeezed then the FHR would decelerate immediately and recover as soon as the pressure is relieved (early deceleration).

Similarly, if the cord is squeezed, immediate and precipitous falls in FHR would occur but recovery is equally rapid once the pressure is released.

Also in the sixties, a technique for sampling fetal scalp blood was developed in Germany and it was noted that when the pH of the blood was low (<7.2) (acidotic) there was very little baseline variation of heart rate. A fetus with no reserves and experiencing hypoxia will become acidotic.

Unfortunately, reliable ultrasonic techniques for external FHR monitoring were not available until 1983. Up to that time the only method of achieving a reliable FHR record in the human was to rupture the membranes and to apply a scalp clip. Consequently, information on the normal human fetus, unaffected by contractions or by liquor drainage, was scant prior to the mid-1980s.

Classifications of FHR changes were developed in the 1970s and are still used today in too many quarters. Since the introduction of better ultrasonic Doppler techniques in 1983 it has been possible to determine that the normal healthy fetus demonstrates frequent accelerations of FHR, that a healthy fetal heart will rarely decelerate prior to established labour, and that narrowing of the baseline variability will not last >40 minutes at a stretch in a non-acidotic fetus. This information has led to more appropriate classifications of normality. FHR traces should be used only as a screening tool to determine which fetuses require blood sampling.

The inexactness and poor teaching of FHR monitoring has led to many instances of serious misinterpretation. Recent developments have led to computer-based training programmes to which all professional CTG users should be subjected.

Postpartum care

Postpartum haemorrhage

Bleeding after delivery is known as postpartum haemorrhage—it may occur as a primary phenomenon within 24 hours of the delivery or a week or so later as a secondary phenomenon, a consequence of retained products of conception. The completeness or otherwise of the placenta and membranes should be documented by the midwife who should notify a doctor if there is any doubt. If products are retained then a formal manual removal of placenta should be carried out under spinal, epidural or general anaesthesia.

Pelvic floor damage

A tear of the perineum or an episiotomy should be sutured as soon as possible after delivery. Sometimes the damage will extend beyond the perineum into the anal sphincter (third degree) or even through the recto-vaginal septum (fourth degree). Resuturing of both degrees of extension require expertise and adequate anaesthesia. Failure to recognize a fourth-degree tear will result in a recto-vaginal fistula and the passage of stool from the vagina with considerable sequelae in terms of surgery, pain and suffering, and disfigurement. Delayed incontinence of stool from the vagina suggests a fistula, which has developed through poor blood supply or poor healing following repair.

It is suggested that at least 30% of recently-delivered women will demonstrate damage to the anal sphincter if tested ultrasonically. This startling fact tends to distort the medico-legal aspects of pelvic floor damage as this is not damage which can be detected clinically immediately after delivery.

Counselling

It is important to stress the value of debriefing after a complicated pregnancy or delivery. It clears up many questions in the patient's mind, reduces the chance of complaint and, most importantly, lessens the likelihood of repeat complications in subsequent pregnancies.

Acknowledgement

The authors are grateful to the Department of Medical Illustration at The Ipswich Hospital NHS Trust for preparation of the illustrations.

References

1. Department of Health. *Why Mothers Die: Report on Confidential Enquiries into Maternal Deaths in the UK 1997–1999*. London: The Stationery Office, 2001.
2. Department of Health. *Changing Childbirth: Part I. Report of the Expert Maternity Group*. London: HMSO, 1993.
3. English National Board (ENB). *Advice and Guidance for Local Supervising Authorities and Supervisors of Midwives*. London: ENB, 1999.
4. National Institute for Clinical Excellence (NICE). *The Use of Electronic Fetal Monitoring*. London: NICE, 2001.
5. National Institute for Clinical Excellence (NICE). *Induction of Labour*. London: NICE, 2001.
6. National Institute for Clinical Excellence (NICE). *Induction of Labour* Clinical guideline D (June 2001) www.nice.org.uk/pdf/inductionoflabourfinalguidance.pdf.
7. Royal College of Obstetricians and Gynaecologists (RCOG). *A Consideration of the Law and Ethics in Relation to Court Authorised Obstetric Intervention*. London: RCOG, 1994.

8. Royal College of Obstetricians and Gynaecologists (RCOG). *Supplement to A Consideration of the Law and Ethics in Relation to Court Authorised Obstetric Intervention.* London: RCOG, 1996.

9. Hannah MA, Hannah WJ, Hewson SA, *et al.* Planned caesarean section versus planned vaginal birth for breech presentation at term: a randomised multicentre trial. *Lancet* 2000; **365**: 1375–83.

10. Department of Health. *Why Mothers Die: Report on Confidential Enquiries into Maternal Deaths in the UK 1994–1996.* London: The Stationery Office, 1998.

11 Paediatrics

Harvey Marcovitch

Nature of the workforce

In the UK the NHS employs over 2200 consultant paediatricians and a similar number of trainees in the specialty. Most are employed within hospitals but many are community paediatricians. Unlike the situation in the USA and many European countries, none practises in primary care. Most childhood illness is dealt with by general practitioners (GPs). Even in hospitals, 'adult' surgical specialists and their trainees deal with more than half the children admitted.

General, orthopaedic and ear, nose & throat (ENT) surgeons conduct most surgery on children but there is a small and distinct specialty of paediatric surgery, handling operations on the newborn and small infants, and particularly complex procedures on young children. Paediatric surgery is dealt with in Chapter 12.

The main paediatric subspecialties include neonatology (the largest group), neurology, endocrinology, gastroenterology, nephrology, oncology, respiratory paediatrics, infectious disease, intensive care and rheumatology. In itself, this may raise issues in litigation—namely, whether or not a particular child should have been referred to a specialist rather than cared for by a generalist. In general, the question cannot be answered by reference to guidelines. Many reports have been published on the issue but most consist of 'wish lists' by specialty groups. However, the British Association for Perinatal Medicine has produced authoritative guidelines on who should provide different levels of neonatal care (see http://www.bapm.org/publications.php). For other specialties see *Commissioning Tertiary & Specialized Services for Children*, 2004 (www.rcpch.ac.uk).

Consultants normally work with a team, which may include senior house officers (SHOs), specialist registrars (SpRs) and staff grade doctors (often referred to as 'juniors'). The first of these are relatively inexperienced, undertaking general professional training leading, usually, to entry into general practice (GP vocational trainees or GPVTs) or paediatrics. The second have been accepted onto a 5–6-year programme to train as paediatricians, at the end of which time they receive their certificate of completion of specialist training (CCST) and can apply for NHS consultant posts. Staff grade doctors are permanent staff members not trainees, who, for various reasons, have not been accepted onto the national training programme leading to a CCST. Each patient has a named consultant who is responsible for his or her care.

Many claims relate to failure to call a senior member of the team or failure to respond when trainees are out of their depth. It is likely that these claims will diminish as emergency care becomes more and more consultant provided, which is current Department of Health policy.

As an aside, the author's experience is that claimants (and solicitors) commonly refer to the junior doctors whom they (or their clients) have seen as 'paediatricians'. On receiving an expert's report they are often surprised to learn that care was given by a trainee.

Nature of the specialty

Children become ill more rapidly than do adults. They are also more likely to recover since chronic (long-term) illness is less common than in adults. The most common reason for acute (sudden) illness is infection. Children suffer far more infections than adults because of the relative immaturity of their immune system; the younger the child the more vulnerable they are. Failure to recognize the severity of illness or to predict the speed and extent of likely deterioration is a frequent cause for complaint or litigation, e.g. in claims regarding failure to diagnose meningitis.

Very young children (under a year) respond to acute illness in a stereotyped manner. Unlike in adults, the symptoms and signs of many different illnesses may be virtually identical, and so difficult to separate, and, of course, young children may not be able to help their doctor by explaining what they are experiencing. For example, lethargy and abdominal pain with evidence of dehydration may be diagnosed by a GP or an accident and emergency SHO as due to gastroenteritis when the cause is actually diabetic precoma. The key is whether the doctor remembered to test the patient's urine and blood for sugar. Headache may be diagnosed as a simple consequence of a raised temperature and indeed is usually no more than that, but the same symptom may be experienced by a child with raised intracranial pressure due to meningitis, brain abscess or a tumour.

Newborn babies are an especially vulnerable group. Death is more likely in the first 24 hours after birth than on any other day (except, of course, the last 24 hours). Acute severe illness not leading to death may result in permanent damage to the developing brain, leading to cerebral palsy. The technical procedures necessary for successful treatment are difficult and may demand exceptional skills, e.g. the insertion of intravenous or intra-arterial lines. The most expensive claims relate to alleged misdiagnosis or mistreatment of newborn infants immediately before, during, or soon after delivery, particularly with regard to hypoxia (reduction in tissue oxygen supply). There is much contention regarding how to determine how severe hypoxia might have been and whether or not it has been responsible for (i.e. caused) any subsequently diagnosed disability.

Chronic illness may lead to claims because its rarity means some doctors may be unfamiliar with the illness itself, with techniques of diagnosis or the necessary treatment. For example, in certain inherited metabolic disorders, coincidental commonplace (and normally unimportant) infection or moderate dehydration may lead to a previously unrecognized (because it is asymptomatic), longstanding but stable situation becoming dangerously unstable.

A further role for paediatric SHOs working with newborn babies, some community paediatricians, and many GPs is to conduct screening examinations for handicapping conditions during early childhood. Screening implies performing a standard examination on the whole population at risk to divide it into a group at low risk and another at high risk for the condition in question. Claims arise alleging failure of screening, e.g. with regard to such conditions as developmental dysplasia of the hip (also called congenital dislocation of the hip), congenital heart disease, congenital hypothyroidism and phenylketonuria.

Some doctors, found by the courts to have failed in their duty of care, have expressed alarm that the law sometimes has a different perspective from medicine on the validity of screening tests, apparently finding the concepts of false negatives and false positives difficult to comprehend. It is important to understand that a screening test is not the same as a diagnostic investigation.

Specific conditions causing problems

Meningitis

This is defined as inflammation of the meninges (membranes surrounding the brain) and spinal cord. Usually there is coincident involvement of the brain itself—meningoencephalitis. Doctors rarely use the latter, more accurate term, so that 'meningitis' now implies that the brain is also involved. Confirmation of diagnosis is by laboratory examination of cerebrospinal fluid (CSF) taken by lumbar puncture.

Viral meningitis is generally benign and litigation is uncommon as no specific treatment is available for most viruses (herpes virus is an exception).

Of the bacterial varieties, the diagnosis of pneumococcal meningitis is often subject to litigation: it may have a slow onset or even supervene unobtrusively during the course of a non-specific, and apparently harmless, upper respiratory tract infection ('a cold'), so diagnosis may be delayed. On the other hand, meningococcal disease often provokes litigation because of its extraordinary rapidity of onset and progression. From first signs of illness to imminent death may be a few hours only and the early signs may be missed or misinterpreted.

Group B streptococcal meningitis specifically affects newborn infants because their mothers commonly carry the bacteria in their genital tract. In the USA, protocols demand screening of pregnant women, followed by anti-biotic treatment and preventive measures when the baby is born. Currently there is no national protocol in the UK, but there are many local guidelines.

Litigation with regard to meningitis usually relates to death or serious sequelae, including deafness and structural brain damage, resulting in mental or motor incapacity (or both), and/or epilepsy. Arguments around cau-sation frequently centre on the 'window of opportunity' during which treat-ment might have been effective. There is a particular difficulty in proving liability (causation) with regard to hearing loss as this occurs very early in the course of the illness, often before even the most astute doctors recognize that the child is significantly ill.

Septicaemia

This implies that bacteria multiplying within the normally sterile blood stream have activated the child's immunological system. In turn, this results in the production and release of so-called cytokines, proteins that attach themselves to body cells and dramatically alter their function. Sometimes it coexists with meningitis.

In its early stages, septicaemia provokes little more than fever and non-specific signs of infection such as lassitude, irritability, anorexia and vomiting. Every year, many thousands of infants and children are infected in this way. Often the condition is self-limiting, the organisms being killed by the body's defences, or by prescribed antibiotics, before the cytokine system is irreversibly activated. Such children may be ill for only a day or two, and then only mildly. Treatment of *early* septicaemia (sometimes termed bacter-aemia) using antibiotics alone is usually successful. As a result there are various protocols advising 'care pathways' for febrile infants. For example, one that is commonly used mandates intravenous broad-spectrum antibiotics for any *ill-looking* child under two years of age with a fever $>39°C$ and a white blood count $>15,000$ (another quotes 20,000). The problem is that 'ill-looking' is a somewhat subjective criterion. It means something quite different to a parent than to a paediatrician. Claims may depend upon a court's decision on whether or not an infant was 'ill-looking'. Lawyers need to be aware that doctors often use the term 'ill' to mean what a lay person would call 'seriously ill' and 'well' to mean what a lay person might reason-ably describe as 'mildly ill'.

Pneumonia and other respiratory disorders

The most common reason for hospital admission of a sick child (and of GP consultations) is a respiratory infection. They are often defined as upper respiratory tract infection (URTI) or lower respiratory tract infection (LRTI). The former may be no more than the common cold, but also includes ear and throat infections (otitis and tonsillitis or pharyngitis). LRTI implies inflammation of bronchi, the larger air tubes (acute bronchitis); of their smaller branches, bronchioles (bronchiolitis); or of lung tissue itself (pneumo-nia). An individual child may have any combination of these, as they are ana-tomically congruent.

Doctors often use the generic term 'chest infection' for any or all of these conditions. The author's view is that they do so euphemistically as many parents see pneumonia as a serious disease; in fact it may vary from life threa-tening to virtually asymptomatic. Chest infection sounds commonplace and so provokes less parental anxiety.

Wherever the anatomical site of inflammation, competent management looks first at whether or not there is respiratory distress or decompensation. Clinicians have to ask themselves: 'can this baby exchange gases adequately?' They mean: 'can this baby absorb sufficient oxygen through inflamed lung tissue or obstructed airways to oxygenate blood properly, and dispose of suffi-cient carbon dioxide to preserve the body's acid–base equilibrium?'

Many respiratory infections are complicated by the fact that the child has inherited a propensity to asthma (15–20% of the population). This may further compromise breathing and demand its own specific treatment with bronchodilators and steroids.

Litigation in respiratory illness often involves alleged mismanagement of bronchiolitis, a winter epidemic disease of infants, 95% of whom recover with little intervention but 5% of whom may need to be ventilated artificially. A few of the most severely affected infants may die or suffer hypoxic brain damage if the need for artificial ventilation is not anticipated in a timely manner and the infant is not transferred to intensive care.

Common errors include

- not realizing the extent of impaired gas exchange by failing to monitor or act upon oxygen saturation readings
- paradoxically, failure to recognize clinical deterioration by over-reliance on saturation measurements (SO_2), which may be misleading, and failure to use the more accurate method of measuring arterial blood gases (pCO_2, pO_2, pH)
- failure to recognize the presence of an unstable foreign body (such as a sweet or a piece of apple) in the airway and thus obtain immediate attention from a senior anaesthetist and/or surgeon.

Gastroenteritis

This implies inflammation of the stomach (gastritis), which is likely to cause abdominal pain, nausea, loss of appetitie and vomiting; and inflammation of the intestines (enteritis) which results in diarrhoea. Viruses (rotavirus, enterovirus) cause most gastroenteritis in the UK but bacteria, such as *Salmonella*, *Campylobacter* and enteropathogenic *E. coli* may be involved. The mainstay of management is keeping the child well hydrated and preventing electrolyte disturbance.

Pitfalls include:

- failure to recognize the degree of dehydration, so underestimating how much rehydrating fluid to give
- failure to recognize that there may be coexisting electrolyte imbalance that requires more careful choice of rehydrating agent (e.g. hypernatraemia, a high serum sodium)
- misdiagnosing some other intestinal disease (e.g. appendicitis) as gastroenteritis because the latter is common and usually easy to deal with
- failure to investigate for inflammatory bowel disease (Crohn's disease and ulcerative colitis) in a child who does not recover at the conventional rate.

Febrile seizures

About three in 100 children aged six months to six years will convulse during an illness with a raised body temperature. Some children have multiple febrile seizures. Certain infecting organisms are more commonly associated with the problem, there is a genetic component, and the rate of temperature change is probably a factor. In general, febrile seizures are benign and of little consequence (except in scaring parents who witness them). It is common in less busy hospitals to admit overnight a child with their first febrile seizure but not subsequently.

Pitfalls include:

- misdiagnosing epilepsy as febrile seizures, but this is usually of little consequence as the correct diagnosis eventually becomes obvious in most cases
- diagnosing a febrile seizure in a child with meningitis or encephalitis, and so failing to treat appropriately
- missing a brain tumour in a child, who happens to have a fever from a coincidental illness when he has a fit as a result of raised intracranial pressure from the effect of the tumour.

Cancers

Rarity can lead to delayed diagnosis. The author's experience of litigation in this area is that failure to diagnose brain and spinal cord tumours makes up the majority of cases. Other childhood cancers, such as leukaemia, bone cancer and 'solid tumours', are usually diagnosed quickly because their manifestations are acute or easily seen or felt by the examining doctor.

Central nervous system tumours often present subtly and gradually, frequently leading parents to present their child late to the GP; also the latter may be slow to refer on for a specialist opinion, and the paediatrician may add to the delay by chasing more common diagnoses.

The major pitfall is that a prime symptom of a brain tumour is recurrent or persistent headache, which is far more commonly due to tension (stress) or migraine. Spinal tumours may provoke back pain (misdiagnosed as minor injury), urinary frequency or incontinence (misdiagnosed as anxiety or secondary enuresis of unknown cause), and difficulty with defaecation (misdiagnosed as simple constipation).

Other common childhood disorders

Table 11.1 lists the particular diagnoses in relation to which the author has provided expert evidence on more than four occasions.

TABLE 11.1 Diagnoses in relation to which the author has provided expert evidence

Cerebral palsy	Alleged mismanagement of labour or neonatal care
Congenital disorders	Spina bifida
	Hydrocephalus, including complications of ventriculoperitoneal shunts
	Congenital heart disease (usually failure of detection by screening)
	Developmental dysplasia of the hip (usually failure of detection by screening)
	Down's syndrome and other chromosome disorders (wrongful life)
	Torticollis (wry neck) allegedly related to birth injury
Infections	Meningitis and/or septicaemia
	Pneumonia
	Encephalitis (usually due to herpesvirus, so potentially treatable)
	Gastroenteritis (dehydration, hypernatraemia and other complications)
	Bronchiolitis (with hypoxic brain damage)
Tumours	Brain and spinal cord tumours (usually delay in diagnosis)
Surgical	Appendicitis (delayed diagnosis)
Neurodevelopmental disorders	Sudden infant death syndrome (preventability thereof)
	Behaviour problems and/or learning disability
	Epilepsy, including psarrhythmia (a rare form in infants causing severe brain damage)
	Head injury (failed monitoring with delayed referral for neurosurgery)
	Inborn errors of metabolism
Treatment	Extravasation of fluids from an intravenous line ('drip') causing skin loss
	Drug overdoses or toxicity

12 Paediatric surgery

Lewis Spitz

The paediatric surgeon has the responsibility for the overall management of general surgical conditions from the prenatal period through the neonatal period and infancy, to the age of 14–16 years. There are two categories of paediatric surgeon. One is the *specialist* paediatric surgeon whose primary responsibility is for the newborn infant (up to 44 weeks postgestational age), for the management of complex conditions requiring surgical expertise, for paediatric urology, as well as 'straight forward' surgical conditions in children with an associated disorder. Specialist paediatric surgeons work in centralized specialist units serving a population of around 2.5 million. The other category is the *general* paediatric surgeon, who undertakes the surgery of relatively common conditions that do not require a major operation or complex perioperative care, e.g. hernias in the older child, surgery for undescended testes, circumcision and emergency surgery for acute appendicitis, torsion of the testis and minor trauma.

The issues which may confront the paediatric surgeon are discussed under the following headings

- prenatal diagnosis and management
- neonatal period
- childhood problems
- intravascular infusions
- consent.

Prenatal diagnosis and management

The specialist paediatric surgeon should form an integral part of the fetal medical team. The detection of a surgical abnormality in the developing fetus will have been established by the ultrasonographer and confirmed by the fetal medical specialist. One role of the paediatric surgeon is to provide accurate counselling to the parents. Although the paediatric surgeon will be aware of the prognosis for the condition *after* birth, fetal loss during gestation will alter the ultimate survival rate. Prior to counselling, it is important to perform chromosomal analysis and to carry out tests to detect additional mal-formations, such as cardiac anomalies.

Congenital diaphragmatic hernia detected before 24 weeks' gestation has a mortality of around 60% compared with a 70–80% survival for infants born at term with a diaphragmatic hernia. Of fetuses with oesophageal atresia detected *in utero*, only 25% survive, primarily due to chromosomal anomalies, while the overall survival of infants born with oesophageal atresia is 90%.

Prenatal diagnosis introduces the option of elective termination of the preg-nancy. This action will clearly be advantageous in cases of lethal chromoso-mal disorders, anencephaly and bilateral renal agenesis. Parents may also opt for termination in less clear-cut conditions, particularly when the condition will inevitably result in chronic disability or major deformity.

Prenatal diagnosis also allows the obstetrician to determine the time, place and method of delivery. A fetus with a large sacrococcygeal teratoma (a tumour at the base of the spinal column) must be delivered by elective Caesarean section, preferably at around 38 weeks' gestation, as vaginal deliv-ery may result in obstructed labour or the teratoma may be traumatized and lead to exsanguinating haemorrhage. In other conditions (e.g. diaphragmatic hernia) the newborn infant may require intensive care after delivery and there are distinct advantages of the delivery taking place in a centre with Level 3 neonatal intensive care on site.

Neonatal conditions

Careful physical examination of the newborn infant will disclose signs or symptoms indicative of major problems.

Imperforate anus

A cursory examination may fail to detect the abnormality, particularly when the infant is able to pass small amounts of meconium through a small opening (fistula) alongside the closed-off anal orifice.

Tachypnoea

Rapid breathing (>60 breaths per minute) in association with tachycardia (heart rate >160 per minute) and cyanosis is a sign of respiratory distress which mandates taking an X-ray of the chest to exclude a pneumothorax or a diaphragmatic hernia.

Bilious vomiting

This should be regarded as a sign of intestinal obstruction until proved otherwise.

Delayed passage of meconium

Delayed passage of meconium ($>$24 hours postnatally) in an otherwise full-term healthy infant is an indication of possible Hirschsprung's disease (absence of nerve cells in the rectum). Delay in diagnosis can result in entero-colitis (a life-threatening complication), or chronic constipation, abdominal distension and failure to thrive. A rectal biopsy is diagnostic.

Failure to pass urine

Failure to pass urine for $>$24 hours after birth may be a sign of a bladder outlet obstruction (posterior urethral valves). Although the kidneys may already be damaged due to prolonged intrauterine obstruction, drainage of the bladder is essential to prevent further damage.

Childhood conditions

Problems arise when the doctor fails to carry out an appropriate examination or to take the necessary action.

Strangulated hernia

Inguinal hernias in infants are susceptible to becoming irreducible and if left untreated the blood supply to the intestine contained within the hernia becomes obstructed, resulting in gangrene of the bowel. In addition the blood supply to the testis on the side of the hernia can be compromised and lead to testicular atrophy. The policy should be to repair all inguinal hernias in infants aged under six months as soon as possible and not to place their names on waiting lists with inevitable prolonged delays in repair.

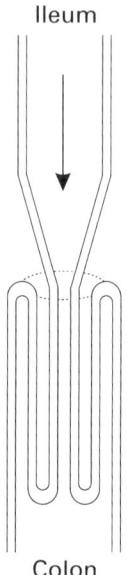

Ileum

Colon

FIGURE 12.1   Diagrammatic representation of an intussusception.

Intussusception

Intussusception (when a segment of bowel infolds on itself) usually affects infants aged between six months and two years, with a peak incidence at 8–9 months. The infant experiences severe colicky abdominal pain and vomiting. Blood mixed with mucus is generally passed per rectum. The diagnosis is confirmed on ultrasound scan and if treated early reduction by air-enema is successful in most cases. Delay in diagnosis results in complete intestinal obstruction and gangrene of the intussuscepted intestine, and can lead to shock and death. In these cases urgent resuscitation is required before surgical treatment (Figure 12.1) – this may take the form of pneumatic or hydrostatic reduction by a paediatric radiologist, or surgical reduction or resection depending on the state of the intestine at operation.

Appendicitis

This classically presents with colicky central abdominal pain, which soon localizes in the right lower quadrant of the abdomen. It is associated with nausea and vomiting and mild pyrexia. There is point tenderness in the right lower abdomen. If left untreated, acute appendicitis rapidly progresses to gangrene, perforation and abscess formation. In children under five years of age, the classical presentation does not occur and they generally present with perforation and acute peritonitis which, if untreated, soon leads to hypovolaemic shock and septicaemia. Urgent resuscitation is necessary before surgery is undertaken.

Testicular torsion

Testicular torsion (twisting of a testicle within the scrotum) is heralded by the sudden onset of excruciating pain in the scrotum. There are two peaks in incidence: first in the neonatal period, and second in the early teenage years. So-called neonatal torsion almost certainly occurs *in utero* prior to birth and the affected testis is unsalvageable. It is mandatory that the contralateral testis is 'fixed' to prevent torsion occurring in the remaining functional testis. In older children, diagnosis and treatment should be carried out within six hours to prevent irreversible damage and, again, the contralateral testis must be fixed. A common error is to diagnose torsion as epididymo-orchitis and to delay treatment while investigations such as Doppler ultrasound or radioisotope studies are carried out.

Adhesion intestinal obstruction

This can develop after any prior abdominal operation. Bilious vomiting, colicky abdominal pain, abdominal distension and absolute constipation are the classical features, and delay in treatment can result in gangrene and perforation of the affected part of the intestine, ultimately leading to peritonitis and shock.

Intravascular infusions

The increased use of intravascular infusions has given rise to large numbers of extravasation injuries—skin necrosis, scarring around tendons and joints, and contractures—due to leakage of a drug or fluid into the subcutaneous tissues. Solutions which are particularly harmful include hypertonic solutions (e.g. parenteral nutrition, 10% dextrose), ionic solutions (e.g. potassium chloride, sodium bicarbonate, calcium chloride), chemotherapeutic drugs (e.g. vincristine, doxorubicin) and vasopressors (e.g. dopamine). Extravasation is recognized by pain and swelling at the infusion site and leakage of fluid at the point of insertion of the cannula. Regular surveillance of the infusion site with immediate cessation of the infusion pump will avoid irreversible damage.

Intra-arterial cannulae for monitoring of arterial blood pressures and blood gases are particularly hazardous. They can lead to arterial spasm, intimal damage of the arterial wall, or thrombosis with profound effects on the distal limb, e.g. gangrene of fingers or toes, or occasionally loss of a limb.

Central venous catheters are essential for long-term venous access for intravenous feeding or the administration of drugs. They are prone to infection, dislodgement and blockage. Strict criteria are needed for their safe insertion and continued maintenance.

Consent

The legal age of majority is 18 years. Children over 16 years old have the power to consent by virtue of Section 8 of the Family Law Reform Act 1969. For children under 16 years, the child needs to be 'Gillick competent' to be able to give consent. This means that the child should understand:

- the nature and purpose of the treatment
- the risks and benefits of the procedure.

Should a child refuse treatment which is judged to be in their best interest, the parents or the surgeon may overrule the child and provide the necessary consent, but an application to the High Court may be necessary.

13 Orthopaedics

CDR Lightowler

'Bones are not filled with red marrow but black ingratitude.' Sadly, this is as true today as it was when the words were written. Doctors bury their mistakes, as the saying goes, but orthopaedic patients limp painfully around to their solicitors clutching the all-revealing X-rays. In spite of this problem, orthopaedics represents one of the most exciting branches of surgery. The word 'orthopaedic' is derived from two Greek works meaning 'straight children'. The term has been adapted to include the management of all pathological conditions of bones and joints. Not all orthopaedic treatments are surgical, and much of the medical management of joint disease is undertaken by rheumatologists. For descriptive purposes orthopaedic problems can be divided into two categories—congenital or acquired. Acquired conditions are traumatic, infective, degenerative, inflammatory, malignant and metabolic; but before we consider these it is important to have some idea of the structure of the bones with which we are dealing.

Figure 13.1 shows the various parts of the bone, which may need further description. A long bone, such as the tibia (shin bone) or humerus (the upper arm bone), or short long bones, such as the metacarpals (the bones you see on the back of the hand) and metatarsals (in the feet) are divided up into several parts for descriptive purposes. At either end is an epiphysis. The periosteum is an outer membrane of bone-forming tissue and this assists with growth during the growing period and is also responsible for laying down bone during fracture healing throughout the patient's life. Endosteum is a similar lining of tissue within the bone between the compact (or hard) outer bone and the spongy bone of the medullary cavity (the marrow of the bone). Where a bone takes part in a joint it is covered by what is known as articular cartilage. A bone derives its nutrition from the nutrient arteries that reach it either by perforating the hard outer bone (the cortex) or by way of the joint capsules, which are connected to the bone near the edges of the joint.

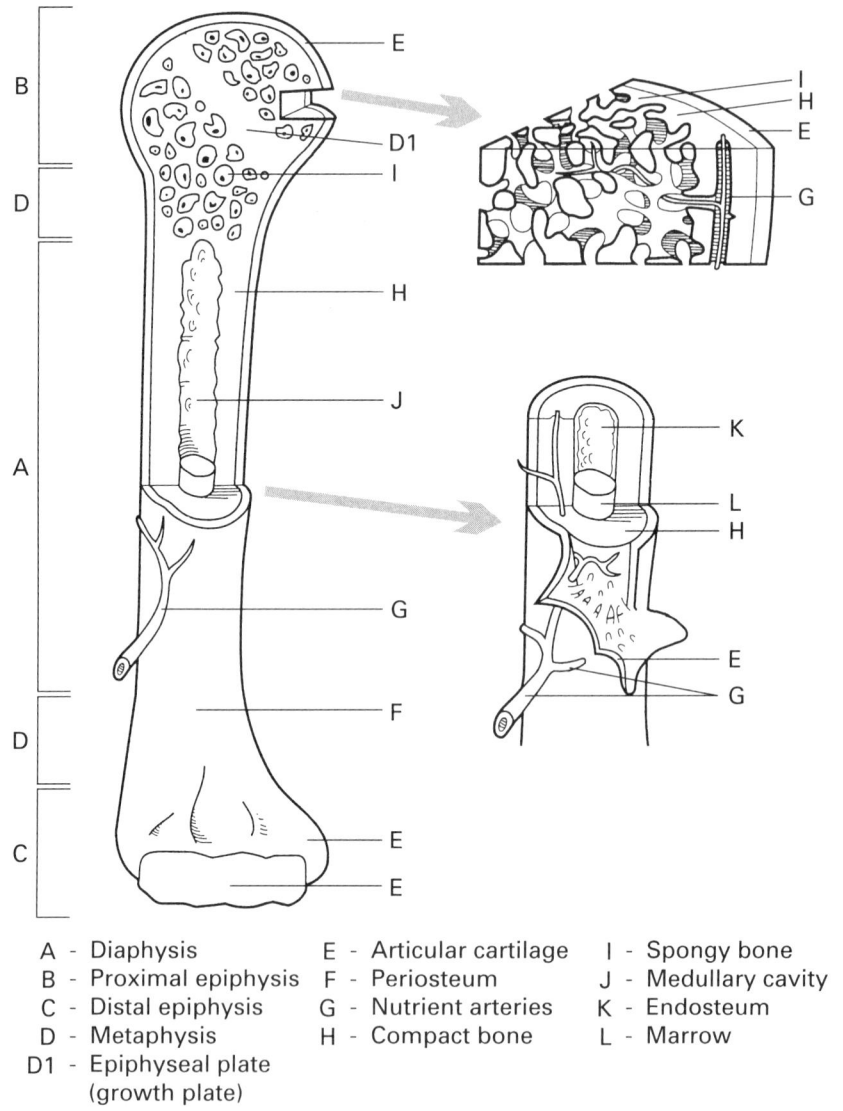

A	-	Diaphysis	E	-	Articular cartilage	I	-	Spongy bone
B	-	Proximal epiphysis	F	-	Periosteum	J	-	Medullary cavity
C	-	Distal epiphysis	G	-	Nutrient arteries	K	-	Endosteum
D	-	Metaphysis	H	-	Compact bone	L	-	Marrow
D1	-	Epiphyseal plate (growth plate)						

FIGURE 13.1 Anatomy of a long bone

Congenital conditions

These conditions are present at birth as their name suggests. Perhaps the best-known example is the limb deformity caused by the drug thalidomide. Included in this category is congenital dislocation of the hip, although nowadays the condition is thought to develop after birth and it is now known as developmental dislocation of the hip. In this condition the femoral head or ball does not fit within the acetabulum or socket. It is an interesting condition. It occurs in certain populations, e.g. Northern Italians; it is more common in the left hip than the right and in girls more than boys. It runs in families. If detected soon after birth, and the hip is reduced and that reduction maintained for six weeks or so, the child will have a normal hip. If missed, often nothing is noticed until the child starts to walk, which they will do with a limp. By this time the hip will have become deformed and the acetabulum or socket will be shallow and filled with dense tissue. The femoral head (or ball) will be small and will be twisted to point forward. The shaft of the femur (or thigh bone) will be thin. Reduction, i.e. putting the head back into the acetabulum, will almost certainly require extensive surgery to clear out and possibly deepen the acetabulum and to rotate the femoral head so that it lies within the aceta-bulum and the child's foot is pointing in the correct direction. No matter how good the surgery, the child's hip is never normal and will almost certainly develop early osteoarthrosis. The shallow acetabulum, the altered angles of the hip, the narrow femur, and previous surgery all render later total hip replacement more difficult. As early detection is so important for this condi-tion, all newborn babies are screened for the problem, generally by examin-ation, and in doubtful cases with ultrasound scanning. In spite of this care a few children with the problem are missed and have to have the major surgery. If the condition is not noticed until the child is seven years of age or older, the hip is generally left dislocated until a hip replacement is required. This is very difficult surgery.

Acquired conditions

Trauma

Bones are the levers which enable lifting, pulling, walking, etc, and joints are the hinges that allow the levers to be positioned so they can be used. Bones are tough and require a lot of force to damage them, whereas joints are less strong and are more easily injured. A door or gate can be damaged, but normally it is the latch or the hinge which goes first. The more mobile the joints, the more easily they are damaged. This is why rugby players damage their knees, shoulders, and ankles but not their hips.

Fractures

A break in the continuity of bone is known as a fracture. Unless the bone is weakened by some other condition, it requires a great deal of force to cause it to break. Clinically, a fractured limb is painful, swollen and deformed, and movement causes crepitus—a grinding sensation. Local soft tissues may be damaged.

There are several types of fracture:

- open or compound
- closed or simple
- spiral
- oblique
- transverse
- comminuted
- greenstick
- traction or avulsion
- compression
- pathological.

An *open fracture* occurs when the bone pierces the covering membrane. This is usually skin but a fracture of the mandible (lower jaw) frequently tears the mucous membrane of the mouth, creating an open fracture into the mouth. Bony infection is the most serious consequence of such a fracture. A *closed fracture* does not pierce the skin or other lining membrane. When a long bone fractures, the fracture line can lie straight across the bone, or run obliquely down the bone, or twist down the bone. These are *transverse*, *oblique* and *spiral fractures*. A *comminuted* fracture is a fracture in which there are more than two parts. A *greenstick fracture* occurs only in children. Only one cortex of the bone breaks and the bone is bent. The same thing happens when you snap a small living branch of a tree, as those who made bows and arrows in childhood will remember—'a green stick bends but does not break'. Restoring the bone to its normal shape requires manipulation, which should include breaking the intact cortex so the bone does not spring back to its deformed position. A *traction* or *avulsion fracture* occurs when a portion of bone is pulled off by the tendon attached to it. A mallet finger, goalkeeper or wicketkeeper fracture is an example of this. For example, the finger tip is hit by a cricket ball and forcibly bent, causing the extensor tendon (which straightens the digit) to pull a portion of bone off the base of the distal phalanx or finger tip. *Compression fractures* are a crushing injury to bone. They occur in the heel bone (os calcis) when patients fall from ladders or in the spine following a fall onto buttocks and in pilots who have ejected. *Pathological fractures* occur in bones weakened by a disease process, such as tumours, either benign or malignant, or osteoporosis.

Orthopaedic management of fractures is aimed at saving the patient's life, relieving pain, correcting deformity and restoring function.

In the last few decades of the 20th century surgeons managing trauma realized that a severely injured patient had a greatly increased chance of surviving a major injury if their initial treatment was good. This period was known as the 'golden hour' and the protocol laid down for patient management in this hour is known as the advanced trauma life support (ATLS). It is as simple as A B C:

- A—Airways. Clear the patient's airways or make sure that they are clear, at the same time stabilizing the patient's neck.
- B—Breathing. Make sure the patient is breathing or help him to breathe.
- C—Circulation. Maintain the patient's circulation. This includes infusions, cardiac massage, etc.
- D—Deficit. Check that the nerve supply to the patient's body is functioning adequately. This is particularly important in spinal injuries.
- E—Exposure. The proper assessment of a severely injured patient requires total exposure of the body; therefore all clothes must be cut off.

Once these procedures have been completed, and the patient is stabilized, three standard X-rays are taken of the neck, chest and pelvis. The neck X-ray is quite difficult to obtain as it must demonstrate all seven cervical vertebrae and the upper thoracic vertebrae and must be taken from the side. It reveals any fracture or dislocation of the cervical spine and indicates whether there is, or is likely to be, any damage to the spinal cord. Until this X-ray is checked and cleared the neck should be stabilized either by a collar or manually.

The chest is X-rayed to ensure that the lungs are properly expanded, and the pelvis is X-rayed to exclude a fracture. Severe pelvic fractures cause a great deal of blood loss, which has to be replaced and can cause severe soft tissue injuries whose detection requires detailed and careful examination. The presence of such a fracture alerts the surgeon to the possibilities of these injuries. This protocol of course can be modified for the less severely injured patient, but it does ensure that nothing in the patient's management is overlooked. Once the patient's condition is stabilized the specific management of their fractures can be started. Once again treatment follows a very simple protocol. If it is open, close it. If it is closed, reduce it; if it is reduced, immobilize it; if it is immobile, start rehabilitation.

An open fracture is serious as it exposes the bone to the risk of infection; therefore, an exposed bone should be covered by a sterile dressing at the accident site, and antibiotics should be given to the patient as soon as possible. After the ATLS stabilization (see above) the patient should be taken to the main operating theatre and under anaesthetic and ideal circumstances the wound should be explored, thoroughly cleaned, and all dead tissue (such as skin and muscle) removed. This last procedure is essential because anaerobic bacteria, which live without oxygen, can grow in this tissue; the organism causing gas gangrene is such a bacterium. The surgeon knows when enough tissue has been removed as the cut edges of healthy tissue bleed. Once this stage is complete the fracture is reduced under direct vision and the skin is closed. Skin grafting may be required if debridement leaves a large defect. If the fracture is a closed fracture then the above procedures are unnecessary. If the fracture is displaced it should be reduced and returned to its normal alignment—this should be undertaken under appropriate anaesthesia, general or local, using an image intensifier.

Once the fracture has been reduced to a satisfactory position it should be immobilized to maintain the position until healing takes place. There are many ways of immobilizing a fracture depending on its site and severity. Strapping is sufficient to immobilize some fractures, e.g. of the fingers, toes, hands and feet. A sling is sufficient for fractures around the shoulder and upper arm and plaster of Paris, or its modern equivalent, will immobilize fractures of the elbow, forearm, knee, lower leg, wrist and ankle. Traction is still used to immobilize certain fractures, often as a temporary measure while the patient is made medically fit for surgery. Traction is when a weight is attached to the patient's limb below the fracture, generally by a system of pulleys, with the patient's body weight being used as a counter-balance. Traction is either skin traction, where the weights are attached to the patient's skin with strapping, or skeletal. In skeletal traction a pin is drilled through an appropriate part of the patient's skeleton and weights are attached to that pin. This is not as unpleasant as it sounds and can be used for long-term (several months) traction. It used to be essential for the management of fractures of the shaft of femur (thigh bone) and is still used in developing countries where other methods of internal fixation are not readily available. Skin traction does damage the skin and therefore can only be used short-term and particularly in children. All these methods are external methods of fracture immobilization.

There are two other groups of fixation devices: internal fixation and the use of external fixators as a sort of 'half-way house'. The fracture is reduced and two or more screws are passed through the skin and deep into the bone above and below the fracture site; this is external fixation. The fracture is reduced and the screws are attached to a rigid bar connecting all of them. If this is not sufficient to stabilize the fracture another series of screws and connectors are inserted at right angles. Not all fractures can be treated like this but it is a very useful method for fixing a fracture if access to the limb is required, e.g. for skin grafting. Fractures can be fixed internally with wires drilled across the fracture site, screws, plates and screws with or without compression, and nails passed down the medulla (marrow) of the bone. These nails can be inserted into the bone, which is unreamed or reamed; a reamed bone is one that has been drilled out to prepare it to receive the nail. These nails can be locked or unlocked. A locked nail has one or two screws passed through the bone at the top and bottom of the nail to prevent the fracture sliding up and down.

Not all fractures require internal fixation. This procedure is required if conservative treatment fails, in poly-trauma when the patient has many fractures to control, where there is major soft tissue damage (e.g. to major arteries and nerves), in pathological fractures, and in severe head injuries. Fractures unite at varying speeds, but all fractures are deemed to have united or joined up when there is clinical and radiological evidence of bony union. Complications of fractures themselves are non-union and malunion:

- Non-union is multifactoral and occurs if there is excess movement at the fracture site, devascularization of the tissues at the fracture, infection and interposition of soft tissues. Treatment is bone graft and fixation of the fracture after clearing the ends of the bones for any soft tissue. If all else fails, occasionally the limb has to be amputated.
- Malunion occurs if the fracture is not adequately reduced and the reduction maintained. Treatment is re-manipulation with or without osteotomy (bone division) and then reduction, grafting and adequate fixation.

Joint injuries

Joints are more easily injured than bones and the more mobile the joint, e.g. knee, shoulder and ankle, the more easily it is damaged. Damage is either a fracture, ligamentous injury or meniscal damage (the layman's term for a meniscus is a cartilage). A major fracture involving a joint should be very carefully reduced and accurately fixed. The joint should be drained to prevent blood accumulating and early mobilization undertaken to reduce stiffness. Even with this regime the patient will be faced with an increased risk of degenerative arthritis in later life because of the damage to the lining cartilage of the joint. Small portions of bone and cartilage, or just articular cartilage, may be fractured. These are called osteochondral and transchondral fractures and they may go unnoticed, especially as the patient will have a very swollen knee and its drainage and immobilization will demand urgent treatment. These small fractures may also not be noticed radiologically, especially if there is very little bone in the fragment. Although some of these bodies attach themselves within the joint and cause no trouble, some remain loose in the joint and are a cause of true locking. (True locking is deemed to have happened when the knee jams in a bent position and cannot be straightened. It is generally associated with pain and the joint is straightened by the patient manipulating it and normally it frees with a clunk. It is pathognomonic of a torn meniscus or a loose body.) The treatment is to remove the loose body, tidy up its place of origin, or if possible put the loose body back in its original site and pin it there. These are called loose bodies. They are not foreign bodies. A foreign body, by definition, is introduced from outside and is a rare event. The only other cause of true locking is from a torn meniscus. Menisci are present in the knee and temperomandibular joint of the lower jaw only. If a meniscus is torn, the torn portion should be removed arthroscopically to allow free movement of the joint. These menisci have an important function and as little as possible should be removed. Ligament damage is treated with gentle mobilization and physiotherapy for minor injuries. Joint aspiration (or removal of fluid) may be required for the more severe injuries, and in the most extreme cases ligament repair, replacement or augmentation is undertaken. Excellent though modern surgery is, all these procedures require a great deal of hard work from the patient to develop and maintain adequate muscles controlling the joint.

Infection

Infection in orthopaedics is a disaster and therefore must be avoided at all costs. It occurs differently in children and adults. In children it is blood borne. It arises from some focus on the body, e.g. a boil, and spreads to the long bones near the growth plate (epiphyseal plate). The child gets very sick and will not let the affected limb be touched. Urgent hospital admission is necessary to rest the patient and the part. Appropriate blood tests and swabs must be taken and then immediate treatment should be commenced. Treatment should be started at once and not delayed until the test results are available. As 90% of these infections are caused by the bacterium *Staphylococcus aureus*, fucidic acid is the first antibiotic of choice as it penetrates bone well and works successfully against this bacterium. For safety's sake, however, a broad-spectrum antibiotic is given at the same time. These antibiotics can be changed if necessary when the results of the tests are obtained. It is essential that antibiotics are given intravenously because they are not absorbed when given orally to a patient who is very ill.

Oral administration should be commenced when the child's temperature has been normal for 48 hours and maintained for six weeks. Surgery is only used to drain any pus which might accumulate near the bone. With such vigorous management the scourge of chronic osteomyelitis has been virtually eradicated from children in the UK.

In adults bone infection is introduced either via open fractures or by surgical procedures. It may be eliminated by the usual surgical techniques of clearance of all the infective material and all the implants, and large doses of antibiotics. Sadly, in spite of such vigorous treatment, recurrence is likely.

Degenerative disease

Degenerative disease of a joint is destruction of the lining articular cartilage. It occurs as a result of old age or secondary to any process which destroys this cartilage, namely trauma, infection or inflammatory disease (such as rheumatoid arthritis). The treatment is conservative or operative. Conservative treatment is pain relief, physiotherapy, walking aids for lower limb problems and splints for upper limb problems. Operative treatment is used for patients with severe pain, particularly when it disturbs sleep. The procedures include osteotomy, arthrodesis, and arthroplasty. In an osteotomy the bone near the joint is divided and the angle of the joint altered so that a less damaged portion of cartilage bears the weight. It relieves pain in about 60% of patients. An arthrodesis stiffens the joint so no movement occurs. It relieves pain most successfully but, of course, puts an extra strain on the joints above and below it. It should only be undertaken if these joints are normal.

With the advent of total joint replacement surgery, osteotomy and arthrodesis are rarely undertaken nowadays. Joint replacement is very successful but it has its own problems caused by infection, loosening of the implants, implant wear and leg length inequality in the lower limb. Although 90–95% of these procedures have a good to excellent result, most surgeons prefer to reserve their use for the over 60s when the life expectancy of the implant may be longer than that of the patient.

Inflammatory conditions

Conditions such as rheumatoid arthritis affect the joints, especially the small joints of the hands and feet, causing pain, swelling, loss of function and secondary osteoarthritis. The condition is treated by rheumatologists, surgery is involved only to aid diagnosis, relieve pain, restore function and, in the last extreme, for joint salvage. These patients are prone to many problems. They are run down by the disease and are often anaemic, they are prone to infection, and their bones are softer. They are also younger than the average patient needing joint replacement and have many joints affected. Fortunately for the surgeon, but not the patient, as they have multiple joint disease they have their own built-in brake. Even when a joint is replaced, the patient cannot move around quickly and therefore is less likely to wear the joint out, which means that joints can be replaced at a much younger age.

Because the surgical management of these patients is so complicated it has become a subspecialty in its own right.

Malignancy

Malignant tumours of bone can be primary—occurring in or arising from the bone—or secondary—arising elsewhere and spreading to the bone. Primary bone tumours are rare, often occurring in young people. In order to improve the expertise in management, all these tumours are now referred to specialist centres for treatment. Tumours arising from the blood-forming tissues within the bone marrow are managed by haematologists; orthopaedic surgeons being required only to treat any pathological fractures. Similarly, secondary tumours of bone, which are far more common than primary tumours, are treated by the staff treating the main tumour, the orthopaedic surgeons managing fractures only. Tumours of the breast, thyroid, lungs, prostate and kidney traditionally spread to the bones.

Metabolic conditions

There are several metabolic disorders which affect bone, e.g. hyperparathyroidism and osteomalacia. Again, these are treated by doctors, the orthopaedic surgeon is only used to treat the problems that arise in the bones and joints. Much is written about osteoporosis, the morbidity it produces, and its management. This is particularly appropriate today as many young girls exercise little and eat poorly; they are not laying down an adequate bone mass in childhood and will have poor reserves when they start to lose their bone mass around the menopause. Future generations of orthopaedic surgeons are likely to be very busy repairing the pathological fractures arising in these women.

14 Neurology

Peter Harvey

Neurologists have three roles in medico-legal work: they advise the court on liability in alleged neurological negligence, on neurological damage inflicted in other specialties and its causation, and the assessment of victims of trauma. The neurologist is concerned with physical disorders of the nervous system, which comprises the central nervous system (brain and spinal cord), peripheral nervous system, and autonomic nervous system (which controls subconscious functions such as heart rate, gut motility, and sweating).

The nervous system is built of many millions of interconnecting nerve cells (neurones) of varied shapes and sizes, but all possessing a basic structure comprising a nerve body which receives messages from many other neurones and which itself gives rise to an elongated projection (the axon) which transmits a message to another nerve body (see Figure 1.2, page 7).

The message transmitted by the axon is essentially electrical, created by chemical change; the message passes from axon to nerve cell body by chemical transmitters which may excite, depress, or modulate the activity of the recipient cell. Most drugs which influence neural activity work through either altering the transmitter activities or through influencing the excitivity of the cell membrane.

Neurological investigation

The most important aspect of the neurological investigation of a patient is the history, taken from the patient, and possibly even more importantly, from a relation or friend. This is followed by a clinical examination, the details of which should be dictated by the history, and at the end of the examination the neurologist usually has an anatomical diagnosis, and more often than not a pathological one as well. Much use is made of scanning—computerized tomography (CT) or magnetic resonance imaging (MRI); other investigations commonly administered are neurophysiological studies, angiography (imaging blood vessels), and examination of the spinal fluid by lumbar puncture.

CT scanning was the first of the revolutionary advances in brain imaging. Even with the best CT scanners the detail is not nearly as good as that obtained in the later-developed MRI, but CT still has its place. It is relatively inexpensive, easy to use, is very good at demonstrating bony abnormalities (MRI is not), and is invaluable in the early detection of bleeding in or around the brain. It is now widely available nationally. MRI scanning on the other hand gives far greater detail of structure and of how brain tissue functions.

The brain

The nerve cells of the brain largely lie at the periphery, forming the cerebral cortex (grey matter) crenulated into ridges and valleys to permit more room in a confined surface. The axons pass deeply to form defined tracts, which connect to other parts of the brain, and to pass down the spinal cord. The axons are covered by an insulating material called myelin, a white material, and collectively this deep part of the brain is referred to as 'white matter'.

Sensory information collected from the body passes up the spinal cord into the brain through similar tracts.

The brain is divided into two halves. The cerebral cortex in each half is responsible for motor and sensory function on the opposite side of the body. It sits astride a central, deeply-placed portion of the brain known as the brain stem which, apart from acting as a conduit for the long nerve fibre tracts that pass to and from the spine, also contains a number of important nuclei (nerve relay stations). The cortex is divided into four lobes (on each side): frontal, parietal, occipital, and temporal. The motor cortex, controlling movement, lies at the back of the frontal lobe and, immediately behind it, in front of the parietal lobe, lies the sensory section of the cortex, which is important in the perception of sensation. The primary visual area is at the back of the brain, in the occipital cortex. Speech is in the left hemisphere in right-handed people and half the left-handed population. The frontal lobe has important functions in behaviour and important cognitive 'executive' functions (Figure 14.1). The corollary is that focal damage to the brain often produces easily recognizable clinical syndromes.

The soft brain is separated from the hard skull by a space containing fluid—cerebrospinal fluid (CSF)—itself contained within a series of membranes, of which the innermost is called the arachnoid and the outermost, a tough, fibrous layer densely applied to the skull, the dura mater. CSF is manufactured

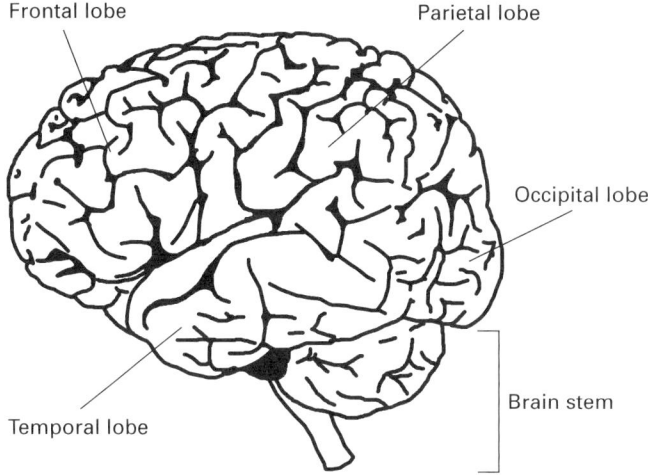

FIGURE 14.1 Left lateral view of the brain to show the pattern of gyri and sulci on the superolateral aspect of the cerebral hemisphere.

inside the ventricles, deep-lying caverns within the brain, which link to expel the spinal fluid near the base of the skull, whence it passes up in the subarachnoid space (and also down the spinal canal) to be absorbed at the top of the skull (Figure 14.2). Obstruction of the flow of CSF in the ventricular system leads to a condition known as hydrocephalus (water on the brain), which can cause progressive neurological impairment, culminating in death if not recognized and treated.

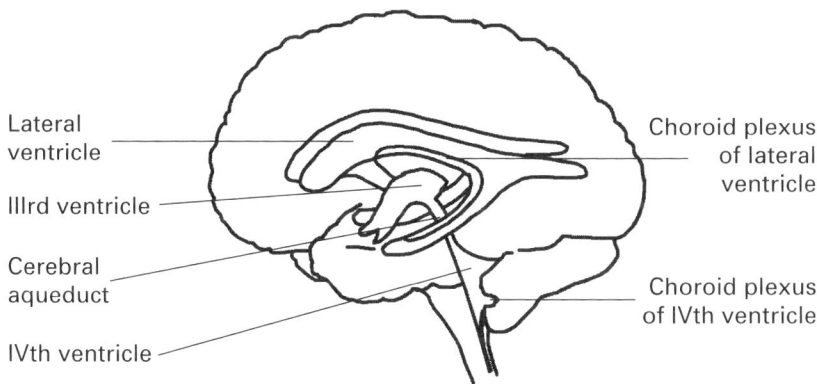

FIGURE 14.2 Organization of the ventricular system in the human brain (sagittal view).

The brain is supplied by blood from arteries that enter the skull from the neck, the two in front being carotid arteries, and the two at the back are the vertebral arteries (the 'circle of Willis'). The arterial (fresh, oxygenated blood) supply to the brain is very compartmentalized and there is very little overlap between adjacent arterial territories. The brain is very sensitive to cessation of blood flow and damage can result from anoxia (no oxygen). Blockage of single arteries produces well-recognized clinical syndromes—'strokes'.

After oxygen and nutrients have been exchanged in the tissues, the 'dirty', deoxygenated blood is collected in veins. Blood in the arteries is under high pressure and blood in veins is at low pressure.

Trauma to the head

Diffuse axonal injury

Head injury producing loss of consciousness may be followed by a period of post-traumatic amnesia. The intervening period may be punctuated by lacunae of retained memories. The residual cognitive and behavioural deficits are common, usually due to trauma to the white matter of the brain, a pathological process known as diffuse axonal injury which, unless very severe, does not show up on MRI. There is controversy over whether relatively mild brain injury can produce lasting cognitive and behavioural disturbances due to damage to the frontal lobes.

Extradural haematoma

A fractured skull may rupture a meningeal artery lying between skull and dura, which will pump out high-pressure blood, creating a large clot that strips the dura off the skull, invaginates the brain, causes pressure on the brain, and can rapidly cause deterioration in conscious level and then death unless rectified. This is a neurosurgical emergency. The cardinal signs of a rapidly increasing raised intracranial pressure due to an extradural haematoma are a fall in conscious level, a dilating pupil on one side, increasing weakness down one side of the body, a rising blood pressure, and a falling pulse rate. Emergency surgery is life-saving and there may not be time to transfer the patient to a neurosurgical unit.

Subdural haematoma

Skull trauma can cause rupture of veins that cross from the dura to the arachnoid, causing a slower leakage of blood, which produces much the same effect as an extradural haematoma, but over a longer time. There may be hours or sometimes even weeks before the typical effects of the subdural haemorrhage are noted. This is particularly so in the elderly population, when a subdural haematoma may be responsible for intellectual and behavioural decline without any focal neurological signs; the removal of the blood clot can be curative.

Subdural haematomata can be fairly acute in onset (a 'boxing' subdural haematoma is always relatively acute). Alcoholics are prone to falling, head injury, and subdural haematomata because they have shrunken brains, but the signs of a subdural haematoma may be missed by medical staff on the grounds that a drunk will 'sleep it off'. Both extra- and subdural haematomata are easily recognized in the acute stage on CT scanning, which should now be readily available to all Accident and Emergency departments.

Intracranial haematomata

Individuals may bleed into the brain itself as a result of a fall, and unless a CT scan is performed the bleeding will be missed and overlooked. It is important to recognize these bleeds because intracerebral bleeding carries a risk of developing epilepsy of at least five-fold the patient's residual lifetime risk of developing epilepsy. (If combined with a subdural haematoma the rate ratio rises to $12:1$.)

The Glasgow coma score is an important clinical aid to the assessment of the unconscious person. It comprises a series of very simple tests. The best responses are recorded and scored. The ability to open the eyes—spontaneously, to speech, to pain, or not at all—is scored respectively from 4 to 1. The best verbal response—orientated, confused, inappropriate words, incomprehensible sounds or none—is similarly scored, from 5 to 1. The best motor response—obeys commands, localizes pain, withdrawal to pain, flexion to pain, extension to pain and none, are also scored. Many add up the score. The maximum score is 15, the worst is 3 and the scores correlate well with outcome after head injury. It must be stressed that a patient can be in the throes of a dense post-traumatic amnesia and still have a Glasgow coma score of 15; that the main use of this scale is the detection of *change*; and that it can be administered by relatively junior and inexperienced staff.

Subarachnoid haemorrhage

This is the sudden bursting of a blood vessel, usually from a bulge in an artery (berry aneurysm), sometimes from an abnormal collection of blood vessels in or on the surface of the brain—an arteriovenous malformation (AVM), causing a sudden headache. This is described, even by the most modest and self-abnegatory individuals, in the most extreme terms—'violent, as if somebody had hit me with a sledgehammer'. It is associated with nausea and vomiting in about 50% of cases; some patients lose consciousness, most develop a stiff neck within minutes or hours, and between 5 and 10% die at the moment of the bleed. Many (15–50%) have a smaller subarachnoid haemorrhage, a premonitory bleed, thought by some to be due to stretching of the aneurysm rather than actual leakage from it. Delays in diagnosis and treatment give rise to allegations of negligence against general practitioners (GPs) (who it has to be stressed will perhaps see only one or two cases in a professional lifetime) and against hospital medical staff. Causation presents difficulty in these cases and advice should be sought from neurosurgeons and neuroradiologists.

The initial diagnosis is often one of migraine, with which it may be confused. Two rare forms of migraine present very much like subarachnoid haemorrhage. The so-called 'thunderclap' headache, like subarachnoid headache, is a severe headache of sudden onset, but it is much briefer, self-limiting, not associated with a stiff neck, and not usually associated with nausea and vomiting. A similar headache can occur at orgasm and this too may present diagnostic difficulty, as berry aneurysmal subarachnoid haemorrhage may occur during sexual intercourse.

Strokes (cerebrovascular accidents)

There are a number of types of stroke but the one of particular interest in medico-legal circles is the stroke due to the passage of blood clots into the brain as a result of hardening of the carotid artery. This is often preceded by a brief episode of neurological dysfunction—disturbed speech and vision, and weakness (which may be dismissed by the GP), and which is followed days or even weeks later by a catastrophic stroke. It is often argued that the early event, called a transient ischaemic attack (TIA), should have been recognized and treated. The problem is that the conventional treatment, the administration of aspirin, reduces the risks of a further stroke, but not sufficiently to satisfy the requirement of a balance of probabilities.

There is a further stroke related to trauma in which damage to the lining of a blood vessel leading to the brain can cause a blood clot to fly off, and this is increasingly commonly recognized. This is called arterial dissection.

Tumour

Tumours can grow from the brain (from non-neuronal supporting cells called glia) and can vary from the indolent and non-aggressive to those that are highly malignant and rapidly fatal. Of more concern in medico-legal circles are the tumours of the dura—meningiomas, slow-growing benign tumours developing from the dura mater—which cause damage by slowly squeezing brain tissue. These can present with subtle intellectual and behavioural decline that may be easily attributed to 'ageing', and which is potentially reversible with the early removal of the tumour. The larger the tumour the more difficult they are to remove. Clinical failures to recognize the presence of such tumours are well recorded, and the poor clinical results of late surgery have resulted in successful litigation. The failures of diagnosis frequently involve a failure to listen to the patient and to take a detailed history. In such cases a psychiatric diagnosis has been proffered by the GP, general physician, or even neurologist, before the physical aspects of the patient's condition become obvious.

Headaches

Many individuals have headaches. Headache is one of the most common reasons for general practice attendance, and it is the most common cause of referral to the neurologist. A very small proportion of patients suffering with headaches have brain tumours, but many patients with headaches are worried that they have a tumour. The characteristic headache of raised intracranial pressure occurs on awakening, is worsened by movement and coughing, is associated with nausea and vomiting, and usually improves on the assumption of the upright posture. This is, however, by no means always the case; patients with such histories will not all have tumours, but to ignore the development of such a headache without further investigation represents a poor standard of care.

Meningitis

Acute meningitis

This is caused by the invasion of the meningeal membranes immediately adjacent to the brain and the intervening spinal fluid by germs, sometimes viruses, more often bacteria, occasionally yeasts and fungi. It is the acute bacterial meningitides that raise most concern. They are eminently treatable with appropriate antibiotics, if caught early enough, but if left untreated for too long, and if the patient survives, serious residual neurological disability may ensue. These disabilities include mental retardation, epilepsy, weakness, clumsiness, and numbness of trunk and limbs. Hydrocephalus is a common sequel. The initial brunt of much litigation is borne by the GP, in whose defence it has to be said that the diagnosis of early acute meningitis, particularly in the very young, can be extraordinarily difficult. The classical symptoms and signs (headache, photophobia, stiff neck, fever, and the typical rash) may be absent. The child may simply be querulous and 'off colour' before the more overt and dramatic symptoms and signs develop.

Although it is true that very often the initial symptoms of meningitis are non-specific and that meningitis can develop as a result of an upper respiratory tract, ear or sinus infection, the suspicion of meningitis should lead to the immediate administration of antibiotics. It is now firmly established that irrespective of the risk of masking subsequent culture from the blood or spinal fluid of the responsible organism, the morbidity of acute purulent meningitis is substantially diminished by the very earliest administration of antibiotics, and 'blue light' transfer to hospital. There is no harm in over-diagnosis, but there tends to be a policy of prevarication.

The literature gives no help in the consideration of causation, it is simply accepted that 'the earlier the better' and each case must be assessed on how well or badly the patient did when treatment was finally instituted.

Chronic meningitis

Meningitis of a more indolent nature has many causes, including cancer and sarcoidosis (a mysterious inflammation that can affect many tissues of the body), but the most common delays are seen in the development of two treatable conditions, tuberculous meningitis and fungal meningitis. The onset is insidious, development of signs of meningitis is slow, headache is predominant, intellectual and behavioural changes may predominate, and physical signs may be sparse or non-existent. Later sequelae of these meningitides are damage to the various nerves that come out of the brain and which control organs in the head, such as eye and facial movement, swallowing and hearing, as well as the development of hydrocephalus and the impairment of function of the spinal cord and the nerves that come out of it. These are not usually reversible once they have been established, and if unreasonable delay in the diagnosis is established, the quantum of damages is substantial. Again, it is often the primary care clinicians who bear the brunt of allegations of negligence.

The drugs that treat tuberculosis and fungal infections are slow to act and advice on causation is always difficult and should be sought from an expert in infectious diseases.

Multiple sclerosis

Multiple sclerosis is a condition caused by inflammatory patchy destruction of the myelin and axons in the central nervous system, producing a variety of clinical patterns, relapsing and remitting disease, progressive disease, or a mixture of the two. Misdiagnosis and treatment are of legal note.

Benign tumours of the lower part of the skull and of the spinal column can mimic the onset of multiple sclerosis, as can abnormalities of the blood vessels of the spine—AVMs. MRI scanning excludes these possibilities, but to make a diagnosis of multiple sclerosis in this day and age in the absence of such scanning is unacceptable.

Relapsing remitting disease may be treated according to strict criteria by the administration of a group of drugs called 'β-interferon'. The drugs are expensive, and it should be stressed that a number of neurologists are extremely sceptical over the long-term advantages of the administration of these drugs and are highly suspicious of the claims made for them.

Epilepsy

Epilepsy is a common condition—one person in 200 suffers from it. The diagnosis is difficult to make. The differential diagnosis includes irregular beating of the heart, faints, psychological problems, sudden attacks of low blood sugar, transient ischaemic attacks, migraine, hyperventilation, panic attacks and disturbances of the balance mechanism.

A misdiagnosis of epilepsy leads to loss of a driving licence, often to loss of employment, and social disruption. The electroencephalogram (EEG) is of limited value in the diagnosis of epilepsy, and is often over-interpreted by the neurologically naïve, with unhappy consequences. If specifically epileptic in appearance it may help to diagnose the type of epilepsy, and it increases the possibility of epilepsy in somebody with suspicious episodes, but the diagnosis must remain a clinical one. However the main problem for somebody diagnosed as suffering from epilepsy is the problem of driving.

It is worthwhile commenting on some of the current regulations:

- All epileptic attacks, even a minor 'aura' occurring in isolation, will disbar a patient from driving on an ordinary driving licence until they have been completely free from all clinical manifestations of epilepsy for one year. There are entirely different regulations for HGV and PSV drivers, who have to show that they have been free from all clinical epileptic manifestations for 10 years, off all treatment, before they can go back to driving.
- A patient who has epilepsy that only manifests itself while they are asleep may drive after three years of continuing to have epileptic attacks, as long as those epileptic attacks are solely while they are asleep.
- A patient is obliged to inform the DVLA of their relevant disability, which is epilepsy, and if the doctor knows that they are continuing to drive they

may be obliged to inform the DVLA (General Medical Council and British Medical Association advice).

Many antiepileptic drugs (AEDs) can lower the effectiveness of the contraceptive pill, to the extent that an unwanted pregnancy may occur. It is the responsibility of the GP and hospital consultant to warn the patient of this and to amend her treatment.

A number of AEDs are teratogenic, i.e. they produce malformation of the growing fetus. Phenytoin was the first so recognized, then sodium valproate, which causes an increased risk of spina bifida and other neural tube defects, but it is now realized that this is a very widespread problem. Also recent papers suggest that some of the drugs and possibly in many of them, there may be the risk of intellectual retardation in children born to mothers taking these drugs during pregnancy. This presents an enormous quandary to the mother as the risks of uncontrolled epilepsy are not theoretical —there is a finite morbidity and mortality, and a risk of losing the baby, which the mother has to balance against the risk of damaging her unborn child.

The spine

The spinal cord is an extension of the brain and passes through a large hole at the bottom of the skull, called the foramen magnum, to pass down the spinal canal. The newborn baby's spinal cord fills more of the spinal canal than the adult, but as the child grows, the vertebral column grows more rapidly than the spinal cord, with the result that in the adult the spinal cord ends at the lower end of the 12th thoracic vertebra, or the 1st lumbar vertebra (Figure 14.3).

Within the spinal cord, nerve pathways carry messages to and from the brain. The principal pathway ordaining movement is called the pyramidal tract. These nerve fibres arise in the brain and pass down the spinal cord where they impinge at each segmental level on nerve cells, which give rise to further nerve processes. Similarly pathways carry sensation from the nerves of the body to the brain. These peripheral nerves pass out from the spinal cord, traverse the CSF-filled space and leave the spinal column between adjacent vertebrae at each vertebral or segmental level. Sensory information travelling along the peripheral nerves is organized within the spinal cord into pathways that travel up to the brain.

Because the spinal cord finishes at the junction between the dorsal and lumbar spines, but the nerve roots still leave the spinal cord at their appropriate segmental level, the spinal canal between the lower end of the spinal cord and its termination in the sacrum is filled with nerve roots. These bear a resemblance to a horse's tail, hence the name 'cauda equina', with each nerve

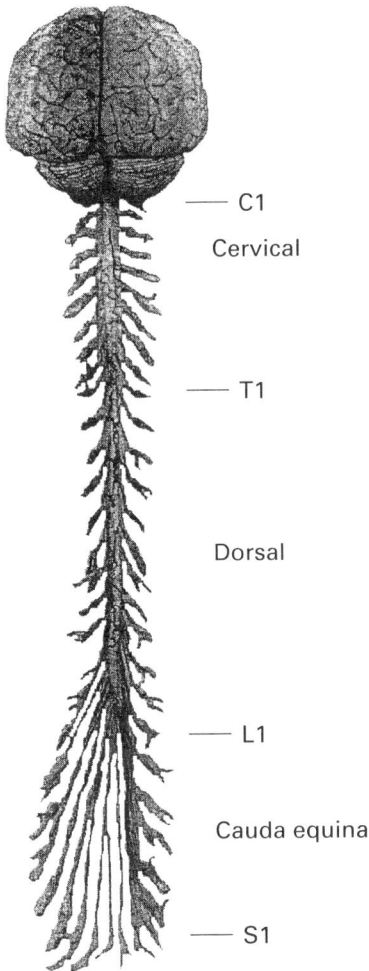

C1
Cervical

T1

Dorsal

L1

Cauda equina

S1

FIGURE 14.3 External structure of the spinal cord from the rear. Reprinted from *Gray's Anatomy, 39th edition.* ©2004 Elsevier Ltd.

root, as it were, 'peeling off' in pairs, to leave in an ordered fashion at each intervertebral foramen. It should be noted that the last nerves to leave the spinal canal travel in its centre, thus the nerves subserving bladder, rectal, and sexual function are in the middle of the spinal canal at the lower lumbar and upper sacral levels of L4/5 and L5/S1, the levels at which prolapsed intervertebral discs are the most common.

There are seven cervical (neck) vertebrae, twelve dorsal or thoracic vertebrae (chest), five lumbar (low back), and five sacral vertebrae which are fused into one bone called the sacrum.

The spinal column comprises a series of bones known as the vertebrae, superimposed one on top of the other, forming a centrally placed strut running vertically up and down the trunk, bearing the load of the trunk, arms and head. Each vertebra comprises a cylinder of bone known as the vertebral body, separated from its neighbour by a buffer, the intervertebral disc, which comprises an outer fibrous tough coat, and a rather more gelatinous interior. Pointing out straight back from each vertebral body is an arch of bone, the vertebral arch. These vertebral arches form, by their superimposition, the vertebral canal through which the spinal cord travels. The 'gaps' between the vertebral arches are filled by a series of membranes of varying toughness and complexity—a continuation of the dura mater—this forms a continuous enclosed canal in which the spinal cord and the emergent spinal nerves float in the CSF, the space of which is in continuity with the fluid surrounding and penetrating the brain in the skull above.

A 'slipped disc' is actually a prolapsed intervertebral disc, in which a dehydrated damaged disc interior has bulged through a weakening in the outer fibrous coat. This is most common between L5 and S1, next most common between L4 and 5, and less common at higher levels. Most prolapses occur more laterally, and if they are going to impinge on a nerve do so on the next nerve to exit below that level, but occasionally, and dangerously, a central prolapse occurs.

Central prolapse of the lumbar disc and the cauda equina syndrome (Figure 14.4)

A prolapsed intervertebral disc causes pain in the back, often due to associated disruption of other structures, in particular the small facet joints. If it presses on a nerve going to the leg it may cause sciatica (pain down the leg), weakness of appropriate musculature, and tingling or numbness. If the disc is a central prolapse it may damage the central rootlets of the cauda equina. Any patient presenting to any doctor with a history of recent onset of low back pain (which may be minimal) but of pain down *both* legs, alteration of sphincter function, and any sensory symptoms whatsoever around the anus, buttocks, genitalia, or back of the thighs, comprises a surgical emergency and should be admitted immediately to a spinal surgical centre. Failure to do so may lead to devastating, permanent disability of weak legs, numb soles of the feet which are prone to ulceration and infection, permanent incontinence of urine and faeces, which requires surgical intervention and usually bypass procedures, and loss of all sexual function. Causation arguments abound as to the precise injury attributable solely to the delay in diagnosis.

Intervertebral disc

Sub-arachnoid space

Dura mater

Anterior

Posterior

Body of
vertebra

L4

A central disc at L4/5 is
capable of damaging all
roots below L5. In fact the
most anterior roots (L5–S2)
are the most vulnerable

L5

S1

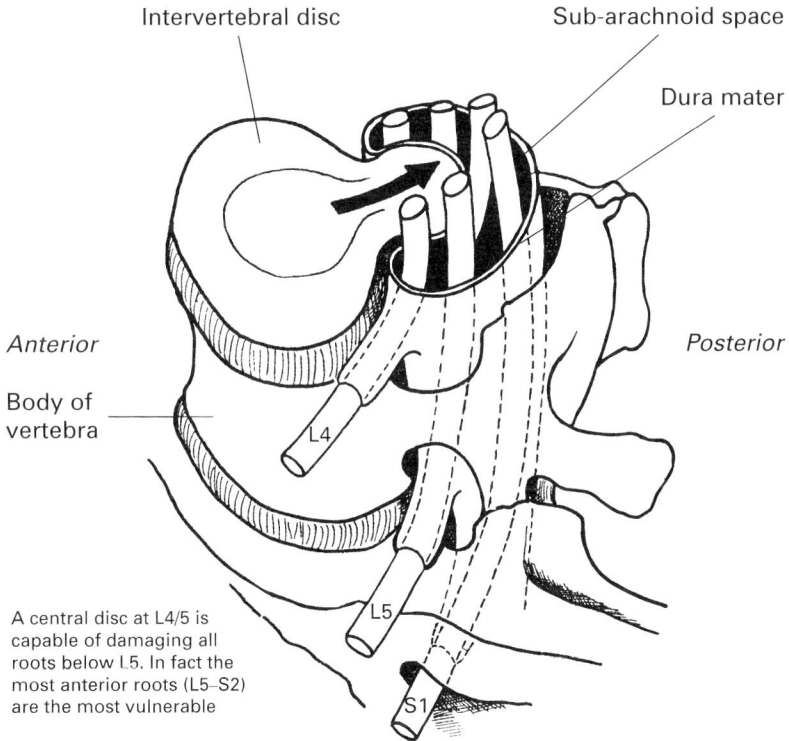

FIGURE 14.4 Central disc prolapse. Reproduced with permission from Patten J. *Differential Neurological Diagnosis*. London: Springer Verlag, 1996.

The dorsal disc

The spinal cord in the dorsal region, the part of the spinal column supporting the ribcage, is relatively poorly supplied with blood, and the prolapse of an intervertebral disc compressing the spinal cord at this level can cause paraplegia (paralysis in both lower limbs), of insidious onset and gradual development. Unless the surgeon is aware of the diagnosis and the surgical approach is from the front (possibly from the side), permanent paraplegia will often ensue.

Other spinal pathology

Spinal cord compression from tumours, which may be benign or malignant, may be missed because it is assumed that they are due to degenerative spinal column disease. MRI scanning is mandatory.

Anaesthetists performing epidural and spinal injection of anaesthetic for childbirth may place the needle too high and damage the last part of the spinal cord, with clinical results similar to those of cauda equina compression.

Peripheral nervous system

Man is derived from a segmental structure, rather like an earthworm. During development in the womb, the human form is twisted and moulded in such a way as to render the initial segmental pattern very difficult to detect in many places. However, it persists in the spinal column, and in the arrangements of the nervous system. Each spinal segment, characterized by one vertebra, has an equivalent segment in the spinal cord, which has one spinal nerve on each side. In the cervical and lumbar regions the nerves supplying the arms and legs form the brachial plexus and lumbar plexus. These plexi are formed by the amalgamation and division of the nerves in a fashion somewhat reminiscent of a 'cats cradle'. Ultimately, the plexi form the definitive nerves that travel down the limbs.

The pattern of innervation of muscles and skin for each level of organization from the nerve root through the plexus (nerve network) and then to a named nerve is very consistent from person to person, and thus a nerve root lesion will produce a similar pattern of weakness in various muscles, and a similarly identifiable pattern of loss of sensation in the skin. By identifying patterns of weakness and the distribution of areas of numbness in the skin it can be stated with a fair certainty whether a peripheral nerve, plexus, or nerve root had been damaged.

A nerve is akin to a post office telephone wire running between the exchange and the telephone. It carries electrical messages from the brain and spine to muscles, instructing the muscles to contract. If the nerve is cut the muscle is obviously paralysed and then wastes away because, for reasons that are not wholly understood, the anatomical integrity of the muscle depends upon an intact nerve supply to it.

Nerves also carry sensory messages from the periphery to the centre. These messages concern the state of the outside world as it affects the body: pain, temperature, touch, and the ability to discriminate and to sense the body's position in space—postural sense. Damage to the sensory part of the peripheral nerves can produce a number of symptoms, such as numbness, tingling and burning to name but a few.

Peripheral nerves comprise a central core, the axon, akin to the metallic core at the centre of an electrical wire, and an insulating sheath of fat called myelin wrapped around it.

Peripheral nerve damage

Causalgia

Causalgia is defined as 'a syndrome of sustained burning pain after a traumatic nerve lesion, combined with vasomotor (vascular) and sudomotor (sweating) dysfunction and later trophic changes'. Pain is felt in and very often beyond, and sometimes widely beyond, the distribution of the injured nerve. It has characteristic features: burning and intractable, helped by cooling, and may be associated with other phenomena. Depression is common. There may or may not be associated disturbances of sweating, blood supply to the skin, and skin texture, which indicate alteration of the sympathetic nerve supply to the skin.

The condition must not be confused with what used to be referred to as 'reflex sympathetic dystrophy', a condition that is often taken by the neurologically naïve to be synonymous with causalgia, but which is probably a different entity, in which there is not necessarily any damage to peripheral nerve tissue. It often occurs in broken limbs, but sometimes without any cause at all, and is characterized by similar pain to causalgia, and marked sympathetic changes in the limb, but without the clinical hallmarks of peripheral nerve injury. This is now called 'complex regional pain syndrome type I' and causalgia is now referred to as 'complex regional pain syndrome type II'.

Before considering the most common cause of nerve damage, namely peripheral nerves that have been squeezed, cut, burnt or pierced, by anaesthetists, surgeons or venepuncturists, some particular conditions should be noted.

Radiotherapeutic nerve damage

Excessive X-ray therapy can damage nerve tissue; this is seen particularly after irradiation of the armpit (axilla) and base of the neck for cancer of the breast. Damage occurs to the brachial plexus after a delay, causing weakness, wasting, numbness, tingling and causalgic pain, which is very difficult to treat. Liability is a matter for oncologists and radiotherapy experts.

Neuralgic amyotrophy (brachial neuritis, etc)

A condition of unknown cause in which severe diffuse pain, usually around the upper quadrant of the body, lasts for days, at the most weeks, and then ceases, to be followed by profound muscular wasting of certain muscles, usually in the upper limb, but it has been described elsewhere. The condition is thought to be an allergic attack on the brachial plexus or nerves, and can be precipitated by trauma, infections, and surgical procedures. The giveaway is the gap in the onset of the weakness—traumatic perisurgical nerve damage produces immediate weakness, while neuralgic amyotrophy produces weakness after a delay.

Guillain Barré syndrome

This is the progressive loss of function of motor and sensory nerves through-out the body. It is probably an immunologically-mediated condition, which can paralyse patients. Most patients recover but there is a definite mortality and morbidity. The patient may present with shortness of breath and weak-ness, which is diagnosed as 'psychological' and is treated with sedatives, with potentially disastrous results if breathing is compromised. Sensory loss is often minimal initially.

Post-phlebotomy median nerve damage

The median nerve supplies a number of muscles in the forearm and hand, and sensation to the front of the thumb, index, middle and half the ring finger. It lies in the mid line at the front of the elbow and is overlain by a large vein, a common target for the venepuncturist taking blood. If the needle is dug in too hard and too deep it may puncture the median nerve, producing immediate pain, tingling and numbness in the hand, which may then go on to produce per-manent weakness and, in particular, causalgia.

Nerves prone to damage by injection

The sciatic nerve is a major nerve in the buttock, which is occasionally injured by direct injection—this is indefensible and can produce major motor and sensory disability in the leg.

Nerves liable to be damaged during clinical procedures (Table 14.1)

Peripheral nerves are liable to be damaged by:

- fractured bones
- cutting during surgical procedures
- phlebotomists (see above)
- pressure on the nerve in an unconscious, supine patient compressing the nerve (e.g. when drunk or anaesthetized on an operating table).

A rare but very disabling peripheral neuropathy causes weakness, wasting, and numbness of the arms and legs following sepsis. The fault lies not in the intensive care unit, but in the reason for the patient being in the ITU with germs in the blood, often as a result of abdominal keyhole surgery (a

TABLE 14.1. Nerves that are prone to damage during surgery

Ulnar nerve at the elbow	The 'funny bone' nerve – can be damaged during anaesthesia by the anaesthetist failing to protect the nerve as it passes round the elbow. Can lead to weakness of the hand and often causalgia affecting the ring and little finger adjacent parts of the hand. Damage to this nerve represents an unacceptable standard of care. It occurs frequently and unless it heals spontaneously and rapidly, is recalcitrant to treatment.
Brachial plexus	These nerves can be injured during open heart surgery when the surgeon splits the breast bone and stretches the ribs apart. This action stretches the brachial plexus and although most patients recover spontaneously, some are left with permanent motor and sensory damage. The brachial plexus can also be damaged when the arm drops off the operating table when the patient is paralyzed and anaesthetized.
Common perineal nerve (in the leg)	Injury to this nerve causes dropped foot. Damage occurs during anaesthesia by pressure, often from 'stirrups'.
Sural nerve	This nerve supplies sensation to the outside of the foot and back of the lower third of the calf. It can be injured during careless varicose vein surgery.
Intercostals nerves	These run around the ribcage and supply sensation to the skin. They are damaged by the insertion of instruments during 'keyhole surgery' and can produce intractable causalgia.
Intercosto-brachial nerve	This nerve supplies sensation to the armpit and the inside of the upper arm. It can be damaged during breast surgery, usually without effect, but sometimes with the production of intractable pain.
Facial nerve	Runs through the carotid gland in the face. Surgery on this gland can result in permanent facial weakness.
Accessory nerve	Runs across the base of the neck and is frequently damaged by inexperienced surgeons biopsying adjacent lymph nodes. Damage produces weakness of muscles around the shoulder, a significant motor disability and very often continuous dull nagging pain because of the altered anatomy of the shoulder joint.
Sciatic nerve	Can be damaged during hip surgery. The motor and sensory deficit is permanent and can be a major disability.
Musculo-cutaneous nerve	This nerve supplies motor instruction to the biceps muscle and paralysis of the nerve causes serious disability. It is often injured in fractures and surgery around the shoulder joint.

similar but less well-recognized process that affects the brain and leads to intellectual impairment).

A number of nerves around the groin are liable to be injured during gynae-cological surgery, often causing localized pain and sensory disturbances that can be permanent.

Psychiatry

John O'Grady

Psychiatrists and lawyers inhabit different worlds. Lawyers are concerned with proving a case, fact finding and the attribution of guilt. Much of the decision-making in law is dichotomous (e.g. guilty or not guilty). Psychiatrists deal with illness and its treatment, and use diagnostic systems that require significant subjective judgement without any clear demarcation between illness and health. When the two worlds come together, they are uneasy partners. It is as if both speak foreign languages and need to have their concepts translated into the other's language (legal or medical). This chapter introduces the lawyer to the conceptual framework the psychiatrist utilizes to make a diagnosis. Post-traumatic stress disorder is used as an example to demonstrate how that diagnostic category is used in civil courts. The chapter ends with consideration of how litigation may itself contribute positively or negatively to a patient's clinical outcome.

Psychiatric diagnosis and illness

'I don't know what you mean by 'glory',' Alice said.
'I mean there's a nice knock down argument for you!'
'But 'glory' doesn't mean a nice knock down argument,' Alice objected.
'When I use a word,' Humpty Dumpty said, in a more scornful voice, 'it means just what I choose it to mean, neither more nor less.'

Psychiatry is essentially like Humpty Dumpty. It utilizes words (diagnostic terms) to label certain combinations of symptoms. There are, however, no objective tests (X-ray, blood tests, genetic tests) that can independently verify the diagnosis. Therefore, in the sense that Humpty Dumpty uses words, psychiatrists invent diagnostic categories to describe their patients' experiences. The diagnostic categories used are not entirely arbitrary as indirect validation for them is provided by studies of patient populations, follow-up of patients over time, response to treatment, and family studies.

Because psychiatry deals with human behaviour, emotions, and cognition, there are basic problems with psychiatric diagnosis. For example, when does normal unhappiness become a depressive illness? This is by no means a trivial issue as, for example, normal unhappiness would not allow a defence of diminished responsibility in a murder trial but a diagnosis of clinical depression might. Where an employee alleges undue stress and unreasonable behaviour by employers, the question of whether the employee is simply unhappy and disgruntled or has been pushed to develop a depressive illness is crucial to consideration of compensation. Should deviant sexual behaviour, such as found in paedophilia, which could be construed as deviating statistically from normal sexual behaviour, be considered an illness, which if accepted might mean a shift to welfare rather than criminal justice disposal?

When is a person's condition due to mental disorder?

It is surprisingly difficult to define what illness or disease is. Kendall provides a thorough overview of the various approaches taken to defining mental disease.[1] These approaches include socio-political definitions, consideration of biomedical disadvantage, and extension of the latter to include handicap. *Socio-political approaches* to diagnosis employ two stems. The first is that the person has an undesirable trait or function and, secondly, that medical technology is best able to deal with it. Severe personality disorder exemplifies a diagnosis potentially utilized for socio-political purposes. The 'dangerousness' exhibited by some is an undesirable trait and society might consider that medical technology rather than imprisonment or other means of control is the best way of dealing with such individuals. As it is only the mentally disordered who can be held in preventive detention, it may be convenient to label certain deviant people as personality disordered to justify preventive detention. Medicine should be independent of political systems and most people are rightly horrified by the abuse of medical technology, say, to incarcerate political prisoners or to justify torture. Socio-political definitions of mental disorder for this reason receive little support. However, the recent controversy about dangerous severe personality disorder suggests that there is an ever-present danger that defining mental disorder in socio-political terms will be a convenient means of justifying social control.

Defining mental disorder as a *biomedical disadvantage* requires: (1) demonstrable biomedical dysfunction; and (2) a value judgement that 'handicap' accrues from that biomedical dysfunction. Take, for example, personality disorder. There is good evidence of a genetic component to at least some personality disorders and increasing evidence of basic dysfunction within brain systems regulating affect, pleasure response, or impulsiveness. Individuals with this label have a high mortality rate from such things as suicide or accidents. They suffer themselves and make others suffer and have an increased propensity to co-morbid mental illness. The former constitutes the biomedical dysfunction and the latter the 'handicap' associated with it, making it reasonable to conclude that personality disorder is properly classified as a mental disorder.

There are three stages in making a psychiatric diagnosis:

- describe precisely the abnormal phenomena displayed by the individual, i.e. symptoms (including biomedical dysfunction)
- draw together those symptoms, which are known to occur together in recognized patterns, i.e. clustering the abnormal phenomena
- put a name to the cluster of symptoms, using an accepted set of diagnostic criteria.

Without utilizing a mutually agreed classification system, each psychiatrist would employ their own idiosyncratic classification. This would make it impossible to communicate, render research impossible, and every clinician would have to write their own textbook! For legal purposes, requiring each expert to employ the same set of diagnostic rules allows for a common language that both sides can understand. It gives both sides in court the opportunity to refer to standard textbooks[2,3] for descriptions of the condition and allows for focussed cross-examination. The two most important diagnostic systems employed in psychiatry are:

- the International Classification of Diseases, now in its 10th edition, abbreviated as ICD-10.[4]
- the diagnostic and statistical manual of the American Psychiatric Association, edition 4, abbreviated as DSM-IV.[5]

Both systems are rapidly converging but there remain some important differences. In British psychiatry, ICD-10 is the recognized classificatory system. Standard British textbooks are structured around ICD-10.[2,3] That classificatory system is essentially a stem and branch tree system—broad categories with many subdivisions. The basic division is between:

- developmental disorders, such as learning disability, autism, and personality disorder. These disorders are rooted in the person's development from childhood into adult life. In that sense, the disorder is 'hardwired' into the person

- disorders which have their origin in adult life. These include the familiar mental illnesses of depression, schizophrenia, and anxiety disorders.

Post-traumatic stress disorder

The example of post-traumatic stress disorder (PTSD) is used to illustrate the structure of psychiatric diagnosis and problems encountered in presenting psychiatric findings in the civil court.

PTSD occurs when individuals are overwhelmed by exposure to a traumatic event that is not encoded properly in memory so that the traumatic event is not recalled in the usual way but comes back in the form of a 'flashback', i.e. a reliving as if in the present. Such exposure alters an individual's cognitive map of the world. Most people believe that the world is reasonably predictable and that they will survive into the future. Exposure to a sudden catastrophic life-threatening event shatters that perception of the world, especially if the traumatic event is due to the malign influence of fellow human beings. The central problem in PTSD is the individual's inability to integrate the traumatic event into their life so far, and this results in repetitive replaying of the trauma in images, behaviours, feelings, physiological states, and within interpersonal relationships. Failure to process the event results in hyper-arousal where innocuous stimuli, which would normally not lead to a reaction, lead to severe anxiety when they are associated with the trauma.

This clinical description employs both biomedical disadvantage and handicap and is brought together into the ICD-10 F43.1 diagnostic criteria for PTSD — 'The disorder should not generally be diagnosed unless there is evidence that it arose within 6 months of a traumatic event of exceptional severity. A probable diagnosis might still be possible if the delay between the event and the onset was longer than 6 months, provided that the clinical manifestations are typical and no alternative identification of the disorder is plausible. In addition to evidence of trauma there must be repetitive intrusive recollection or re-enactment of the event in memories, daytime imagery, or dreams. Conspicuous emotional detachment, numbing of feelings and avoidance of stimuli that might arouse recollection of the trauma are often present but are not essential for the diagnosis. The autonomic disturbance, mood disturbance, and behavioural abnormalities all contribute to the diagnosis but are not of prime importance.'

PTSD is by no means rare. There is a life-time likelihood of exposure to a life-threatening trauma of around 13%.[6] Amongst prisoners of war, it is estimated that between 50 and 70% develop PTSD; 60% of victims of rape may develop PTSD. Exposure need not be direct, as exemplified by some 20% of residents of Lockerbie developing significant symptoms whilst not being directly involved in the air crash.[7] The persistence of PTSD over many years has been reported in the children involved in the Aberfan disaster.[8] These figures also illustrate that not everybody exposed to a severely threatening traumatic event will develop PTSD.

Pre-existing vulnerability

It is clear that individuals react differently to identical traumas with some individuals being severely affected whilst others do not exhibit any symptoms.[9] Genetic endowment may account for 30% of variants between individuals and may reflect a basic difference in the reaction of the neuroendocrine system (the biological regulatory systems within the brain for stress and response to danger). Pre-existing personality and temperament have an effect upon how trauma is assimilated by a particular person. Pre-existing psychiatric disorder may make an individual more prone to the development of PTSD. Exposure in childhood to trauma, such as physical or sexual abuse, may make the individual more sensitive in adult life to the effects of violence or sexual assault. Poverty, poor parenting, low educational attainment, and lack of a cohesive social network may all contribute to vulnerability to trauma.

As well as the effects of PTSD *per se*, an individual may experience many secondary psychiatric problems, such as substance misuse, anxiety/ depression, impairment in social relationships, impairment in physical health, and impairment in cognitive functioning.

Legal implications

What appears on the surface to be a relatively straightforward psychiatric disorder, namely a syndrome that is directly related to trauma, has many dimensions and is complicated by pre-existing vulnerability and subsequent psychiatric morbidity. For example, an individual may not pass the threshold for compensation if their reaction occurs outside the stipulated time scale. Certain individuals may have very severe symptoms in one cluster but not in others, leading to significant disability but not meeting the diagnostic criteria. The type of trauma allowed for the diagnosis is very specific. However, the nature of a trauma is a very subjective one and individuals may have a set of symptomatic responses which are identical to those of PTSD but which follow a traumatic event outside the definition of PTSD.

Pre-existing vulnerability and subsequent mental illness leave room for argument about how much the traumatic event contributed and how much can be attributed to pre-existing vulnerability. In some cases it may be impossible to say whether the psychiatric condition would have occurred 'but for' the traumatic event.

Psychiatric aspects of litigation

Going to court and the possibility of gain through compensation has led to the suspicion that the legal process causes the psychiatric condition itself. After World War I the availability of pensions for 'shell shock' was considered to be responsible for the severity of a soldier's disability. This led in Germany to a policy of not compensating those with psychological symptoms after trauma. Kennedy, a lawyer, summed up a common view of psychological disability in those seeking compensation after injury:

> 'A compensation neurosis is a state of mind borne out of fear, kept alive by avarice, stimulated by lawyers, and cured by a verdict.'

There is surprisingly little research into the psychiatric effects of being involved in litigation. The best studied cases concern those involved in seeking compensation after road traffic accidents, in particular whiplash injuries. The traditional view has been that court action to seek compensation is associated with a poor psychological outcome. However, independent of being involved in a court action, following whiplash injuries patients experience a cluster of psychological problems persisting for >6 months and, whether a litigant or not, does not influence psychiatric disability.[10] Studies have shown that there is indeed improvement after compensation but that many patients show persistent disability after legal resolution.[11] However, cause and effect is difficult to disentangle as Mayou et al further found that the more severely injured sought compensation more often.[11] Thus, most of Kennedy's assertions are incorrect. For patients with PTSD the legal process itself may impair recovery through re-traumatizing the victim. The adversarial system may require the victim (during robust cross-examination) to recall and provide details of the traumatic event they have actively sought to suppress, causing significant distress. Many commentators observe that the motivation to seek compensation may be driven by a desire to seek acceptance of responsibility by others, an explanation of 'what went wrong', or an altruistic desire to prevent the trauma happening to others. The adversarial system may add to a patient's distress by a perception that they are 'on trial' rather than the defendant, or that the defendant is seeking to avoid responsibility. Thus, there are numerous reasons why the legal process may be associated with a worsening of symptoms besides that of secondary gain from the compensation itself.

In a six-year follow up of claimants following road traffic accidents it was found that compensation claims were often prolonged and final settlements modest.[12] There was little evidence that claims were exaggerated. Most settled early and many preferred not to claim. There was no evidence that settlement led to improvement in clinical state. Significantly, subjects were often more concerned with recognition of their suffering rather than the size of the final settlement.

It seems reasonable to conclude that prolongation of legal proceedings is likely to be associated with a worse prognosis for the patient and it is important that legal proceedings are brought to an end as soon as is practicable. No fault speedy resolution procedures employed in some countries for medical negligence might be associated with a better outcome for the patient and merit careful assessment. Lawyers need to be aware that the adversarial legal process may itself be traumatic to the victim.

References

1. Kendell RE. The distinction between personality disorder and mental illness. *Br J Psychiatry* 2002; **180**: 110–15.
2. Gelder MG, Lopez-Ibor JJ, Andreasen N. *New Oxford Textbook of Psychiatry*. Oxford: Oxford University Press, 2000.
3. Gelder M, Mayou R, Cowen P. *Shorter Oxford Textbook of Psychiatry*. Oxford: Oxford University Press, 2001.
4. World Health Organization. *The ICD-10 Classification of Mental and Behavioural Disorders*. Geneva: World Health Organization, 1992.
5. American Psychiatric Association. *Diagnostic and Statistical Manual of Mental Disorders (DSM-IV)*. Washington: American Psychiatric Association, 1995.
6. Kessler R, Jonnega A, Bromet E, *et al*. Post-traumatic stress disorder in the national co-morbidity survey. *Arch Gen Psychiatry* 1995; **52(12)**: 1048–60.
7. Brooks N, McKinlay W. Mental health consequences of the Lockerbie disaster. *J Trauma Stress* 1992; **5**: 527–43.
8. Morgan L, Scourfield J, Williams D, *et al*. The Aberfan disaster: 33 year follow up of survivors. *Br J Psychiatry* 2003; **182**: 532–6.
9. McFarlane A, Yehuda R. Resilience, vulnerability and the course of post-traumatic reactions. In: van der Kolk B, McFarlane A, Weisaeth L (eds), *Traumatic Stress*. New York: Guilford Press, 1996.
10. Mayou R, Bryant B, Duthrie R. Psychiatric consequences of road traffic accidents. *Br Med J* 1993; **307**: 647–51.
11. Mayou R, Tyndel S, Bryant B. Long term outcome of road traffic accidental injury. *Psychosom Med* 1997; **59**: 578–84.
12. Bryant B, Mayou R, Lloyd-Bostock S. Compensation claims following road accidents: a six-year follow-up study. *Med Sci Law* 1997; **37**: 326–36.

Further reading

Basic medicine: physiology

Ganong WF. *Review of Medical Physiology*, 13th edn. Norwalk: Appleton and Lange, 1987.
Guyton AC, Hall JE. *Human Physiology and Mechanisms of Disease*, 6th edn. Philadelphia: WB Saunders, 1997.

General anaesthesia

Harper NJN, Pollard BJ. *Muscle Relaxants in Anaesthesia*. London: Edward Arnold, 1995.
Healy TEJ, Pollard BJ. *Aids to Anaesthesia*, 2nd edn. London: Churchill Livingstone, 1991.
Rushman GB, Davies NJH, Cashman JN. *Lee's Synopsis of Anaesthesia*. Oxford: Butterworth-Heinemann, 1999.
Vukmir Rade B. *Airway Management in the Critically Ill*. New York: The Parthenon Publishing Group, 2001.

Midwifery and obstetrics

Clements RV. *Risk Management and Litigation in Obstetrics and Gynaecology*. London: RSM Press, 2001.
Clinical Risk including *AVMA Medical and Legal Journal*. London: RSM Press (see particularly March 1995).
Harpwood V. *Legal Issues in Obstetrics*. Aldershot: Dartmouth Press, 1996.

Paediatrics

Cerebral palsy

Blair E, Stanley F, Hockey A. Intrapartum asphyxia and cerebral palsy. *J Pediatr* 1992; **121**: 170–1.
Crichton JU, Mackinnon M, White CP. The life expectancy of persons with cerebral palsy. *Dev Med Child Neurol* 1995; **37**: 567–76 (commentary Hall DMB 1032–3).
Eyman RK, Grossman HJ, Chaney RH. Survival of profoundly disabled people with severe mental retardation. *Am J Dis Child* 1993; **147**: 329–36.

Hagberg B, Hagberg G. The origins of cerebral palsy. In: David TJ, ed. *Recent Adv Paediatr* XI. Edinburgh: Churchill Livingstone, 1993 pp 67–83.

Hutton JL, Cooke T, Pharoah POD. Life expectancy in children with cerebral palsy. *Br Med J* 1994; **309**: 431–5.

Pharoah POD, Cooke T, Johnson MA *et al.* Epidemiology of cerebral palsy in England & Scotland, 1984–9. *Arch Dis Child Fetal Neonatal Ed* 1998; **79**: F21–5.

Rosenbloom L. Diagnosis and management of cerebral palsy. *Arch Dis Child* 1995; **72**: 350–4.

Rutherford M, Pennock J, Schweis O. Hypoxic–ischaemic encephalopathy: early and late magnetic resonance imaging findings in relation to outcome. *Arch Dis Child* 1996: **75**: F145–51.

Williams K, Alberman E. Survival in cerebral palsy: the role of severity & diagnostic labels. *Dev Med Child Neurol* 1998; **40**: 376–9.

Meningitis

Bonadio WA. Medical-legal considerations related to symptom duration and patient outcome in bacterial meningitis. *Am J Emerg Med* 1997; **15**: 421–5.

Booy R, Kroll S. Bacterial meningitis in children. *Curr Opin Pediatr* 1994; **6**: 29–35.

Radetsky M. Duration of symptoms and outcome in bacterial meningitis: an analysis of causation and the implications of a delay in diagnosis. *Paediatr Infect Dis J* 1992; **11**: 694–8 (commentaries 698–701).

Richardson MP, Reid A, Tarlow MJ *et al.* Hearing loss during bacterial meningitis. *Arch Dis Child* 1997; **76**: 134–8.

Wright T. Bacterial meningitis and deafness. *Clin Otolaryngol* 1999; **24**: 385–7.

Septicaemia

Browne EJ, Ryan JM, McIntyre P. Evaluation of a protocol for selective empiric treatment of fever without localising signs. *Arch Dis Child* 1997; **76**: 129–33.

Pollard AJ, Britto J, Nadel S *et al.* Emergency management of meningococcal disease. *Arch Dis Child* 1999; **80**: 290–6.

Hip dislocation

Baronciani D, Atti G, Andiloro F *et al.* Screening for DDH: from theory to practice. *Pediatrics* 1997; **99**: e5.

Committee on Quality Improvement and Subcommittee on Developmental Dysplasia of the Hip. Clinical practice guideline: Early detection of DDH. *Pediatrics* 2000; **105**: 896–905.

Congenital heart disease

Gregory J, Emslie A, Wyllie J *et al.* Examination for cardiac malformations at 6 weeks of age. *Arch Dis Child Fetal Neonatal Ed* 1999; **80**: F46–8.

Wren C, Richmond S, Donaldson L. Presenctation of congenital heart disease in infancy: implications for routine examination. *Arch Dis Child Fetal Neonatol Ed* 1999; **80**: F49–53.

Cancer

Edgeworth J, Bullock P, Bailey A *et al.* Why are brain tumours still being missed? *Arch Dis Child* 1996; **74**: 148–51.
Parker A, Robinson R, Bullock P. Difficulties in diagnosing intrinsic spinal cord tumours. *Arch Dis Child* 1996; **75**: 204–7.

Neurology

Biller J. *Iatrogenic Neurology*. Oxford: Butterworth-Heinemann, 1998.
Garfield J, Earl CJ, eds. *Medical Negligence. The Cranium, Spine and Nervous System*. Oxford: Blackwell Science, 1999.

Glossary

Acetabulum:	socket of the 'ball & socket' hip joint
Acetylcholine:	a chemical nerve transmitter
Acidosis:	raised acid levels in blood
Acute:	of sudden onset
Adhesions:	fibrous bands, usually within the abdomen and often as a result of surgery
Adnexum:	group of structures next to the uterus (tube, broad ligament and ovary)
Affect:	mood
Afferent (nerve fibres):	towards the centre of the body
Agenesis:	failure to develop
Alopecia:	loss of hair
Amniocentesis:	withdrawal of amniotic fluid via a **cannula**
Amyotrophy:	wasting of muscle
Anaesthesia:	loss of sensation
Analgesia:	absence of pain
Anaphylactic:	sudden and severe allergic reaction, due to the release of chemicals into the bloodstream
Anastomosis:	a connection of two tubes to form a single continuous tube
Anencephaly:	congenital absence of the brain
Aneurysm:	weak point of blood vessel wall, producing a swelling
Angiography:	examination of blood vessels by means of a dye (injected into the bloodstream) that shows up on X-ray film
Anoxia:	lack of oxygen
Anterior:	to the front (of the body)
Arachnoid:	one of the thin coverings of the brain and spinal cord with a 'spider's web' appearance

ARM:	artificial rupture of membranes
Arterio-:	of an artery
Arthrodesis:	an operation to fix a joint in a rigid position
Arthroplasty:	operation to re-fashion a joint
Arthroscope:	an **endoscope** for looking inside joints
Articular:	relating to a joint
Asphyxia:	inability to breathe
Atheroma:	fatty deposit in the walls of blood vessels
Atresia:	congenital absence of a hollow organ
Autonomic:	without voluntary control
Autonomic nervous system:	the part of the nervous system outside voluntary control
AVM:	arterio-venous malformations
Axon:	long fibre of a nerve cell that connects with another cell
Brachial:	pertaining to the arm
Bradycardia:	slow heart rate
Bronchus:	a branch of the trachea to and within the lungs
Cannula:	fine hollow tube, usually for introduction of fluid into the body
Carcinoma:	malignant growth or cancer
CAT:	computerized axial tomography
Catheter:	hollow tube inserted into a body cavity or blood vessel, often for drainage
Caudal:	pertaining to the tail/towards the base of the spine ('tail')
Cephalic:	relating to the head
Cerebral cortex:	outer layer of the brain
Cerebrum:	the brain
Cervical:	of the neck
Cervix:	the neck (of an organ, e.g. the uterus)
CHAI:	Commission for Health Audit & Improvement
Chemoreceptors:	cells stimulated by chemical change
Cholecystectomy:	surgical removal of the gall bladder
Chorionic villus:	part of the placenta
Chronic:	long-standing
Colposcope	a magnifying instrument to examine the uterine cervix
Contralateral:	opposite side
Coronal:	a vertical plane through the body or an organ from side to side

Cortex:	outer layer of an organ e.g. of a bone/the cerebral cortex
CSF:	cerebral spinal fluid
CT:	computerized tomography
CTG:	cardiotocograph
CVA:	cerbrovascular accident ('stroke')
Cyanosis:	dusky purple colour of the skin due to lack of oxygen
Cytotoxic:	poisonous to cells
Debridement:	surgical removal of dead or infected tissue
Dendrite:	short fibres of a nerve cell
Diastole:	the stage of the cardiac cycle when the heart dilates and fills with blood
Differential diagnosis:	alternative diagnoses
Dissection (of an artery):	separation of the layers of the walls of an artery
Distal:	furthest from the centre
Dorsal:	towards the back of the body
Dura mater:	tough membrane covering the brain and spinal cord
Dystocia:	difficult labour
ECG:	electrocardiograph, a recording of the electrical activity of the heart
Ecto-:	outside/outer
-ectomy:	surgical removal
Ectopic:	outside the normal site e.g. tubal pregnancy
Ectopic pregnancy:	pregnancy that develops outside the womb
EEG:	electroencephalogram, a recording of the electrical activity of the brain
Efferent (nerve fibres):	away from the centre of the body
Embolism:	blockage of a blood vessel by a plug of tissue, usually a blood clot, which has become detached from the site of its formation and travelled in the bloodstream to a distant site
Encephalitis:	inflammation of the brain
Encephalopathy:	disease of the brain
Endo-:	within
Endocarditis:	inflammation of the heart
Endocrine gland:	ductless gland that secretes hormones directly into the blood
Endoscope:	an instrument ('telescope') for visual examination inside a body cavity

Endothelium:	single layer of cells, usually lining a hollow structure
Epididymo-orchitis:	inflammation of the testis and spermatic cord
Epiphysis:	growing point of a bone
Erythema:	redness of the skin due to increased blood flow
Extradural:	outside the dura mater
Fallopian tube:	the tube between the ovary and the uterus (womb)
Fibrinolysis:	dissolution of blood clots
Fibroblast:	a cell that produces fibrous tissue such as collagen
Fistula:	opening connecting two adjacent hollow structures, or to the outside
Ganglion (plural ganglia):	a knot of nerve cells (neurones)
Glottis:	vocal cords and muscles
GMC:	General Medical Council
Haematoma (plural haematomata):	swelling due to bleeding into the tissues
Hemiplegia:	paralysis of one side of the body
Hepatic:	of the liver
Histopathology:	study of diseased cells
Hormone:	chemical messenger in the blood
Hyper-:	high/raised
Hyperparathyroidism:	excessive parathyroid hormone, causing a disturbance of bone metabolism
Hypertension:	raised blood pressure
Hypo-:	low/below
Hypotension:	low blood pressure
Hypothyroidism:	low levels of thyroid hormone
Hypoxaemia:	reduced oxygen in the blood
Hypoxia:	reduced oxygen in the tissues
Hysteroscopy:	endoscopic examination inside the womb
Idiopathic:	disease of unknown origin
Idiosyncracy (drug):	unusual reaction (to a drug)
Ileostomy:	surgical opening into the small intestine (**ileum**)
Infarct (infarction):	death of tissue due to loss of blood supply
Intracranial:	within the skull
Intrapartum:	during childbirth
Intussusception:	infolding (of the bowel) within itself
Ipsilateral:	the same side
Ischaemia:	lack of blood
-itis:	inflammation (of a part)

Labium (plural labia):	lip
Lacunae:	abnormal spaces in a structure
Laparoscope:	an **endoscope** for examining inside the abdominal cavity
Laparotomy:	operation to open the abdomen
Larynx:	voice box
Lateral:	to the outer side (of the body)
Lesion:	change in the tissues due to injury or disease
Liquor amnii/ amniotic fluid:	the fluid surrounding the infant in the womb
LSCS:	lower segment Caesarian section, i.e. delivery of infant via surgical opening in the lower part of the uterus through the abdominal wall
Lumen:	cavity in a hollow structure
Lumpectomy:	surgical removal of a breast lump
Lymphoma:	cancer of the lymphatic system
Macrosomia:	large body
Mammogram:	X-ray of breast
Mastectomy:	surgical removal of the breast
MDDUS:	Medical & Dental Defence Union of Scotland
MDU:	Medical Defence Union
Meconium:	first faeces of the newborn infant
Medial:	towards the mid-line
Medulla:	inner core of an organ e.g. bone/brain
Meniscus:	crescent-shaped cartilage (gristle) in a joint, especially the knee
Menorrhagia:	heavy menstrual blood flow
Metastases/metastatic disease:	the spread of malignant disease to other parts of the body
Morbidity:	illness or disease
MPS:	Medical Protection Society
MRI:	magnetic resonance imaging
Multigravid:	a pregnant woman who has previously been pregnant
Multiparous:	relating to second and subsequent childbirths
Myelin:	fatty sheath covering the **axon** of a nerve fibre
Myocardium:	heart muscle
Necrosis:	death of tissue
Neonatal:	newborn, relating to the first 28 days of life
Neoplasm:	benign or malignant tumour
Nephrology:	study of renal disease

Neuro-:	of a nerve
NICE:	National Institute for Clinical Excellence
NMC:	Nursing and Midwifery Council
Neuritis:	inflammation of a nerve
Neuroendocrine:	hormone affecting the nervous system
Oedema:	retention of fluid in the tissues
Orchitis:	inflammation of the testis
Os (external os):	opening
Osteomalacia:	softening of the bones due to lack of vitamin D
Osteomyelitis:	infection of bone, esp. the marrow
Osteotomy:	cutting into a bone
-ostomy:	surgical opening into a tubular or hollow organ
-otomy:	a cutting operation
Oxytocic:	stimulating labour by increasing contractions of the womb
Paraesthesia:	abnormal sensation e.g. tingling, 'pins & needles'
Paraplegia:	paralysis of both legs and the lower part of the body
Pericardial:	around the heart
Perinatal:	relating to the first seven days of life
Peritoneum:	thin layer of cells, covering the **viscera** of the abdomen and lining the abdominal cavity
Phalanx:	one of the bones in the fingers or toes
Pharynx:	the throat, above the gullet and windpipe
Phenylketonuria:	brain disease due to an inherited lack of a specific enzyme
Phlebotomy:	withdrawing of blood
Platelet:	a constituent of the blood, important in the clotting mechanism
Pleura:	membranous lining of chest cavity and covering of the lungs
Pleurisy:	inflammation of the pleura
Plexus:	network of nerve fibres
Pneumothorax:	air within the chest cavity, outside the lungs
Posterior:	to the back (of the body)
Primigravid:	a woman in her first pregnancy
Primiparous:	relating to first childbirth
Proximal:	nearest the centre
Pulmonary:	of the lung
Purpura:	bruising into the skin
Purulent:	filled with or discharging pus
Pyrexia:	raised temperature/fever

Quadriplegia:	paralysis of all four limbs
RCM:	Royal College of Midwives
RCN:	Royal College of Nursing
RCOG:	Royal College of Obstetricians and Gynaecologists
Reduction (of fracture):	re-alignment
Resection:	cutting out
Sagittal:	a vertical plane through the body or an organ from front to back
Salpingectomy:	surgical removal of the **Fallopian tube(s)** [oviduct(s)]
-scope:	an instrument for visual examination
Seminoma:	cancer of the testis
Somatic:	pertaining to the body
Speculum:	instrument allowing inspection of a canal or orifice
Sphincter:	circular muscle closing an aperture
Subarachnoid:	beneath the **arachnoid** membrane covering the brain
Subdural:	beneath the dura mater
Systole:	contraction of the heart muscle to expel blood around the body
Tachycardia:	rapid heart rate
Tachypnoea:	rapid breathing
Teratogenesis:	abnormal development of foetus
Teratoma:	tumour of cells of mixed origin, formed during foetal development
Thrombocytopenia:	reduced **platelets** in the blood
Thrombosis:	formation of a blood clot within a blood vessel
TIA:	transient ischaemic attack
Tocolysis:	relaxation of the womb to slow or stop childbirth
Tomography:	X-rays taken in a cross-sectional plane of an organ or area
Torsion:	twisting
Trachea:	wind pipe above the bronchi
Tracheostomy:	surgical opening in the front of the trachea
Tracheotomy:	incision into the trachea through the front of the neck
Trophic (changes):	characteristic changes seen (in the skin) when the nerve supply to the area is severed
Ureter:	tube carrying urine from kidney to the bladder
Urticaria:	'nettle rash' or hives

Uterus:	the womb
Vascular/vaso:	pertaining to a blood vessel
Vasopressor:	substance that causes constriction of the blood vessels (and a consequent rise in blood pressure)
Venous:	of a vein
Ventral:	towards the front, especially abdomen
Viscera:	internal organs of the body
Vulsellum:	grasping forceps

Index